HEADS, YOU WIN!

How the Best Companies Think

Quinn Spitzer
and Ron Evans

TOUCHSTONE BOOKS
LONDON . NEW YORK . SYDNEY . TOKYO . TORONTO . SINGAPORE

First published in Great Britain by Simon & Schuster UK Ltd, 1997
This edition first published by Touchstone, 1999
An imprint of Simon & Schuster UK Ltd
A Viacom Company

1 3 5 7 9 10 8 6 4 2

Simon & Schuster UK Ltd
Africa House
64-78 Kingsway
London WC2B 6AH

Simon & Schuster Australia
Sydney

A CIP catalogue record for this book is available from the British Library

1 3 5 7 9 10 8 6 4 2

ISBN 0-684-85159 8

Printed and bound in Great Britain by Cox & Wyman Ltd, Reading

To our wives, Tina and Karen.

You demonstrate that smart people can make a poor decision at least once and then spend years honing their problem-solving skills.

Contents

Introduction

We have suspected for some time that what really drives businesses and their leaders is not money or power. It is the deep and abiding fear that someone somewhere has discovered the elusive Holy Grail of business—competitive advantage!—and that these leaders don't have it. Books, seminars, articles, and speeches, all detail the management secrets of companies whose success suggests that the grail of competitive advantage is at last in their grasp, and other companies worldwide line up to emulate the practices of these chivalrous knights. Motorola espouses "Six Sigma" quality, and dozens of companies quickly adopt it as their business mantra. Southwest Airlines soars on no-frills, high-performance transportation, and the skies begin to fill with "wannabes." Rubbermaid makes headlines for its product innovation process, and within months identical approaches appear in scores of companies. Everywhere, it seems, companies and their leadership are looking for someone else's star to hitch their wagons to. As the saying goes: Just because you're paranoid doesn't mean they're not out to get you!

Looking back over the last several years, we have seen consultants propound new business management theories with captivatingly clever names, while we were still immersed in thirty-five-year-old processes for making decisions and solving problems developed by Benjamin B. Tregoe and Charles H. Kepner. This is not to suggest that we were not very proud of our work. We took an enormous amount of satisfaction from the list of our long-term clients, including lasting relationships with companies such as Hewlett-Packard, Corning, Chrysler, Sony, Johnson & Johnson, Siemens, and others among the world's best enterprises. Yet we had no unique name for the organization of the 1990s. We had not developed a manifesto for business in the twenty-first century. We hadn't even developed a catchy new acronym—a mortal sin if there ever was one in the field of management.

In 1994 we were discussing our concerns over a pint of Guinness in McHugh's, a small pub in the tiny Irish town of Liscannor. A local patron, overhearing our conversation, upbraided us for talking business in a pub, a serious breach of Irish etiquette. He then offered the following observation: "You lads seem too concerned with fancy phrases and such that normal people don't really care about at all. You'd do well to learn to express yourselves plainly and stick to the basics."

His admonition struck a resonant chord with us. We have seen many management techniques that were overly complex and seemed to fail when put into practical application. We had invested so much time in critical thinking processes like problem solving and decision making because for us they were simple and practical. They were the "basics." These processes had endured and not fallen victim to the "fad" label because they were fundamental to every business. For this reason, we theorized, they would continue to attract the attention of the world's best businesses.

The notion that these critical thinking skills might be as vital to business success as the more ephemeral nostrums for management was more than reassuring. It was cathartic. There was no doubt in our minds that the critical thinking skills we had worked with for almost two decades were as valid as ever, and the four areas of business activity to which they can be applied remain of central concern to every business: Situation Appraisal—a means to assess, simplify, and prioritize complex business issues; Problem Analysis—nothing more or less than a process for finding out why something has gone wrong; Decision Analysis—a methodology for making choices that ensures adequate consideration of the many facets of benefit and risk; and Potential Problem and Potential Opportunity Analysis—planning approaches that can help avoid future problems and capture future opportunities. These are the activities that still dominate the business day, and the use of critical thinking skills is still essential to overall success. Whatever the business, whatever its size or complexity, they provide, in and of themselves, a basis for competitive advantage.

While Kepner and Tregoe's landmark best-seller, *The Rational Manager*, explains how individuals can develop their personal critical thinking skills, Kepner-Tregoe, the management consulting firm, has as its mission improving the effective organizational use of these processes. Consequently, over the past thirty-five years we have had the opportunity to learn a great deal about how organizations approach the business of making decisions and solving problems, and we have formulated three premises:

PREMISE ONE—*Critical thinking skills are the foundation on which all other organizational improvement practices and theories rest. Without an underlying competence in assessing complex situations, solving problems, making decisions, and planning for future problems and opportunities, an organization is unlikely to advance any other initiative successfully. Consequently an organization that can build a proficiency in these critical thinking skills will have a platform for achieving competitive advantage.*

PREMISE TWO—*While these critical thinking processes have endured in their current articulation for more than thirty-five years, they have done so in a dramatically changing business environment. Thus the way critical thinking skills are deployed in business is also changing, making it increasingly hard for businesses to build competence in these fundamentals.*

PREMISE THREE—*A number of outstanding organizations have succeeded in building an organizational proficiency in problem solving and decision making. Learning from their approaches can help other organizations build a similar proficiency in critical thinking.*

To test the validity of these premises, we have supplemented our own experiences with three distinct research methods. First, we asked the well-known research firm Yankelovich Partners to examine the state of problem solving and decision making in business today. We chose this outside firm to avoid the "contamination" we ourselves might bring to the research due to our biases on the subject. We wanted to learn if others felt as we did, that critical thinking skills were fundamental to business success. We were also curious to understand the views of businesspeople about the underlying competence in these skills exhibited by today's organizations. We must confess to a little trepidation when Yankelovich Partners presented its findings. We knew that if it reported that most people felt these skills weren't that crucial to business success or that businesses were already extremely competent in these skills, we would be on the next flight back to Ireland. Fortunately the results confirmed our beliefs.

Our second research method involved a detailed examination of some of our best clients, companies committed to being more effective in problem solving and decision making despite the fact that they were already arguably among the best businesses in the world. We wanted to know how they were developing proficiency in critical thinking. The top executives of these fine organizations talked with us at length about their views on problem solving and decision making.

The list of people willing to participate is, in our opinion, an honor roll of business leadership. These names include:

Roger G. Ackerman, Chairman and CEO, Corning Incorporated
Norman P. Blake, Jr., Chairman, President, and CEO USF&G Corporation
Sir Michael Heron, Chairman, The Post Office, United Kingdom
Jay F. Honeycutt, Center Director, NASA, Kennedy Space Center
James R. Houghton, former Chairman and CEO, Corning Incorporated
Ralph S. Larsen, Chairman and CEO, Johnson & Johnson
Robert A. Lutz, President & COO, Chrysler Corporation
Sir Colin Marshall, Chairman, British Airways Plc
Jeffrey J. O'Hara, President and COO, Darden Restaurant Inc.
Edward Snider, former Chairman, Spectacor Corporation; currently Chairman, Comcast-Spectacor
Richard F. Teerlink, President and CEO, Harley-Davidson, Inc.

As we fleshed out the book's thesis, we recognized that we could also profit greatly from the insights of some of today's great management thinkers and commentators. Kenneth H. Blanchard, Alan Kay, Joel Kurtzman, Ray Marshall, Henry Mintzberg, Tom Peters, C. K. Prahalad, Peter Senge, Noel Tichy, and Stuart A. Varney all were extremely generous with their valuable time.

What follows are our arguments in support of these three premises. Drawing from our own experience as well as from these three research sources, we not only argue that these critical thinking skills are fundamental to sound management and, hence, competitive advantage, but we also offer our view that the absence of sound decision-making and problem-solving skills may be the most probable cause for the multitude of failed change efforts. We examine the critical thinking skills themselves in successive chapters, and in each case, because we believe that there have been profound changes in the way these skills are used, we have attempted to describe why these changes have taken place and how effective organizations are adjusting their problem-solving and decision-making approaches to accommodate them. Then we examine the issues in the business environment that have the most significant impact on how well critical thinking skills are used. These issues—teams, intuition, questioning, systems, data management, and values—have each been the subject of dozens of books and articles. We have limited our examination of them to their relationship to effective problem solving and decision making, and, in the process, we believe we have added a new perspective.

Given our strong belief in the necessity and effectiveness of these processes, we were, quite candidly, hoping to find a formula for developing critical thinking skills in organizations. That would have at least allowed us to lay claim to having a single answer to the perplexing question of what constitutes competitive advantage. We found, however, that there was no single approach to deployment. So instead we have described the factors we observed as common among those companies that have achieved a proficiency in critical thinking. Their experience provides a guide or road map to achievement of a similar proficiency. Finally, because the critical thinking processes described in this book are firmly wedded to the concepts and processes first presented by Kepner and Tregoe in *The Rational Manager*, there is a brief review of the practical application of these processes in the Appendix. Any reader who becomes intrigued with these processes will find *The Rational Manager* an important reference.

As we were beginning to write this book, returning to Philadelphia on a flight from Charlotte, we noticed that a neighboring passenger had pulled from his briefcase a copy of the latest best-selling management book. Minutes later, the plane's landing gear fully retracted, we saw that our fellow traveler, book on chest, had fallen into a deep, seemingly untroubled sleep. For us, this confirmed a long-held suspicion that business books are often better soporifics than stimulants. We hope this book will be an exception to that rule.

Becoming a world-class organization without a proficiency in the critical thinking skills is a virtual impossibility. For that reason, this book was instructive for us as we wrote it. It caused us to examine our own organization and reflect on the possibility that by taking these ideas for granted, we could become "the shoemaker's children." We hope that *Heads, You Win!* will encourage our readers to undertake a similar examination of their organization's proficiency in critical thinking and to focus on it as the most enduring source of competitive advantage.

CHAPTER 1

The Primal Manager

I ask people who know American business well to name three or four chief executives who really made a difference: not short-term, but who really sustained superb performance. Almost never does anybody mention a Harvard MBA, let alone any MBA.

HENRY MINTZBERG
Bronfman Professor of Management,
McGill University

The topic of change has, for many of us, become a major irritant. Hundreds of articles, dozens of books, and cloying phrases like "Change is the only constant" have alerted us that a lot has been happening during the 1990s. Yet one of the most important changes in the business world has gone largely unnoticed: the changing of the guard in business leadership.

During the 1990s virtually an entire generation of top executives left their businesses, retired, or passed away. Many of these executives had achieved legendary status—Packard at Hewlett-Packard, Morita at Sony, Jones at ICI, Walton at Wal-Mart, and Carlzon at SAS, to name a few. These leaders shared some notable characteristics that differentiate them from their successors. They lived through the Great Depression, which crippled the world's economy in the 1930s; they experienced the horrors of World War II; they served their business apprenticeships in the postwar rebuilding period of the late 1940s and early 1950s. But what may differentiate them most from their counterparts of today is the issue of management.

This "old guard" was the last of a breed of executives who developed their management skills almost entirely in the workplace. They were building businesses while management "science"—if it can be called that—was still in its infancy. While there was the stray management theory in the corridor—Mayo on group dynamics, Taylor on scientific managing, Bernard on executive functions—the idea that managing an organization required an associated body of knowledge was only beginning to evolve.

In 1948, for example, when the careers of these executives were moving to full speed, the *Harvard Business Review* had a robust circulation of fifteen thousand. That number had reached nearly two hundred fifty thousand by the mid 1990s. The Harvard Business School itself and the few other graduate business schools in existence in 1948 awarded 3,357 MBAs—a far cry from the 75,000 MBAs awarded forty-five years later. Even McKinsey, the best known of consulting companies, was a relatively small firm with annual revenues of under $2 million, compared with 1994 revenues of more than $1.2 billion. Management guru Peter Drucker was a youngster of thirty-nine. Seven-year-old Tom Peters was probably "in search of" a new bike.

The executives of this period were not uneducated—in fact, many were extremely well educated—but they did not learn their approach to business from a business school, a management expert, a celebrated management book, or an outside consultant. Options such as these were not generally available. These executives learned their business skills in the industrial jungle. They were the last of the "primal managers."

The forty-year-old executive of the 1990s, by contrast, probably holds one of the tens of thousands of MBAs awarded each year. His formal management education is supplemented by dozens of business periodicals and hundreds of management books. If, however, a situation seems resistant to even this mass of management wisdom, there are several hundred consulting firms and more than a hundred thousand consultants ready to provide additional management skill and knowledge. In 1993 businesses around the world spent $17 billion for consultants' recommendations, and AT&T alone lavished $347.1 million on outside expertise. That does not necessarily mean that the business executives of the past were superior to those of the present. Obviously each group has had its share of successes and failures. It is undeniable, however, that many of these "primal managers" were successful without the massive body of knowledge about business, management, and organizations that we have come to view as so critical for business effectiveness.[1] Of course, today's business executives operate in a very different economic and geopolitical climate. There is an avalanche of information to absorb and assess. They must keep up with an accelerating rate of change in every aspect of their businesses. Their marketplace is international. Still, we suspect that if those "primal managers" of years gone by found themselves at the helm of any of today's extraordinarily complex and competitive business enterprises, they would steer a straight and successful course.

What They Knew That We Don't

This conclusion creates a major conundrum for those of us trying to solve the business problems of today. If Sam Walton built Wal-Mart without an MBA, if David Packard made Hewlett-Packard an industry leader without "business process reengineering," if Akio Morita created the Sony empire without Kenichi Ohmae as his guru, then how did they do it? Is there something more fundamental at the core of organizational success than the theories found in business schools, management books, and consulting reports? The answer to that question is as close to self-evident as exists in the world of business. These executives were not just people of action, but people of thought—critical thought. And with the precision of hindsight, we can conclude that the critical thinking they brought to their businesses was fundamentally

[1] Interestingly enough, it was the primal managers themselves who supplied much of the impetus and the financing for MBA programs. Their support for such programs may, in fact, have emanated from a sense that their own learning experience had been too arduous, haphazard, and protracted.

more effective than that of their colleagues and competitors at the time. Further, because we now have the benefit of convincing research into what such critical thinking skills entail, we can presume to say that these leaders were especially proficient in four such processes, all of which contributed to their business success:

1. They effectively assessed a complex economic environment, allowing them to identify and plan quick responses to the most critical business issues. *We call this process "Situation Appraisal."*
2. When problems surfaced, they accurately identified the cause and quickly implemented corrective action. *We call this process "Problem Analysis."*
3. They made good decisions, balancing the benefits and risks associated with their choice. *We call this process "Decision Analysis."*
4. They implemented their chosen actions effectively by circumventing problems and seizing opportunities. *We call this process "Potential Problem Analysis and Potential Opportunity Analysis."*

These four thinking processes are often cited as distinguishing features of successful executives. Saying that they are fundamentally superior problem solvers and decision makers is a little like the radio commentator who noted during the 1992 Olympics, "Carl Lewis, what a good runner. . . . All his arms, elbows, and knees moving in the same direction."[2] But consider the real implications of this premise. What it suggests is that executives may hold degrees from the most prestigious business schools, be schooled practitioners of the most celebrated management theories, and receive advice from respected consultants, yet they will probably fail without an underlying competence in these four areas, which we have collectively identified as problem solving and decision making.

---

[2] Ross and Kathryn Petras, *The 776 Even Stupider Things Ever Said* (New York: Harper Perennial, 1994), p. 176.

What Happened to My Magic Bullet?

This premise contrasts sharply with the prevailing view of management excellence. Today's executives are expected to have a devotion to quality and customer service. They must ensure that their organizations are lean. Their approach to business must be time based. They must develop a value-driven strategy. They must optimize their core competencies. They must strengthen the supply chain and distribution management. They must always dress for success and exercise regularly. And, dress and personal fitness aside, they usually build a corporate initiative around each of these areas because, they believe, they are the keys to success. It's not surprising that a study we conducted in 1993 showed that nearly half the executives surveyed had undertaken eleven or more such initiatives in a three-year period.[3]

Yet when viewed in their most elementary form, it seems apparent that all of these initiatives—as well as nearly every other fabled management palliative of the last fifty years—are nothing more than a collection of decisions to be made and implemented and problems to be solved. Consider two engaging business concepts: reengineering and the learning organization. Both call for businesspeople to cast off the shackles of narrow, historically based business thought and acquire new knowledge and perspectives about their organizations. Using the language of problem solving and decision making, these concepts can be viewed from a very different perspective.

Reengineering, for example, requires teams of employees, and perhaps consultants, to identify the key outputs required to achieve strategic objectives, choose the most efficient steps to produce those outputs, and plot the actions necessary to move from the current outputs and steps to the proposed outputs and steps. While there is some suspicion in organizations undergoing reengineering that it is a semimystical experience, in which

[3] Kepner-Tregoe, *House Divided: Views on Change from Top Management—and Their Employees*, typescript (Princeton, N. J.: Kepner-Tregoe, Inc., 1994), pp. 7–9.

teams are led hypnotically by fanatical sects of consultants in pinstripes, the reality is that a group of people is making a series of complex business decisions about work processes. Executives are balancing risks and consequences in order to choose the most predictably successful approach. Most important, reengineering suggests that we broaden the range of alternatives for how we do our work. Unfettered by the historical options that have driven business for decades, we can now look at entirely new ways to construct processes and align resources. In reality, reengineering combines Situation Appraisal, Potential Opportunity and Potential Problem Analysis, and Decision Analysis under a different, more au courant guise.

It should therefore come as no surprise to find that the success ratio of reengineering efforts seems as spotty as the success ratio for decision making in general. Even reengineering's gurus Michael Hammer and James Champy estimate that 50–70 percent of reengineering attempts will fail. Or, as Robert L. Ecklin, Corning, Inc.'s senior vice president, put it, "In our experience, the only real difference between successful and failed reengineering efforts is the quality of decision making and decision implementation."

The "learning organization" achieved a similar cultlike status shortly after the publication of Peter Senge's *The Fifth Discipline.* Senge's explication of the "Five Disciplines" of the learning organization suggests that competitive advantage comes to those who build knowledge and, indeed, wisdom in their organizations. The vistas and new perspectives gained from this wellspring of knowledge can produce an excitement and introspection, both personally and organizationally, that can propel organizations to success. The "Zen" overtones to Senge's theories can hardly be ignored. The ultimate learning organization might, in fact, be a monastery of Buddhist priests who have dedicated their lives to acquiring wisdom. (Imagine the CEOs' top team decked out in orange robes, chanting mantras at their next executive retreat.)

The real dilemma of the learning organization is, "What do we do with all this knowledge?" Some would argue that the acquisition of knowledge is a noble goal unto itself. But unless it is utilized and implemented effectively, the learning organization is nothing more than an engaging cloister. Christopher Lorenz of the *Financial Times* put it well: "Most Western managers suffer from rampant confusion about the nature of information. They fail to use knowledge effectively. . . ."[4] The organization must, in fact, use knowledge to make new and better decisions, resolve previously intractable problems, and better anticipate the problems and opportunities of the future. Senge's brilliant ideas in systems thinking and personal mastery all lead inexorably to decision making and problem solving as the enabling mechanisms that turn these theories into desired outcomes.

Reengineering and learning organizations, as well as most "magic bullets" in management practices, are, in this context, intriguing business activities that depend for their ultimate success largely upon the quality of the decision making and problem solving inherent in them. Robert Chia, a lecturer at Lancaster University's innovative Master of Philosophy in Critical Management program, takes the argument one step further by examining the origin of these practices. "Fashionable concepts such as Total Quality Management or Zero-Based Budgeting emerged from radical approaches to problem solving. But people get hooked on the system instead of the style of thinking behind it."[5] Business thinking ultimately traces back to the skills of problem solving and decision making.

Foundation Processes and the Leaky Basement

The decision-making and problem-solving skills that grounded the primal manager, and that underlie many of the great management nostrums of today, form the foundation for business success. In a 1995 Yankelovich/Kepner-Tregoe study of three hundred senior executives, 92 percent of the executives inter-

[4] Christopher Lorenz, "How to Turn Signals into Knowledge," *Financial Times* (London), 9 September 1994, p. 11.
[5] Peter Aspden, "A Philosophical Approach—A Post-Graduate Course with a Difference," *Financial Times* (London), 22 July 1994, p. 11.

viewed rated problem-solving and decision-making skills as "absolutely critical" or "very important" to the company's success.[6] If, therefore, these skills are so pivotal to business achievement, we come face-to-face with a compelling question: Are executives any good at these processes? The anecdotal evidence is not encouraging.

Certainly there have been problem-solving and decision-making blunders throughout history, with the business world providing some of the most breathtaking examples. Consider a few whoppers from the period before 1970:

- In the 1940s the E. R. Squibb Co. held the patent on the oral contraceptive. It decided to swallow it.
- Around this time Great Britain developed the jet engine but gave the patent to General Electric. For decades the only thing "special in the air" was American.
- In the 1950s Finnish engineers developed technology that used microwaves to instantly heat substances in an oven. They left it on the shelf.
- Also in the 1950s the Ford Motor Company set out to "revolutionize" its automobile design. It rolled out the Edsel.
- In 1964 Xerox introduced the first fax machine but failed to exploit its market potential. Its profits and market share were instantaneously transmitted to shrewder Japanese competitors.

These examples would be astonishing even if they were not just the "tip of the iceberg," so to speak. While there is, arguably, a similar list of rousing successes from this era, it is apparent that decision making in business prior to 1970 produced mixed results. And not surprisingly, there is an equally embarrassing host of blunders from the 1970s on, after management science had reached adulthood:

---

[6] Yankelovich Partners, "A Study of Decision Making and Problem Solving in Today's Business Environment," typescript (Norwalk, Conn.: Yankelovich Partners, Inc., 1995), p. 48.

- Swiss watch companies in the early 1970s decided to ignore Japanese quartz watches, a technology invented in Switzerland. This seriously damaged the crown jewel of Switzerland's exports.
- IBM's failure to anticipate the workstation and minicomputer revolution and its decision to maintain focus on mainframes contributed to a drop in the value of its stock in the billions of dollars, while it gave up market share to more nimble and opportunity-minded competitors. Big Blue was singing the blues.
- Coca-Cola, armed with millions of dollars of marketing studies, launched New Coke. After an astonishingly negative public reaction, New Coke lost its effervescence. And Coca-Cola returned to its old formula.
- Disney selected a northern Virginia site for its newest theme park, which was to center on American history. An outcry from local residents showed Disney what a small world it is after all. Disney canceled its plans.
- Quaker Oats, thirsting for a profitable acquisition, bought high-flying Snapple, only to find that the deal soured its earning mix.

Obviously, a list of examples of any length doesn't prove that decision making is a business weakness. Even so, big-ticket decisions are always being made, and some of them could turn out to be bad ones. The year 1995 alone provides dramatic examples: Consider CEO Robert Allen's decision to break the $75 billion AT&T Corp. into three separate companies—the largest voluntary corporate breakup ever—after years of major acquisitions. How will this decision be viewed in five or ten years? Or its competitor, Sprint Corp., and its partners—how will their $7 billion acquisition and development of the untested PCS technology fare? IBM jumped into electronic commerce and Internet business with its $3.5 billion acquisition of Lotus. Despite a near lock on the market, Ford redesigned its best-selling Taurus to attract a younger, more affluent buyer—and raised its price dramatically over the competition's. How will these decisions look with the benefit of hindsight?

The Yankelovich/Kepner-Tregoe "Study of Problem Solving and Decision Making" found that senior executives took a dim view of decision-making prowess in large multinational corporations. Eighty percent of the executives surveyed felt that executives in large multinational corporations frequently missed achieving their objectives in decision making. When it came to solving problems, only half the executives felt secure in their company's ability to ask the right questions to get to the root of a problem.

The results of this study reveal an underlying uneasiness with business capability in problem solving and decision making. If the respondents reflect the views of their peers, our business organizations are, at best, adequate in these most fundamental of skills. From an organizational perspective, have we been dealing with fads and essentially ignoring the core business skills? Is it possible that while we've been painting the house, the basement has been flooding?

Sinners Can Repent. . . .

Even those who are unwilling to accept the notion that we have achieved a plateau of mediocrity in these crucial areas would be hard-pressed to argue against the benefits of improving decision-making and problem-solving skills. A few good or bad decisions can make or break a career—and a business. The benefits of a good decision can be enormous. For example, William Hewlett and David Packard's bold decision to move beyond Hewlett-Packard's niche in test equipment and into the computer industry signaled the beginning of one of America's great success stories of the past twenty-five years. Honda's Tadashi Kume gambled that Americans would believe that Hondas made in America would possess the same quality as those made in Japan. He built a plant in Marysville, Ohio, and then proceeded to ensure that such quality became reality. Honda's success prompted a surge in Japanese manufacturing in the United States.

Conversely, a deterioration in these foundation proficiencies, however slight, can result in business blunders with disastrous personal consequences. Steve Jobs's choice of John Scully as CEO at Apple ultimately led to his forced departure from the company he founded. Strategic differences with his chairman aside, Ernest Mario's decision to take an aggressive posture with the U.S. Food and Drug Administration allegedly doomed him as CEO at Glaxo. In short, the status of an organization's competence in the problem-solving and decision-making processes is or should be a critical issue for today's management, if for no other reason than that the margin required for breathtaking victory or ignominious defeat is often so very narrow.

Vision or Hallucination?

For every doomed decision maker, there seems to be, at least in today's business lore, a "management mystic"—a business leader who through nearly divine inspiration intuits a trend that is beyond the grasp of more mortal business intellects. This trend is then converted into a business, almost instantaneously creating markets that heretofore didn't exist. Was Bill Gates really Gandalf in the *Lord of the Rings*? Or was it the other way around?

This vision, or perhaps hallucination, is so real in the American business psyche that a cottage industry has emerged to create new seers of the future. Ivy League business schools are pitching techniques to "catch the new wave," which conjures up the terrifying notion of platinum-haired business executives in Speedos saying, "Hey, man, that's a really cool new product concept!" Business writers urge management to break "genetic codes" and cultural barriers that restrict creative thought so that they can develop the next breathtaking business idea. This will allow them to create a new market in which they are the leader or even sole provider. What management needs, so says this school of thought, is more creativity, a few more epiphanies, and, perhaps, a better AAA map of the road to Damascus.

We have a few problems with this line of thought. We certainly don't disagree with the importance of creativity and the need for some discipline in spotting potential opportunities, largely because we've devoted two later chapters to those topics. We are, however, uncomfortable with the notion that breakthrough business concepts occur in a flash of inspiration, thus making the quest for that flash a major goal of enlightened leadership. In fact, the lightning of business inspiration is going off all the time in today's business climate and probably always has.

Even a cursory examination of breakthrough business ideas reveals that these ideas were rarely novel by the time they achieved prominence. Hewlett-Packard's RISC technology began at IBM and "migrated" to Hewlett-Packard because IBM wasn't terribly interested. Ray Krok didn't invent fast food, he simply recognized the potential in the concept developed by the McDonald brothers. In reviewing a book by Gerard Tellis and Peter Golder, *The Economist* in March of 1996 noted, "Real success goes to 'early leaders'—firms that entered the market an average of 13 years after the pioneers and now have a market share three times the size of the pioneers.'"[7]

The problem in these and dozens of other cases was not the absence of a breakthrough idea, but a conscious decision by well-intentioned business executives not to "catch the wave." All the foresight being touted by management thinkers is literally valueless if bad decision making leads an organization's leadership to squander its opportunities.

From the Primal to the Proficient Manager

There is little doubt that the mental processes for making decisions and solving problems described by Kepner and Tregoe and many others—Kaoru Ishikawa's theoretical work, for instance, Genichi Taguchi on problem solving, and Amos Tversky on decision science—are both well understood and valid. There is abundant evidence of the universality of these processes and their applicability to organizational issues. The ultimate question, then, is, given *today's* business environment, how effectively have companies been able to implement these concepts throughout

[7] "Why First May Not Last," *Economist*, 16 March 1996, p. 65.

their organizations? Certainly many have failed to do so, with unfortunate consequences, while others have adopted and are using them with great success in making complex decisions and resolving difficult problems.

Like many of the essential attributes of business, problem solving and decision making have, we suspect, become frozen on what we call the Learning Ladder. This ladder (see next page) describes the conceptual evolution experienced by nearly all great management theories.

The climb up the ladder from knowledge of a concept to its proficient application is a step-by-step process. The complaint most often heard against softer concepts of management is that they seldom rise above the level of understanding. Even those that advance to the skill level only rarely go beyond that. And once an organization reaches the capability level, there is often a lowering of urgency. "We've proven to ourselves that we can do it." That is why great concepts like Total Quality Control produce an initial response but are often not sustained. If the concept does reach the competence level, as the ladder illustrates, that doesn't ensure excellence. Most of the members of a losing squad are competent football players, but is competency enough? In any athletic endeavor, skills can be competently demonstrated in practice and in some game situations, but it is their proficient and consistent application that makes the difference between winning and losing throughout a season.

How often do organizations achieve across-the-board proficiency? Indeed, is this even an imperative for most businesses? Probably not. Achieving competence itself is such a grueling struggle that it is difficult to sustain momentum on the ladder to proficiency. Yet in problem solving and decision making, proficiency may very well be the primary determinant of business success.

Unfortunately, few businesses can stake a claim to being proficient at making decisions and solving problems. The explanation for this difficulty lies in the way these foundation processes are used—and the circumstances in which they are used. Both have changed dramatically, reshaping how they are practiced by our best decision makers and problem solvers to build a solid organi-

The Learning Ladder

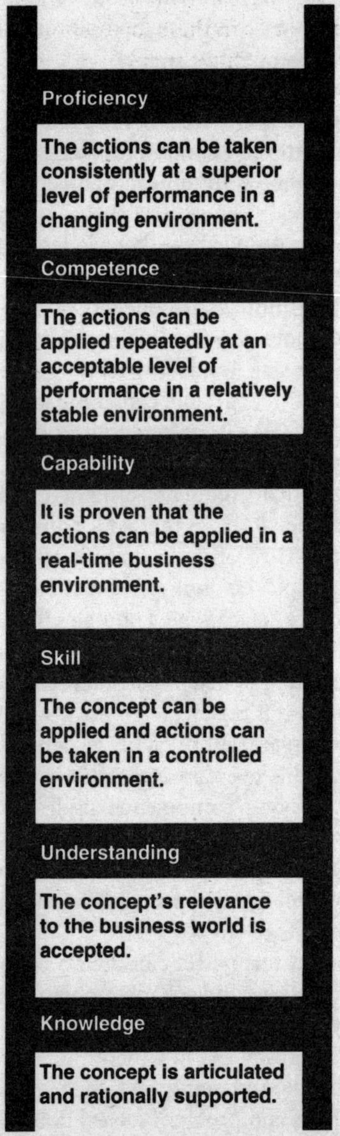
Proficiency
The actions can be taken consistently at a superior level of performance in a changing environment.
Competence
The actions can be applied repeatedly at an acceptable level of performance in a relatively stable environment.
Capability
It is proven that the actions can be applied in a real-time business environment.
Skill
The concept can be applied and actions can be taken in a controlled environment.
Understanding
The concept's relevance to the business world is accepted.
Knowledge
The concept is articulated and rationally supported.

zational capability. Some of the best business leaders and their organizations are already responding to these changes. They are constructing proficiencies in these foundation processes that will provide a powerful competitive strength in the marketplace. The good news for the businesses that aren't there yet is that the map their proficient counterparts have been following is not a secret. It's a map worth examining because it contains the clues to better decisions and fewer problems.

Poor decisions and unsolved problems will always find their way into an organization. But there are tools available that you—or your organization—can use to improve the odds that you will not make one of the business world's biggest blunders. Knowledge of what those tools are is the first step. In the words of the Indian mystic, "Sinners can repent, but stupid is forever."

CHAPTER 2

Situation Appraisal—Clearing the Path

You've got to break down complex issues into more manageable chunks and then set priorities. This is an interactive process with all the people in your organization: those who report to you and those to whom you report.

George B. Cobbe
Vice President,
Hewlett-Packard Company

On any given day, a stroll through Honda headquarters in Tokyo, Japan, would reveal team after team of people meeting in rooms papered with easel sheets. Blue-suited, white-shirted Honda employees are engaged in discussions with such fervor and diligence that surely suggest some moment of truth is about to arrive. The Western observer, hampered by a lack of knowledge of Japanese ideographs, is likely to conclude that critical decisions are being made and important problems solved.

A closer look, aided by a competent translator, proves that the Western observer's assumptions are wrong. The purpose of the meetings is to discuss the broad issues facing Honda in the terrifyingly competitive global automotive market. The meetings will end without conclusions. There will be no list of action items to be typed, distributed, and forgotten. The will be no set of final recommendations from these Honda teams. None of the Honda engineers who constitute the teams will feel the need for an "answer" from the meetings. Most amazingly, they will probably be back at the discussion the next day and won't reach a conclusion then, either.

What's happening here? How does this fit with notions of the legendary productivity of the Japanese? Are they merely slower and more methodical? Or is this scene simply an aberration, the by-product of bad sushi or too much sake the night before?

The reality is that these meetings, often called Nimawashi sessions, are an essential aspect of how Japanese and many other Asian businesses frame complex business issues. The desire to achieve a result, make a decision, form a conclusion, or get to the bottom line so prevalent in Western business practice is subordinated in Japan to the desire to first fully understand the context or the situation within which decisions must be made or problems must be solved. To Westerners the Nimawashi sessions appear tedious, frivolous, and often pointless. But to the Japanese they are the critical foundation for assuring thoughtful, well-implemented action. We call the process used in these discussions "Situation Appraisal."

Sushi or Steak?

The methodology of the Situation Appraisal process—described in detail in the Appendix of this book—is astonishingly obvious, simple, and easy to apply. The environmental shifts that have made other skills like problem solving and decision making so difficult to apply have not plagued a methodology that seeks to appraise rather than analyze. The only problem with Situation Appraisal that we've discovered is that it is hardly used at all.

For example, in our Yankelovich survey we asked executives to rate their organization's ability to identify critical issues in complex situations—a key feature of Situation Appraisal. Forty-nine percent of the executives rated their organizations a "3" or less, with "6" being "Excellent." The reason for this, we suspect, has to do with a lack of understanding of the core process and an even more profound lack of understanding of its value.

The bases for Situation Appraisal are perhaps more philosophical than other critical thinking processes that derive from empirical roots. In fact, the Situation Appraisal process has much of its grounding in Oriental philosophy. In essence, it is a discussion based on a series of six fundamental questions.

1. Why are we doing what we are doing?
2. What are the threats and opportunities that exist in the environment in which we work?
3. How do these issues relate to each other?
4. How can we make these issues simpler to understand and address?
5. Where should we direct our focus?
6. What should we do now?

These questions quickly bring to mind the fundamental tenets of Buddhism, Taoism, and Sufism: the importance of questioning, the need to ask why, the focus on understanding the whole before discussing the parts, the beauty of simplicity, and the balancing of threat and opportunity. They also suggest, in the Western mind, the potential for endless dialogue without any real sense of movement. This contrast in views is more substantive than simply the fear of the excess time required for broad questioning. Western views and Eastern views conflict in several key respects.

Eastern Thinking	Western Thinking
Focus on Questions	Focus on Answers
Issue Is Why?	Issue Is How?
Understanding Is Key Requirement	Being Right Is Key Requirement
Contextual View	Process View
Holistic Perspective	Linear Perspective
Bias for Analysis	Bias for Action
Need for Clarity	Need for Measurement

As with any such comparison, few thinkers fit either mold precisely, nor do the Eastern and Western styles typify all thinkers in those cultures. Neither list of philosophical biases is better or worse than the other. What is important, however, is that these thinking styles pervade the cultures in which they are most evident. They are in evidence not only in the societal norms of the culture, but in the way in which business is conducted.

This dialectic tension between Eastern and Western philosophies of thought often leads to the dismay reflected in the Honda example—dismay that is by no means limited to Western observers. For their part, Eastern businesspeople are puzzled, if not amused, by the ubiquitous lists of action items so visible in Western business meetings. But not surprisingly, there is much to embrace from both thinking styles. The Western penchant for action and movement can energize a business and allows for rapid response to new opportunities. The focus on answers gives real value to the acquisition of expertise. Its pragmatism generates ideas that are easily understood by others.

In contrast, the Eastern approach, by providing decision makers with an opportunity to explore the broad context of situation, spawns greater innovation and brings about a better understanding of the system relationships implicit in every issue. When actions are eventually taken, broad, unpressured involvement encourages teamwork and, in most instances, solidifies commitment.

What Situation Appraisal seeks to do is provide a bridge between these philosophical positions with a "Western-style" process grounded in Eastern philosophy. Situation Appraisal uses three simple steps to produce a synthesis of both of these thinking skills and their benefits.

1. Getting the lay of the land
2. Changing the frame of reference
3. Balancing action and contemplation

Getting the Lay of the Land

Paradoxically, the process of Situation Appraisal, despite its perceived slowness, is essential to real movement in any business environment. It's much like the advice given to outdoorsmen: "Before you make your camp, you'd better get the lay of the land"—an admonition that has saved many campers from involuntary river rafting after a hard rain. Getting the "lay of the land" in business terms means spending the time to investigate the entire array of issues facing the business, the "issue landscape" of the business in which a problem must be solved or a decision made.

Because nearly all issues in a given business relate one to another, they cannot be compartmentalized. As George Cobbe, vice president of Hewlett-Packard, puts it, "I've got eight or nine businesses to deal with in parallel with each other. And I can't stop dealing with the other seven businesses to address the issues of the eighth. I've got to worry about those in parallel with each other." Because of the "parallel processing" phenomenon Cobbe describes, it is impossible to deal effectively with single issues without understanding the whole array of issues that relate to them.

Another reason for creating this "issue landscape" is the need to put the issues into perspective. For example, a line failure in a manufacturing business may delay product shipments and cost some downtime, a significant but manageable event in the life of an automotive supplier. However, when the ripple effect of delayed shipments causes Ford to halt production for even a short period, its suppliers may find they've lost one of their biggest customers. They may also find that their reputation has been damaged to such an extent that this supposedly manageable line failure is, in reality, life threatening. In other words, it is nearly impossible to know the importance of any issue without understanding its relationship to the other issues confronting the business or the business environment. Joseph Keilty, executive vice president of American Express, says of businesspeople today, "The skill set they are missing is the ability to 'disaggregate.' They can't take a set of complex bits of information and disaggregate them into any higher or lower hierarchy of importance. So they treat them all the same, which paralyzes decision making." Situation Appraisal provides the tools to disaggregate effectively.

Without Situation Appraisal, we have discovered that team members often work on different issues without realizing it. A giant consumer products company recently experienced problems in the plastic it used to manufacture disposable diapers. Bubbles were developing in between the laminated plastic sheets, and, after wearing these diapers, babies around the world were left with bottoms that looked like the surface of a golf ball. A team was assembled to deal with the problem, and its members worked unproductively for hours until it was discovered they were actually working on three separate issues without knowing it. Three members thought they were there to find the cause of the bubbling; four members were certain they were there to identify alternative suppliers; and two members thought they were there to find the name of somebody in procurement to blame. Each of these issues may have been worth pursuing, but, without knowing there were three or more issues to consider, they found themselves moving in many different directions. Situation Appraisal would have prevented that. All of the issues related to the problem could have been considered and then, in the words of Keilty, "disaggregated" and thus better understood. A feel for the lay of the issue landscape always allows for well-informed reasoning about the relative importance of the threats and opportunities confronting a business.

At a typical meeting in a conference room at Johnson & Johnson, members of a business unit create lists of issues without discussing all the details. The issues may be a manufacturing improvement opportunity in a Puerto Rico plant, the need to accelerate the development and approval of package inserts for a new therapeutic compound, the finalization of a cross-marketing agreement with another pharmaceutical company, and a financial reforecast given stronger than expected sales for another new drug. What the participants in this meeting now realize is that these issues relate to each other and that there is an order in which they will need to be addressed. Whereas in the past the financial forecast would have been the lead action item, the chief financial officer of this business unit proposes to put it last after the other issues are resolved and their financial implications are determined. They now understand the real priority of these issues because they "disaggregated" them. The Johnson & Johnson people are getting "the lay of the land," and Situation Appraisal is their method for doing it.

Changing the Frame of Reference

According to C. K. Prahalad, "All managers have grown up with a certain process of socialization. There is what I call 'received wisdom' in most companies." While the socialization and received wisdom Prahalad refers to come in part from the culture of the company, they also stem in large measure from the broader context of Eastern or Western cultures. The socialization arising from this cultural orientation is particularly powerful because it pervades both business and social environments.

Such socialization leads, inevitably, to the development of what Prahalad and others have identified as a management "comfort zone," where thinking becomes habituated. Honda's Nimawashi sessions are just as much habit as the action items that paper the conference rooms at Dow Chemical. Prahalad suggests that to ensure future success it is vital for managers to move from this "zone of comfort" into a "zone of opportunity." How is this done? As Prahalad explains, "I think it's easy to articulate, difficult to implement, as every good thing is. I think the first requirement is to break existing frames of reference."

Breaking frames of reference has long been viewed as therapeutic for business in both Eastern and Western culture. Iconoclasm is regarded as critical to stimulating creativity and innovation, and as essential if executives are to avoid stumbling into business traps out of force of habit. Yet, as Prahalad suggests, it's not easy to do. But what Situation Appraisal offers is a way to shift cultural perspective for Western and Eastern businesspeople alike—a key ingredient in acquiring a new frame of reference. Western leaders, when forced to outline the myriad threats and opportunities on the business horizon, find themselves taking a panoramic view that is probably uncomfortably new yet refreshing. Prahalad comments, "Top managers are somewhat distant from the reality of the new things that are happening. For example, I find it interesting to see how few top managers can have a thirty-minute discussion of the implications of the Internet, or virtual reality, or the effects of the young generation growing up on Nintendo. There is a certain amount of intellectual and emotional distance that top managers have from the emerging realities, and, therefore, it is hard for them to relate to what is going on." Situation Appraisal provides the venue for such discussions as well as the opportunity for executives to emotionally and intellectually engage issues that might not arrive in the center of their desks daily.

Sir Colin Marshall of British Airways provides an illustration of the ability to shift perspectives by recounting how his company responded to the Gulf War crisis in 1991. During and after the war, airlines around the world were faced with plunging passenger counts, given anticipated terrorist responses to events in the Middle East. It was easy for any airline to become trapped in the morass of threats and related contingency planning. Even after the end of the war, it was a well-learned behavior, or "habit," in Prahalad's terms, to spend days assessing the financial damage and developing measures to cut more costs to recover profitability.

British Airways took a different route. It looked at the array of issues and broke out of the "comfort zone" by forcing key executives to examine opportunities at a time of real disaster for the industry. The result was the legendary marketing campaign, "The World's Biggest Offer"—essentially a giveaway of airline seats—that catapulted British Airways back to a revenue and profit position even stronger than the one it had enjoyed before the war. This ability to "change the frame of reference" is a hallmark of great companies. It is a difficult task, as Prahalad correctly notes, but using Situation Appraisal makes it easier to shift perspectives, even in difficult times.

Balancing Action and Contemplation

Cadbury's maxim, "Ready, fire, aim," made legendary in Peters and Waterman's *In Search of Excellence,* accurately reflects an enduring bias in Western business toward action. One executive at pharmaceutical giant E. R. Squibb took this view to the extreme and was known for taking morning walks to see who was receiving *The Wall Street Journal,* on the theory that employees who were reading the paper were not "getting things done."

While this penchant for action pervades the business ethos, we are simultaneously counseled by Peter Senge and others to think and learn, explore and inquire. The only irreproducible corporate asset is the intellectual capability of the workforce, and we must ensure that our organizations allow for its growth. In Eastern businesses the need for everyone to participate in the discussion of issues affecting them is well documented. We recall that in one services firm, the corporate offices in the United States asked its division in Japan for approval of a corporate brochure in 1988. Corporate continued to wait for the results of their colleagues' deliberation throughout 1994. The delay apparently was due to the addition of new members in Japan who also needed to deliberate. Finally, with the realization that it might be 2001 before they heard from their Japanese colleagues, corporate determined to proceed without Japanese approval.

Are these two management styles reconcilable? That is a fair question, and more than a few puzzled businesspeople are trying to answer it because both styles have great merit. We believe the trick is not to choose one or the other as an operating business philosophy, but to achieve a manageable balance.

To achieve such a balance, the first necessity is to restrain the natural impulse of some managers to leap into action before all of the issues are on the table. One executive in a large European company fired a subordinate manager for what he thought was a major loss in a derivatives play. When the smoke had cleared from the incident some two weeks later, the executive discovered that the derivatives play had actually netted a handsome profit. He sheepishly rehired his subordinate with suitable apologies and a nice commendation for his contribution to profits. But the story does not end here. Three weeks after the rehiring, the company's auditors confirmed that while the derivatives play was profitable, the manager had made it without authority, thereby putting the company in a position of substantial financial risk. By this point a second termination was virtually impossible.

What Situation Appraisal would have required is a suspension of action and a simple listing of issues without discussion. Since discussion is suspended, the process of laying out the issues is usually quick enough for even the most impatient executive. In the case of our derivatives trader, the decision probably would have been the same—termination. But by putting all the issues clearly on the table, the termination decision would have been made for entirely different reasons and without all the yo-yoing. Instead the company retained an employee it could not trust because of managerial incompetence.

Once the issues have been arrayed, clarified, and put into order of priority, the next challenge is to avoid having them fall into the hands of a task force. Someone once defined a task force as a group of the unwilling brought together by the unknowing to do the unnecessary. Once the issues are consigned to a task force, the potential for endless dialogue and total paralysis is limitless.

Situation Appraisal subjects the most important issues to a "plan for resolution." While action itself may not be taken, commitment to a specific plan to determine those actions is developed. The meeting room at Procter & Gamble may still be covered with easel sheets, but more is going on than just repapering the walls. One executive may leave the meeting with the responsibility to provide, under a defined timeline, a revised production plan to capitalize on a new opportunity, while another executive commits to recharting process flows between two sister plants at the same site. Throughout the process of identifying issues and resolving them, Procter & Gamble found the time for contemplation without abandoning all hope of action.

Try It, You'll Like It

For centuries mothers and fathers around the world have fought with children on the battlefield of dietary habits. The child stubbornly refuses to eat what is offered, forcing the parent to charge into battle with the timeless refrain, "Try it, you'll like it." History is silent on the results of these battles, though we suspect that the fields are littered with vanquished mothers and fathers. What parents fail to recognize is that there is often a significant difference between what we like and what is good for us. As good as green vegetables are for kids, they probably won't like them when they try them. The same can be said in many organizations for Situation Appraisal.

The blend of questions and answers, context and conclusion, analysis and action, threat and opportunity, that makes up Situation Appraisal is clearly beneficial. Yet the discipline of this tool, as with most disciplines, can make those using it feel uncomfortable, particularly when it doesn't yield immediate, breathtaking results. Nonetheless, as the organization matures, just as when the child matures, its capacity for discipline increases. When this increase in capacity for discipline is supported by Situation Appraisal, organizations are better positioned to balance action and thought, doing things right and doing the right things. Parenthetically, Japanese executives in the services firm we mentioned used Situation Appraisal and approved their version of the new corporate brochure within a matter of days. This stuff really does work!

CHAPTER 3

Problem Solving—The Eternal Search for "Why"

One of the reasons problem solving is so difficult today is that historical information is often not available. More assumptions must be made, and these must be rigorously tested through sharp questioning.

SIR COLIN MARSHALL
Chairman,
British Airways Plc.

There is some reason to believe that problem solving may be the most seminal of critical thinking skills. Children, shortly after they learn to talk, start to ask the question that begins the problem-solving process: Why?

"Don't stick your finger into the light socket," cautions the parent.
"Why?" the child asks.
"Because it's dangerous," responds the parent.
"Why?" presses the child.
"Because you could get electrocuted."
"Why?"

The questions continue until the parent realizes he or she is incapable of explaining to the child the relationship between electrophysiology and cardiac arrhythmia. Ultimately the final, definitive answer is offered to the unrelenting child: "Because I said so!"

The child, now flush with success in frazzling and frustrating its parent, realizes that there is something pretty powerful in this question "Why?"

As children grow into adulthood and ultimately enter the job market, the "why" question becomes something more important than an easy way to befuddle parents. The answer to why a project has gone wrong, why a machine doesn't work, or why a proposal has failed is often pivotal to the productivity and success of both the employee and the business. But even in the time it has taken to move that child from Pampers to designer briefs, the nature of problems and the problem-solving process has grown extraordinarily complex.

In Search of Problems Past. . . .

The search for the cause of things gone wrong has, in fact, a history of its own. For decades problem solving has been typified by several enduring features.

1. Problems were about things.

Searching for the cause of problems has traditionally been associated with "things." In their seminal work on the subject,[1] Kepner and Tregoe even suggested that problems be stated as "objects with defects." Problems were essentially defective matcrial, nonperforming or poorly performing machines, broken or failed equipment, and malfunctioning components. The mechanic who had an ability to peer under a car's hood to locate a bad alternator or leaking water pump was the archetypal problem solver.

[1] Charles H. Kepner and Benjamin B. Tregoe, *The New Rational Manager* (Princeton, N.J.: Princeton Research Press, 1981).

2. THE SOLUTION INVOLVED THE REMEMBRANCE OF THINGS PAST.

Problem analysis was fundamentally about change. Everything was fine; machinery and equipment were working. Suddenly—or, more typically, over a period of time—they began to fail, constantly or intermittently, totally or partially. Clearly something had changed from the idyllic days of peak performance. The key to problem solving, therefore, was an examination of the past to discover the change that produced the failure. The electric typewriter is working perfectly and then suddenly shuts off without warning. Could this be related to the power outage last week when the company's maintenance staff pruned two oaks, a rosebush, and a high-voltage line? Gathering historical problem information was relatively easy, as the equipment, component, or part had probably been in use for ten to twenty years. It was even likely that the organization had a person or two who had worked with the object over most of that period.

3. THERE WASN'T ALL THAT MUCH TO REMEMBER.

While every business kept log entries, productivity charts, and statistics, there were still relatively few data points. Often the most critical historical information was lodged in the head of the employees who had maintained the facility and its equipment over the last few years. Thus a big challenge in effective problem solving was the gathering of good data. Often the major roadblock to finding the cause of a failure was the absence of critical information. A major chemical company once had to wait several weeks to solve a serious quality problem because it couldn't get certain supplier specification conformance data.

4. YOU COULD ALWAYS PUT A BAND-AID ON IT.

Certainly no business can afford to let a serious problem fester unresolved. While many problems can be easily solved, there are always those that seem intractable. Rather than let this type of problem cripple ongoing operations, most businesses became adept at interim actions, which allowed them to circumvent, patch, or temporarily mitigate the problem. When time and data became available, the managers could then address the task of finding the root cause and installing a permanent solution. Some companies became so good at such actions that entire plants were jury-rigged. One large plant making automotive components was described by a company executive as an "incomprehensible maze resulting from years of 'Band-Aid-ing' problems."

These four features—problems as objects, the historical nature of data, the relative paucity of good data, and a tendency toward interim action—enabled many problem solvers to approach their dilemmas like industrial archaeologists, slowly and deliberately gathering and sifting historical data to find the hidden treasure of a solution. For most of this century the majority of the problem situations encountered in the business world reflected these four factors. Over the last twenty years, however, while the essential precepts of problem solving have remained constant, the nature of the business world—and thus the nature of problems—has changed profoundly.

If It Ain't Broke, Don't Break It
('Cause We Probably Can't Fix It)

No one needs to be reminded of the impact that information technology has had on the business world. What may have been overlooked, however, is the impact of information technology on how we go about solving problems. While there remain, undoubtedly, problems that lend themselves to a deliberate search of a limited set of historical factors in pursuit of root cause, such problems are proving the exception where they once were the norm. Problem solving today is a totally different animal. Consider the following six factors:

1. "Things" are now part of complex systems.

A brief walk through nearly any factory in a developed economy makes it clear that equipment, machinery, components, and material can no longer be examined in isolation. Everything is linked inextricably with everything else. Equipment, machinery, and materials are all part of a more sophisticated production system. Terms such as "MRP II" and "JIT" reflect a design in which computer technology, employees, the production facility, the equipment, and the material are all part of a new manufacturing pastiche. Gone are the days when problem solvers examined the poor performance of a lonely die press and found a misalignment.

Today, poor performance is more likely to be caused by a system software glitch than a mechanical defect. In fact, the emergence of a large service economy means many problems have nothing to do with machinery, manufacturing, or plant production. They are problems with claims processing, computerized scheduling, automated invoicing, and the like. Even the auto mechanic of today is more likely, in his white lab coat, to resemble a neurosurgeon, as a trip to any Lexus or BMW dealership will attest. Why? Faulty computer systems produce considerably less grease and oil than leaking head-cover gaskets.

2. DON'T KNOW NOTHIN' 'BOUT HISTORY—OR HIGH-TECH EQUIPMENT.

The demise of an old pump in a Philadelphia area chemical plant was an event that produced absolutely zero alarm. As with all old equipment, the pump's failure was easily accepted for three reasons. First, it had been amortized shortly after Harry Truman left office. Second, after a period of time old things are expected to break because nothing lasts forever. Finally, and most important, it had been fixed twenty-eight times before by a mechanic who had worked on it for the last twenty years. Consequently there was a relatively high likelihood it could be fixed again. Such equipment, however, is less and less in evidence in modern manufacturing. More likely it is two years old with few past failures. It is probably tailored for a specific use in that facility so there is no other exact replica elsewhere. Even the operation it performs may not have been in the production process thirty-six months ago. What this means is that when the equipment of today fails, panic sets in! It hasn't been amortized, it's not supposed to fail, and we have no idea how to troubleshoot it. In this increasingly common instance, problem solving doesn't look to history or other properly operating processes or machines, because there simply aren't any. Instead, using manufacturer-provided schematics and perhaps some computer diagnostics, the maintenance engineers try feverishly to solve a problem they've never or rarely seen before.

3. You gather the data, while I go get some more data.

The Western fascination with total quality control of the 1980s undoubtedly did much to produce better products. It also contributed to the deforestation of North America. The mantra of the quality movement was "data." Phrases like "If you can't measure it, you can't control it" sent thousands of Western managers to their computers to develop databases for any and all aspects of their business. The resulting reports, charts, and graphs were so voluminous that the plant manager of a giant high-tech firm in Washington State claimed its plant relocation was necessitated by a lack of storage space for TQC reports. Of course, the dramatic increase in data collection in business during the 1980s was not solely the result of the total quality movement. Equally important was the simple fact that information technology made it so much easier to compile, store, and report data. Sophisticated programs, databases, and spreadsheets, coupled with computer storage capability previously not dreamed of, created a technical incentive to accumulate data.

The effect of this data on problem solvers is significant. No longer is the challenge to seek out missing information from relatively limited data sets. Now the problem solver is awash in data on any problem issue, and the challenge is to find the relatively small portion that can be converted into useful problem-solving information. In the late 1980s Martin Marietta launched a rocket from Vandenberg Air Force Base carrying a state-of-the-art satellite. Shortly after launch, however, a major failure required the launch team to abort the mission and destroy the rocket. The result: A $400 million satellite performed a two-and-a-half-gainer into the Pacific Ocean. For Martin Marietta, one of the world's finest aerospace companies, this constituted an extremely bad day. A bad day turned into a bad month when company engineers, personnel rarely equaled in problem-solving ability, recognized that there were over four million anomalous events during the launch and brief flight—with reams of data available for nearly every one! Problem solving for them was, indeed, a very different type of challenge.

4. JUST DO IT. BUT DO IT RIGHT NOW.

If there was ever any patience in the problem-solving process, it had finally disappeared by the late 1980s. New systems, increasingly sophisticated equipment, and the pressures of time all combined to create a sense of urgency heretofore unknown. Interim actions became less commonplace because problem solvers hadn't enough experience with new systems and equipment to know how to jury-rig them—even assuming that was possible. The cost of problems escalated as a failure in one part often shut down an entire system. These costs are so high, in fact, that the organization demands and rewards immediate action. In response to this high degree of urgency, the standard procedure for computer support engineers in nearly all companies when a problem occurs has become "swapping the board," or a wholesale replacement of major product components, rather than searching for root cause.

The bias for immediate action is so great that thought before action is sometimes overtly discouraged. While working with a client who was experiencing very costly equipment failures, we were consulting with the team responsible for one production system, trying to help them use a common problem-solving process to find the cause of yet another breakdown. As we were huddled around an easel, wrestling with a critical piece of information, the manager burst into the room and said, "It's down again. What are all you people doing sitting around? Get out there and fix it." In fact, when we analyzed why problem solving was not better in this company, we found that the pressure to act immediately upon the occurrence of a problem was the largest single factor.

5. Problem? What problem?

By definition, a problem occurs when performance deviates from a norm or what is expected. When expectations are built over a period of years, discerning problems is a relatively easy task. When the parts are produced five millimeters off spec, it doesn't require the shrewdness of Sherlock Holmes to know that there's a problem. When expectations change, however, particularly when they change quickly and dramatically, it becomes difficult to be sure what is a problem and what is not. In the 1970s it was possible to finish the first three chapters of *War and Peace* while your IBM XT was booting. Years later your Zenith laptop was booting nearly instantly. Today, your Compaq notebook takes longer to boot because you have installed enough applications on the hard drive to manage the affairs of a small third-world country. What constitutes acceptable performance if expectations change constantly and quickly? Without clear, stable expectations, a deviation from those expectations is tough to detect. And without a deviation, where's the problem?

In the case of the computer, most of us would say we don't really care. But how about an issue such as customer satisfaction? Continuous improvement dictates that if we achieve 96 percent today, we should shoot for 97 percent tomorrow. Does that mean that 96 percent becomes a problem the next day? What if we take into account the fact that two years ago we probably didn't measure customer satisfaction at all, or at least in this way? Is 96 percent still a problem? In other words, solving problems is hard enough, yet today it's possible that we're not sure what a problem really is!

6. Can't anybody here fix this thing?

Even if we assume that the entire world of problem solving has remained the same, the problem solvers—the industrial detectives charged with finding the cause of deviations and fixing those problems—have changed in a very fundamental way. They're no longer on the job!

During the early 1990s hundreds of thousands of employees

left their companies. In some cases they had no choice. In others they left because they were offered lucrative packages to retire early as part of a gentler downsizing. At one point in 1993, *Inc.* magazine reported that the rate of forced departures had reached over one thousand per day! No one would suggest that the people who left in the great attrition of the 1990s were the best problem solvers in their business. It would, however, be equally erroneous not to suggest that at least some of them were, in fact, people who had spent the major part of their careers solving their organizations' problems. Noted one IBM executive with major geographical and business group responsibility, "Voluntary retirement is an attractive option only to those near retirement or those who can easily locate another job. In IBM, we've seen that those who could easily locate another job and left were often, in fact, our sharpest employees." One of our clients in the steel industry extended this argument. The company offered early retirement at one of its plants, a continuous flow operation in which a malfunction in the blast furnace could close the plant, fast. Said the group's vice president of operations, "When we offered early retirement . . . we were shocked to learn that one of the people accepting it was the man who had maintained the blast furnace. If there's a problem there now, God only knows how we'll solve it!" Across the board, the brain drain of the past decade means that while problem solving is getting more complex and difficult, the best and most experienced problem solvers are all too frequently walking out the front door forever.

Solving the Problem of Problem Solving

The apparent erosion of problem-solving capability is less a cause for despair than a call to reexamine the essence of one of business's "foundation skills." Today's best executives are already in the process of this reexamination. Chrysler's president, Robert Lutz, tells the story of a problem his company once had with the Jeep Cherokee. He was visiting Chrysler's Toledo plant when he learned that the padded sun visors on the Cherokees were bursting open at the seam after delivery.

"What are we going to do?" he asked product engineers.

"Well, we're reengineering the whole sun visor," he was told. "We're going to a different design with an entirely different seam."

Lutz then asked, "How long have we been building the Cherokee?"

"Since 1984," came the reply.

"And it's been the same design ever since?"

"Yes."

"When did they start bursting open?"

"The first reports were about three months ago, but now it's an epidemic, and the way to solve the problem is to go to an entirely new design."

"Have we asked ourselves why it worked for nine years and six months, and now they've suddenly started popping open?"

"We don't know, but the fix is to go to an entirely new design."

"How long is that going to take?" Lutz asked.

"A month or two for the design, then we've got to test it. Then the supplier will have to tool up for the new design."

"So, for the foreseeable future we'll still be making sun visors that pop open?"

"Well, yes, but that's—"

"Okay, let me try again. Have we ever asked ourselves why they worked for nine and a half years and then suddenly stopped working?"

"Well, no, we haven't asked ourselves that."

"Why don't you check with the supplier and find out if there's been any change in the process or the plastic material that's being used?"

The engineers did just that, and they found out it was a simple case of tool wear. The supplier replaced the tool and the problem was solved. Said Lutz, "It was a problem that could be solved in days rather than months." But the experience did not leave him a happy camper. "[The] absence of rudimentary problem-solving capability on the part of otherwise good and well-trained engineers was just profoundly disturbing," he said.

Lutz believed that Chrysler's quality problem at the Toledo plant was not due to a lack of will or willingness to spend money. "It was a lack of speed in problem identification and resolution," he said, and concluded that "until we had a core competency in problem solving, we were not going to make progress in improving Chrysler's quality performance." He and Chairman Robert Eaton then committed to move ahead rapidly to make changes.

How does a world-class company like Chrysler make good on that type of commitment? The answer is to approach the analysis of problems with some critical modifications in the traditional approaches. To make a foundation skill like problem solving a core competency or key capability in an organization requires more than a rededication to the task. It requires a virtual redeployment of the problem-solving skills and processes throughout the organization. This type of effort can be characterized by a series of "new rules" for problem solving that, in effect, lay out the guidelines for success.

Three New Rules for Effective Problem Solving

RULE 1. THE INITIAL OBJECTIVE OF PROBLEM SOLVING IS NOT TO SOLVE THE PROBLEM, BUT TO KEEP FROM DOING SOMETHING STUPID.

The urgency in problem solving today leads to a keen desire for quick, often erroneous fixes. Such was the case in Surat, India, when in 1994 several suspicious deaths led many to conclude that this heavily populated city was experiencing an outbreak of pneumonic plague. Fearing an epidemic, over five hundred thousand people fled from Surat and the surrounding area. Planes from India were refused entrance in many countries, and intensive immigration health screening was required in others. Pakistani citizens traveling in the area weren't even allowed to return to their own country. The public waited anxiously for a week until it appeared the crisis had passed.

Slowly the population of Surat returned and life regained as much semblance of normalcy as possible after such a massive disruption. The cost was in excess of $1 billion for India alone. The cost in human misery and dislocation was incalculable. And all of this would have been simply another footnote in the long tale of global health crises had it not been for several articles in the respected British medical journal *Lancet.* A team of independent physicians investigating the reported cases of plague found that the cases they observed were not, in fact, plague, but pneumonia. No one has proven conclusively that there was an occurrence, or even the threat of occurrence, of plague.[2]

In an increasingly pressure-packed world, there is little time to find the "true cause" of many problems. Yet as the episode at Surat illustrates, acting on the wrong cause can often have more devastating results than the problem itself. In our consulting we have labeled this the "red herring effect," and it afflicts organizations everywhere.

Problem solving must have as its first objective the quick elimination of possible causes, rather than the discovery of *the* cause. This objective would seem to be counterintuitive, suggesting that the initial reaction to "root out the source of this evil" is often a very dangerous response. Yet in practice this approach may be the one factor that makes the difference between a problem solved and an evil of even greater proportions. Isaiah Owens, manager of manufacturing logistics with the Pepsi-Cola Company, put it best: "Sending the troops out to fix the problem is a recipe for disaster. I tell my people to quickly rule out what didn't cause the problem so we don't start fixing things that aren't broken!"

The notion that the first task of problem solving is to disprove hypotheses is not simply a turn of phrase, but reflects an important pragmatic position. Sir Karl Popper, the celebrated British philosopher, argued throughout his life that we don't properly understand the value of conjecture and hypothesis in the natural world. He insisted that the only truly valid theories are those that can be disproven. In problem solving this argument could be modified to suggest that, while in many cases we will never know the true cause of a problem beyond conjecture, we can validate what didn't cause it. With the complexity associated with problems today, this notion has very practical overtones. Because of the absence of historical data and the massive amount of problem information to be analyzed, there will be more problems for which cause cannot be proven—as illustrated by the tragic 1991

[2] "India: Was It the Plague?" *Economist,* 19 November 1994, p. 38.

crash of a United Airlines 737 in Colorado Springs and the 1995 USAir 737 crash in Pittsburgh. Alternatively, the time and expense required to find root cause may make the search prohibitively expensive, as is often the case in fixing computer hardware. In these cases the best that can be expected from problem solving is a removal of the "red herring effect."

Rule one requires organizations to reconstruct their problem-solving processes by beginning with this "culling" step. Whenever a major problem occurs, a team is quickly established with the specific directive to eliminate possible causes. In problems of extraordinary significance, this team may work in parallel with a traditional problem-solving team assigned the task of determining root cause. Individuals working on problems of lesser importance would be well advised to begin their inquiries with this quick culling process. It will allow them to work without the distraction of favored suspects. It will also allow for immediate progress in what may otherwise prove to be a more drawn-out problem-solving exercise.

This "culling" activity was introduced at Corning, Inc., in 1993, with their "Solutions" program, and the results were not theoretical. At Corning's Pressware plant in Corning, New York, the company's newsletter, *Solutions*, chronicled an example of the rewards of the culling activity.

A $200,000 Case of Mistaken Identity

When a fresh shipment of the raw material, feldspar, was introduced at Pressware, the glass composition variability suddenly deviated from acceptable levels. Of course that meant that feldspar caused the deviation and that a project for increasing its usage had to be abandoned as a potential cost-saving modification, right?

Not so fast! Although at first glance this seemed to be a watertight case against the increased usage of feldspar, Bertrand Charpentier and Dave Anderson from the Raw Materials Technology Group had a strong hunch that this was a case of mistaken identity. Therefore, they assembled a team of plant and staff personnel and used the SOLUTIONS problem analysis tool to investigate further.

"By looking at many events and systematically checking all possible variables and their causes, our team was able to prove that it could not have been the new lot of feldspar that led to the upset," notes Bertrand. "At the same time, we ascertained that, in fact, it was the contamination of the raw materials with another chemical during unloading and storage that led to the problem."

By determining that feldspar was "innocent," the team could continue wth its increased usage project and ultimately recommended full implementation of its use. This little piece of detective work—à la SOLUTIONS—resulted in an annual cost reduction of $200,000 . . . with no lowering of quality standards. Now that's something even good ol' Sherlock would have been proud of!

RULE 2. DON'T GATHER DATA—THROW IT OUT.

Only rarely do consultants have the good fortune to walk into an organization that's in the middle of a catastrophe. In the early 1960s a colleague found that situation at a Fortune 500 chemical company. At that time the company was one of the largest producers of photographic film, and when it had encountered a problem with fogged film in the marketplace, it began a lengthy process of investigation. This process, which lasted months, involved the collection of thousands of pages of data and the completion of dozens of laboratory experiments. Radiation and x-rays were studied in the type of detail found only in government reports. During this laborious process the company lost the confidence of the marketplace, particularly professional users, as well as a market position that to this day it has never regained. The cost to the company was in the millions of dollars.

This story, known to the thousands of participants in Kepner-Tregoe workshops as "the Tamworth saga," is noteworthy as an example of the consequences of failing to solve a problem properly. It is also noteworthy in that the company involved was one of the world's largest and best-run businesses. What really makes it a matter of interest, however, is that all of the thousands of hours of research costing hundreds of thousands of dollars—as it turned out—were totally unnecessary. The chemical company had all of the data needed to solve the problem two weeks after it was first reported. Like many other businesses, the company had fallen victim to a problem-solving failure that is increasingly common in today's environment—"information entrapment."

If quick action taken against the wrong cause can be damaging, delays that result from interminable information assembly can be devastating. There are a number of factors that lead people to become entrapped in their own search for data. The unparalleled ability that exists today to gather data is tremendously seductive. The primary metrics for information are quantitative—MIPs and megabytes—not qualitative; thus emphasis is on more data rather than on good data. Gathering data, for many, becomes an exercise akin to walking in an English garden maze. Once you begin the process, it's often difficult to get out. The task of filing, collating, cross-referencing, sorting, and categorizing information begins to take on a life of its own. Meanwhile the problem remains unsolved, and soon it becomes unclear why all this data gathering was being done in the first place.

Avoiding "information entrapment" requires the deployment of several problem-solving practices. First, before any data gathering is done, there must be a uniform agreement about just what the problem is. It is not sufficient to suggest, for example, that it is a communication problem when some of the problem-solving group understand that to mean that the style of the message is offensive while the others believe that it is simply inaccurate. Second, the problem solvers must agree upon the set of questions that will guide their information-gathering process. (The set of Problem Analysis questions provided in the Appendix is a good place to start.) Third, a referee must be appointed to separate the information that is factual from that which is hypothetical. This referee should also manage an information clearinghouse so that the same information isn't collected several times. All teams or individuals engaged in the assembly of information must align their efforts directly back to the framework established in these three practices.

The deft management of data in problem solving is a hallmark of British Airways. As you might guess, safety at British Airways is an organizational obsession, which puts a premium on collecting and analyzing data relating to just about every facet of an aircraft's operation. The amount of data generated by a single transatlantic flight is almost enough to fill the cargo bin of a jumbo jet. But ground engineers that meet the crews of incoming British Airways flights are carefully trained in problem-analysis questioning. They can cut to the heart of an issue quickly and accurately, without becoming entrapped in voluminous data—and, at times, without being able to re-create the exact conditions under which the problem occurred. If an indicator light flashes during a flight, engineers "question to the data void." Which indicator light was flashing? Were there any other indicator lights flashing? When during the flight was it first noticed? How many times and for how long did it flash? Such questioning channels data and begins to sketch the anatomy of the problem, so cause can be determined.

A postscript to the dangers of information entrapment was found in a memo issued by the New York City Board of Education. It read, "Extant data systems contain an abundance of knowledge which is underutilized due to deficit of knowledge and abilities due to inaccessibility."[3] Judging from this memo, one by-product of "information entrapment" may be a loss of ability to write a coherent sentence.

RULE 3. TAKE ON THE PROBLEM AS A TEAM.

As the American patriot Thomas Paine put it, "We must all hang together, or assuredly we shall all hang separately." "Hanging together" in problem solving simply suggests that problems, like a mutant disease strain, are becoming increasingly resistant to individual attack. Nearly gone are the days when a lone problem solver can, after careful analysis, confidently declare that the cause has been found. The lack of historical data, the systems approach to business, and the huge volumes of available data and information have made problem solving the domain of the team.

The medical specialty of cardiology is an excellent example. In the 1970s a cardiologist would diagnose the problem and prescribe the treatment. Today a cardiologist merely directs the patient to a group of other cardiologists. One specialist might do a

[3] Ross and Kathryn Petras, *The 776 Even Stupider Things* (New York: Harper Perennial), 1994, p. 56.

diagnostic catheterization with dyes to determine arterial blockage. Another may complete an electrophysiography to identify electrical abnormalities. Detailed work will simultaneously be done by an expert in echocardiography. All of these people are part of a team whose job is just to find the problem before any treatment is administered.

Business organizations are no different. Because problems can rarely be neatly delineated by single functions or operations, it is equally rare that they can be solved by individuals or even functional teams. Because of this, the best companies are taking a much more deliberate approach to the deployment of problem-solving skills. First, it is essential that the same methodology be used throughout the organization. When a problem-solving team is assembled from many parts of the organization, each with different methodologies, the process often comes to a standstill. Their deliberations become less about solving the problem and more about agreeing on the approach. Hewlett-Packard recognized this phenomenon some time ago and adopted exactly the same approach for problem solving in its offices in over forty countries. It supplemented this by helping suppliers adopt the approach, and in California the approach has even been transferred to customers. In this context, the actual methodology employed is often less important than the broad distribution and understanding of a common methodology throughout the organization.

A second step is to create a cross-function problem-response mechanism within the organization. Organizations are very adept at placing responsibility for problems with a defined organizational entity, a department, or a business unit. Unfortunately, while the effects of a problem may have been seen in one area, the cause may actually be located in another. Invariably, we have found, problems are "owned" by the area in which the effects are observed—a double whammy if that area doesn't own the cause as well.

Take the example of a financial deviation. If the accounts don't agree, the problem is located in finance because that's where the effects (the financial statements) are observed. Consequently finance is expected to solve it. This is bad news for finance if the cause for the problem is a software defect detectable only by the information services function, a transaction error by the bank, or incorrect data input from field operations. Without a cross-function problem-response process in place, there is little incentive for information services or field operations to step in and help solve the problem. And the bank is likely to be reluctant to help prove it was the culprit. Even in organizations committed to a team concept in business, the locus of the responsibility for a problem can be very difficult to determine.

The best companies, whether committed to a team concept or to a traditional model, have changed this dynamic. They have developed a set of experts in problem solving. These experts are not part of an internal consulting function, but personnel throughout the organization who, in addition to their specific functional work skills, have developed an in-depth competence in problem solving. At Procter & Gamble this approach has been formalized as a process in its "Rational Skills Program," a four-week intensive effort to provide internal problem-solving expertise.

When there is an "unplanned outage" on a machine, say, at a Procter & Gamble paper plant, the problem-solving experts or "process facilitators" jump into action by bringing together a team of workers to think through the problem. With each machine costing millions of dollars, this is not an environment that favors solving problems by hunch. Process facilitators work to pool the intelligence and experience of the workforce in an unrelenting effort to solve problems quickly and systematically.

Once such internal expertise has been developed, a business can nominate an expert from outside the functional area to assume the problem as his or her responsibility. What this communicates is that solving the problem is an organizational issue—not a matter simply for a single area where the effects of the problem are observed. The result is faster and more successful problem solving and less blame placing.

Murphy Lives

When that irascible Irishman Murphy uttered his immortal words of warning, "Anything that can go wrong will go wrong," he was merely observing that the human race has yet to achieve "zero defects." And things may not be getting much better. With the increases in the sophistication with which we approach business comes an increase in the complexity of the problems we confront. The challenge is not so much to prove Murphy wrong because, as another of his laws states, "Buttered bread will always fall butter-side down." The challenge is to be less intimidated by the inevitability of a problem. Building an organizational problem-solving competence allows us to approach problems with confidence in our abilities to resolve them quickly and effectively.

CHAPTER 4

Decision Drag in a Nanosecond World

The ability to have critical thinking skills will allow us to make better decisions quicker. It doesn't mean that someone who doesn't have critical thinking skills won't get to the same decision. But it's going to take them a hell of a lot longer. And they're going to wallow through a lot more.

RICHARD F. TEERLINK
President and Chief Executive Officer,
Harley-Davidson, Inc.

The Judeo-Christian religious tradition can trace its roots to one incredibly bad decision made some number of years ago. As the Bible describes it, a serpent, with considerable marketing expertise, suggested a single alternative with an array of supposedly attractive benefits. Adam and Eve bought the sales presentation and found themselves expelled from the Garden of Eden. That makes them the first decision makers on record to learn the dangers of failing to consider the adverse consequences associated with an alternative.

Since this inauspicious beginning, the human race has continued to be involved in the business of making decisions—billions of them, simple, complex, important, and unimportant. The good ones have been justly celebrated while the bad ones have been vilified. All of this raises an intriguing question. Are we any better at decision making today after a few dozen centuries of practice? Interestingly, while we've gained considerable decision making expertise individually from a number of decision making tools such as those described in the appendix, the quality of decision making in an organizational context may not have improved. The increasingly complex environment in which we work has produced such profound changes in the way we make decisions that even good choices may not produce good outcomes.

What a Difference Twenty Years Makes

One person who had a unique opportunity to experience the changes in decision making over the past two decades is Edward Snider, one of America's most prominent and respected sportsmen. In 1966 he conceived the idea of building a world-class sports and entertainment arena for the city of Philadelphia. The Spectrum would hold concerts, serve as home court for the local National Basketball Association franchise, and be home to a National Hockey League team, which Snider himself would start as part of league expansion in 1967. Snider, the driving force behind the Sol C. Snider Entrepreneurs Institute at the University of Pennsylvania's Wharton School, was a classic entrepreneurial decision maker. He made and implemented decisions quickly based on his uncanny sense of the sports and entertainment needs in the Philadelphia area.

Within a month Snider formulated a plan for the arena; gained the commitment of the National Hockey League, the mayor, and the City Council of Philadelphia; and initiated the development of the project. The entire process from concept to groundbreaking took six months and cost $50,000. The documents involved were contained in a small binder just an inch and a half thick. The arena was built for $6.5 million, and sixteen months after the idea was hatched, Philadelphia would dedicate the Spectrum, a facility that by 1987 was the most active sports and entertainment venue in the United States. People in the Philadelphia area fell in love with the Spectrum, the Flyers hockey team won two championships in the 1970s, and Snider became a multimillionaire. It wasn't hard to see that the Spectrum was the result of his fine instinct and excellent decision making.

Twenty years later, however, Snider was faced with a new challenge: building a new arena. The adjacent state of New Jersey was eagerly trying to capture the sports and entertainment market in the Philadelphia area, just as it had done in the New York metro area to the north. New Jersey leaders began wooing the tenants of the Spectrum to New Jersey by offering a new, modern facility and attractive financial terms. Snider recognized that constructing his own new, state-of-the-art arena was the most powerful defensive move available. Thus in 1987 began the development of a new arena complex for Philadelphia dubbed "Spectrum II."

It would be nine years before Spectrum II became a reality. The project stopped and started at least four times during that period. The cost of *developing* the project alone was over $20 million, more than three times the cost of *constructing* the original building. The new building itself would cost an additional $200 million. The documents required for the project stood over six feet tall and included an archaeological study to insure that professional ice hockey and basketball would not be played over an Indian burial ground. This, despite the fact that the same site had been used for decades for dozens of Army-Navy games and the Dempsey-Tunney heavyweight championship fight. After groundbreaking in 1994, Snider's mood was not one of satisfaction and accomplishment, but one of resignation and relief. He readily admits that Spectrum II—or the CoreStates Center, as it is now called—was a bad decision. "If I had known what was involved, I'd never have built it," he said.

What makes the comparison between Spectrum I and II so intriguing is that the same man made two nearly identical decisions. Both buildings were built on the same site and house the same teams and events. The question is, what accounts for the fact that twenty years later the second decision, similar in so many respects to the first, is one that caused Snider such angst? Did his decision-making abilities atrophy during that period, or did the process of decision making change so much that it is has become difficult for even skilled decision makers to make good decisions?

Changing the Rules of the Game

We suspect that Snider's decision-making skills are as strong today as they were in 1966. Ironically for this sportsman, the reasons why decision making seems more difficult, and the decisions themselves often less successful, are rooted in a fundamental change in the "rules of the game."

Like many dimensions of management, decision making has historically been viewed as a skill. Kepner and Tregoe, in *The Rational Manager,* noted that the skill was, in fact, a mental process. They then examined the process primarily from the viewpoint of the individual decision maker. The purpose of this process was to make the "best balanced choice" that would produce superior decision making (see appendix for details). Implicit in this approach to decision making was the supposition that these good choices were then implemented and the odds of success significantly increased.

While it is hard to quarrel with a process approach to making choices that has proven its worth over decades, it may be insufficient to explain the difficulties that even good decision makers are experiencing today. Best-selling author and leadership expert Kenneth Blanchard offers this explanation: "I think things are moving at such a fast pace today that a decision made today isn't necessarily appropriate a year from now or probably tomorrow." In fact, it now appears possible to make an excellent choice and have the decision prove to be a disaster even before it is implemented. The reason for this is that the fundamental *system* for decision making appears to have changed.

If decision making has been thought of as a system at all, it has been thought of simplistically. In essence, it comprised two parts: making the decision and then implementing it. We call this the "Attila the Hun" Decision-Making System.

This model, while old, has a certain staying power. Our recent survey of top managers shows that while Attila may have been dead for fifteen hundred years, his decision-making style is a living legacy in certain organizations. Asked to choose who in a large U.S. corporation today would be the most effective decision

The "Attila the Hun" Decision-Making System

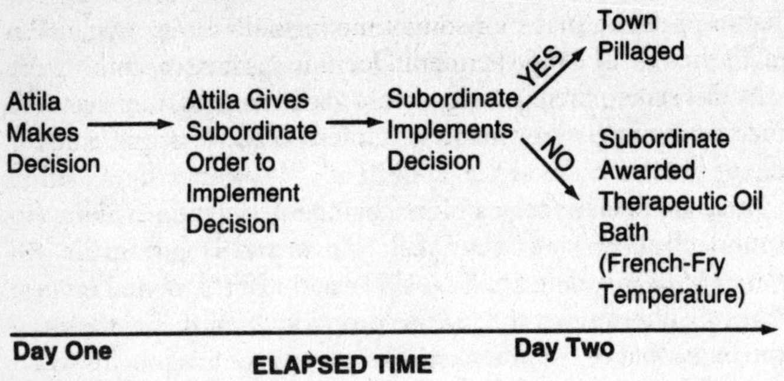

maker, Socrates or Attila the Hun, 37 percent of the executives polled cast their lot with the great barbarian.

Barbaric or not, this simple and straightforward system undoubtedly has appeal. Today, when speed is the mantra of many business executives, it offers time efficiency, especially where implementation is concerned. But even in its more benign form, it represents the decision-making system used in a traditional "command and control" environment—an environment that typified business for many of the past decades. This decision-making approach is central to the attractiveness managers find in the application of sports metaphors to business.

Best-selling books by American football coach Don Shula, British rugby player Will Carling, and basketball coach Pat Riley trumpet the characteristics that make winners in sports and—so say the authors—will also make winners in business. The underlying decision making implicit in these sports metaphors follows the Attila the Hun system. The coach calls the play, the player sees the open man, and the play takes place. Decision and action follow nearly instantaneously. Today's manager, however, rarely finds a similar dynamic because, unlike sports, business for the most part has left behind the command and control model. The traditional view of a decision-making system as simply selecting an alternative and implementing that choice is problematic not only because the world is not a football field, but, more important, because it doesn't accurately depict the real decision system that has been in place for some time in the business world. We call it the Age of Empowerment Decision-Making System.

In this system there is a significant gap in time between when a decision is made and when it is implemented. That gap consists of two primary elements: confirmation and communication. Confirmation is the recognition that most decisions are subject to some type of review. Often times the review is perfunctory, as when a colleague is asked, "Does this sound right to you?" Other times it is more substantive, checking to make sure that the decision is sound or is capable of being implemented rather than simply being an excellent, but ultimately impractical, choice. Communication involves notifying various parties that a decision has been made and conveying enough information about the content of the decision so that implementation can begin.

All of this seems straightforward enough. Decision makers have been confirming and communicating decisions for centuries. What is new, however, is that changes in these two elements of the decision-making system have significantly widened the implementation gap which, in turn, has had a profound effect on both the speed and quality of decision making.

The Age of Empowerment Decision-Making System

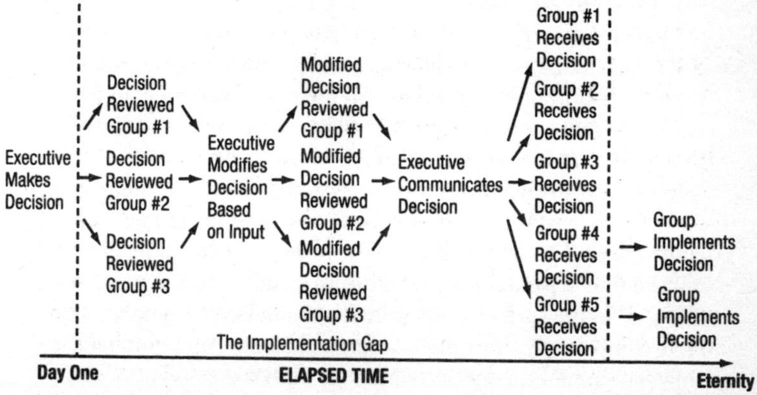

Confirmation

For Attila, as with some of his modern-day counterparts, the confirmation of his decision was relatively quick and easy. He asked if everyone thought his idea was a good one, and at least those who were not enamored with the idea of a bath in boiling oil replied with vigor that it was brilliant and set out to implement it. Attila's staff meetings were probably not appreciably different from those of many corporate executives of the past few decades. Recent years, however, have made the confirmation process a long, complex, and often tedious exercise. Once a decision of any significance has been made and before it is implemented, there are at least five areas in which confirmation may be sought.

1. Consistency with internal policy.

Periodically businesses put greater emphasis on the confirmation process in the wake of a bad decision—locking the barn door after the horse has been stolen. For example, the members of the board of directors of a large eastern property and casualty company may have wished they had kept closer tabs on what their former chairman was thinking in 1987. That year the previous CEO offered an executive vice president with little insurance background an employment contract, which ultimately required the new CEO to pay out more than $4 million in severance fees when the executive was fired three years later. During and immediately after a crisis, businesses may also vow never again to be so cavalier in their decision making, especially where large sums of money are concerned. Their boards begin to take their role in corporate governance far more seriously, and formalized reviews are required to protect against the recurrence of shoddy decision making. The result is that many decisions require several reviews, and some businesses have institutionalized this process with expanded review committees. The new management of the casualty company now require four separate reviews before an employment agreement is allowed. In the past, one was sufficient. One large American high-tech company requires that no fewer than seven committees review any capital expenditure in excess of $100,000.

2. INSURING CUSTOMER SATISFACTION.

One of the favorite phrases of today's generation of business leaders is "Delight the customer"—a notion once confined to the world's greatest amusement parks. A zealous obsession with customer satisfaction has led many organizations to involve their customers in the decision-making system, perhaps on the theory that it is easier to be "delighted" with your own decision than someone else's.

In most cases, however, businesses are unwilling to turn over decision-making authority to the customer. First, customers in competition with each other are difficult to involve in the process. Second, information that is involved in the process, such as profit margin, is not comfortably shared with even the most trustworthy customer. Instead customers are alerted to a decision prior to the start of implementation. Such notification is designed to insure that the decision will not produce any significant or unmanageable adverse customer reaction, and it can be fairly complicated and time-consuming. Customer site visits and focus groups have proliferated to such a degree that many customers believe they have the capability to influence or even reverse any supplier's decision. And in some cases they do. A U.S. auto manufacturer routinely suggests that its suppliers' decisions have not been positively received in Detroit. And its subsequent recommendation to rethink the decision is issued with the same subtle urgency exhibited by members of a Mafia family on the docks of New York City.

3. ACCEPTANCE BY OUTSIDE REGULATORY BODIES.

From Ralph Nader's celebrated condemnation of General Motors' Corvair to the judgment against Exxon for the *Valdez* oil spill, the increasing role of government and public interest groups in the affairs of business is well chronicled. We have all witnessed a broadening of the constituency involved in business decision making, and the involvement of outside agencies probably is warranted. Clearly incidents such as the Union Carbide/Bhopal tragedy put more outside pressure on an organization's internal decision-making apparatus.

The net effect is that substantive decisions are increasingly subject to review and comment by third parties. In the case of government entities, involvement may be coerced by compliance requirements in areas such as health, safety, the environment, and fair employment. The cost of noncompliance is often so high that business leaders will begrudgingly accept the painfully slow pace to which the decision-making system decelerates. Interest groups use the threat of adverse publicity or product boycotts to insert themselves into the decision-making arena. These threats are so powerful that even demonstrably false allegations like that of "devil worship" can bring a giant like Proctor & Gamble to abandon its decades-old "man in the moon" logo. These formal and informal regulatory parties have used power and influence effectively to increase the implementation gap to such a degree that decision making itself may be increasingly ineffective.

4. Support of the implementors.

One by-product of the move toward greater industrial democracy is an increased awareness on the part of the decision maker of the power of the workforce. If the decision is broadly unpopular or misunderstood, the workforce can easily sabotage its implementation or, at a minimum, reduce the efficiency of implementation to such a degree that the decision is no longer viable.

Consider the results of a 1993 survey we conducted on change initiatives. When asked to rate their employees' reaction to organization initiatives, more than 60 percent of the executives polled described employees as neutral, skeptical, or downright resistant. It is difficult to imagine how any initiative can succeed when it faces such a wall of cynicism.[1] The need for support of major decisions has led to significant attempts to alert employees to new initiatives. Red Lobster, the $1.8 billion unit of Darden Restaurants, spent hundreds of thousands of dollars and thousands of hours over nearly two years to ensure that its "Guest First" program, designed to put the chain in the lead in customer satisfaction, reached sixty thousand employees in seven hundred restaurants.

---

[1] Kepner-Tregoe, *House Divided*, op. cit., p. 14.

5. SUPPORT OF THE POWER BROKERS.

The hostile offer for Chrysler made by Kirk Kerkorian in partnership with Lee Iacocca is a reminder that even executives as powerful and successful as Chrysler chairman Robert Eaton have their decisions closely scrutinized by others. These "power brokers" are frequently large shareholders such as Kerkorian or Wall Street analysts who significantly influence those shareholders. "Power brokers" can also be key personnel inside the organization who have significant formal or informal authority. Decision makers realize that while they might have formal authority to make a decision, that authority can evaporate with a negative review from a influential stock analyst or a well-positioned internal executive.

Survival instincts encourage these decision makers to seek out such power brokers for a review of their intended actions before implementation. Joseph E. Antonini, former chairman, chief executive officer, and president of retailing giant Kmart, made the decision to manage Kmart as a retail holding company, with the discount chain being only one of four core companies. The power brokers on the board and the analysts on Wall Street refused to confirm Antonini's decision. This, despite the fact that Antonini was viewed as strongly in control of the corporate governance at Kmart. His decision—and his position—are now history.

Clearly, the influence of power brokers depends on the size, scope, and importance of the decision. But such influence is present to some degree in even less important midlevel decisions. All up and down the line, confirming a decision is no longer as simple as "What do you think about this?" Thus the expanding implementation gap.

Communication

Communication has always been a problem in decision-making systems. An excellent decision can be misunderstood easily by well-intentioned subordinates who proceed to implement something entirely different. During the Civil War, for example, Confederate general John Bell Hood's order to attack was understood by the troops to be a positioning movement. This misunderstanding allowed Union general John M. Schofield to escape and secure a Northern victory at the pivotal battle of Nashville.[2] In recent years, however, the communication of decisions has become the second major cause of the lengthening of the implementation gap. There are several good reasons for this.

1. Cold communication.

The decline of face-to-face communication, the fastest mode of conveying decisions, and its replacement by colder transmission devices—fax machines, E-mail, the Internet, voice mail—has not only increased implementation time in some instances, but also, more problematic, has reduced the certainty of receipt. Cold communication does not always allow for the firm confirmation of understanding that occurs in face-to-face communication. Consequently understanding often is confirmed again and again, "just to make sure."

2. Data overload.

The vast increase in the production of data has made it more difficult to sift the data required for actions from mountains of other data transmitted for informational purposes. One Johnson & Johnson executive, for example, set a personal one-day record recently with forty-seven E-mails and thirty-eight voice mails—a twenty-four-hour total of eighty-five messages, not including face-to-face, telephone, or written correspondence! Blanchard comments, "Now you gather as much information as you can. I think that's impacted decision making. So much information is available. You keep getting more information. At one point, a few years ago, you'd say, 'that's about it.'" This overload is not simply an American phenomenon. Joel Kurtzman, former editor of *The*

[2] Winston Groom, *Shrouds of Glory: From Atlanta to Nashville: The Last Great Campaign of the Civil War* (New York: Grove Atlantic, Inc., 1994), pp. 136–155.

New York Times business section and the *Harvard Business Review*, related this story: "I was talking to the chairman of a very large Japanese trading company. I asked him about decision making in Japan. He said, if anything, decision making in Japan had gotten slower. Their problem, as he described it, is information overload and the inability to sift the wheat from the chaff in terms of finding out what they ought to act on."

3. TEAMING.

The erosion of middle management has markedly increased spans of communication. In days past, a decision was made and a middle manager was summoned, told of the action to be implemented, and assigned responsibility to make sure that others were working to put it into effect. With middle managers increasingly absent in business, executives are now required to communicate with entire teams to ensure that they are aware that a decision needs to be put into effect. This not only geometrically increases the number of messages to be sent; it also removes the control function that ensured that the message was properly acted upon by the implementors.

4. WORKFORCE DISTRIBUTION.

When a commander wanted to implement an action in days gone by, he rounded up the troops, who were told what needed to be done and then hurried off to complete the assignment. Today's business executive is lucky just to be able to locate his troops. The implementors may be in five units strewn across twelve countries, and the resulting coordination and communication problems can make a group meeting as difficult to plan as D-day. Reuters, with a superlative communication network, routinely implements decisions with personnel from five or more countries. Yet even in the case of Reuters, the battle with the clock—finding a time all can confer—can create delay. Amway, one of the largest foreign companies in Japan, with local revenues of $1.8 billion, leases the Tokyo Dome to gather its far-flung distributors to inform them of important decisions.

Communication and confirmation, for all of these reasons, occupy an increasingly large and time-consuming part of the decision-making system. Their net effect is that, while decisions may be made more quickly and implementation may be as efficient as it has ever been, the entire system may be slowing down—or breaking down! It is this "change of pace" that is wreaking havoc with the decision making of top executives.

Most businessmen and -women are already aware of the pernicious effect of the implementation gap. Corporate halls echo with the complaints of leaders who can't seem to get good ideas implemented on a timely basis. Those who long for the halcyon days when the manager gave the order and the minions quickly carried it out will have to find their solace in movies like *Citizen Kane* and *Patton*. In America, at least, those days are gone forever. Blanchard notes, "I used to be able to make a decision and that was done, and then on to the next decision. Decisions today are never done."

At a time when speed is an imperative, decision making itself has speeded up. Our Yankelovich study suggests that decision making—selecting the best choice—has increased in speed, while decision implementation has improved. On the latter point, 74 percent of the executives in our study reported that once a decision was made, they were either "extremely" or "highly" confident that it would be correctly implemented. Yet ours and other research conclude that major initiatives are too time-consuming and often dismal failures. This paradox becomes easily explainable in the context of the implementation gap. Snider made his decision to build Spectrum II in a matter of weeks. The building of the arena was well ahead of plan. But the "implementation gap" extended for eight years. Thus, while decisions are being made more rapidly, the system itself has slowed to a snail's pace because of this widening gap. We call this phenomenon "decision drag."

Does Slow and Steady Really Win the Race?

Is there anything wrong, however, with slowing down the decision-making system? Being quicker, while always offering the illusion of progress, is not always better. Mahatma Gandhi's counsel that "there is more to life than living it faster" remains a valuable bit of wisdom. Nonetheless, there are undeniable benefits for acting expediently in some cases, as well as penalties for acting more slowly in others. It is this loss of available opportunities and threats resulting from delay that concern us most about the slowdown in the decision-making process. We see several troublesome consequences of decision drag.

CONSEQUENCE 1. THE PURPOSE OF THE DECISION CHANGES.

All business executives have, at one point or another, found themselves in a lengthy meeting when suddenly they were struck with an overwhelming sense of confusion. The more verbal of these executives will stop the proceedings and address that most seminal of all questions to the group: "Does anybody know why we are here?" This is usually not meant to initiate a dialogue on the meaning of life, as there are relatively few existentialists in management today. Rather, it is to suggest that the discussion of various courses of action has bogged down because no one is really sure of the purpose of the decision they are to implement.

The uncertainty about the purpose of a decision, coupled with the fact that there is likely to be a chain of other decisions associated with it—when, what, where, who, how much—means that the time between the need to act and the beginning of action can be lengthy indeed. And, as the time elapses, the reason for the decision becomes more and more obscure, because the frame of reference is now historical. It becomes so obscure, in some cases, that the answer to the executive's plea, "Why are we here?" is often, "Damned if we know!" More troubling is the possibility that the decision ultimately made could have little or nothing to do with the originally articulated purpose.

In the early 1990s a large packaging company based in the eastern United States—we'll call it King Packaging—acquired another significant-size packaging company in the Midwest. Each company had its own extensive research and engineering functions, and King's CEO recognized that the combined companies now had the research, development, and engineering functions that a $100 billion company would require. He directed his group to articulate a strategy for these functions, which he believed would lead to the rationalization of excess capacity. The group, comprising all of the top executives of the organization except the CEO, worked individually on the task and then assembled in a local hotel. On the morning of the second day of discussion, an executive vice president—a man for whom an hour-long decision-making meeting was fifty-nine minutes of wasted time—stood up and addressed his colleagues: "I don't have time for all of this analysis. Let's make a decision and get out of here. We all know what to do. Let's just decide and do it." The EVP's lack of patience was refreshing and forced the group to a conclusion. The outcome was a very effective restructuring of the research, development, and engineering function, which eliminated most of the duplication and streamlined their operations. What didn't happen was the fulfillment of the CEO's original purpose of articulating a longer-term strategy for those functions.

This packaging company, because of its exceptional management capability, was able to lose sight of the original purpose of a decision and still achieve an excellent result. Yet three years later there is doubt whether or not its executives have a clear business strategy at a time when Wall Street analysts are demanding more details on their vision. Other businesses aren't as fortunate as King Packaging. Ross Perot is fond of pointing out that, in the process of acquiring EDS, General Motors lost sight of why it was acquiring the business. Some doubt it ever knew.

Consequence 2. Opportunity windows slam shut.

As the pace of change continues to accelerate, there are an increasing number of decision makers who are getting their fingers crushed in slamming windows of opportunity. For years General Mills debated the merits of international expansion and, while debating, acquired companies in furniture (Pennsylvania House), toys (Fisher-Price), sports shirts (Izod), and jewelry (Monet) in a diversification strategy that could only be termed bizarre. By the time it decided that international expansion was important to business growth, the company found Kellogg's, its arch rival, holding a dominant position overseas. General Mills' delay in decision making about the international expansion of its core business put the company in the position of trying to wedge open an opportunity window that its rival had nearly slammed shut through quicker action.

Delayed decisions have been at the core of many business debacles. The Detroit auto industry's legendary delay in responding to the oil crisis by making small automobiles widely available in the U.S. market paved the way for the Japanese automakers. IBM's delay in moving away from its mainframe reliance to establish a position in workstation computing put the company into the position of follower in the fastest-growing information hardware sector. None of these cases was a consequence of slow product development cycles—which today have been deemed the primary culprit in marketplace defeats. The products were available and the decisions had been made to produce them. Nor would implementation have been a problem. There was not a company in their industries that had the production capability of IBM or GM. The culprit was the implementation gap that allowed their decisions to atrophy as they were confirmed and communicated over a period of years. And, while their decision-making systems meandered along, more nimble competitors like Toyota and Hewlett-Packard stepped in.

CONSEQUENCE 3. DELAYED CORRECTIVE ACTIONS ALLOW THE DAMAGE TO MOUNT.

It is often acknowledged that U.S. naval superiority in damage control was one of the biggest factors in the World War II victory at Midway. After taking several devastating blasts, the *Yorktown* was kept afloat by "decisive action," which meant that the implementation gap between the time when the damage control officer decided what to do and the seamen began doing it was probably fairly short. It is hard to envision this officer gathering his men into a briefing room and announcing, " Men, we've just been hit by a torpedo. As we're speaking, thousands of gallons of seawater are pouring into the ship, floating your possessions toward Guam. I want to talk a little about what I'd like to do and get your views on it." Sound farfetched? There are executives taking torpedoes daily in the business world whose response is exactly the same. Respected Intel found a minor defect in its Pentium chip—the heart and soul of its profitability. And while the seawater flowed in, the company delayed the implementation of its damage control strategy. It knew what to do and how to do it, but the decision was confirmed and communicated internally for so long that Intel was treated to mountains of free, front-page negative publicity, tarnishing an otherwise golden image.

CONSEQUENCE 4. LOSS OF ENTHUSIASM FOR IMPLEMENTATION.

Executives may sometimes hide their decisions under a basket, but not the ones in which they take pride. These are often celebrated with the type of hoopla and glitter usually reserved for political conventions. Such was the case with the announcement of the employee buyout of United Airlines. The decision was big news in every media outlet. Terms like "the biggest employee buyout in history" and "Come fly *our* friendly skies" became newspaper headlines. The drama surrounding the announcement was expected to create enthusiasm among passengers and employees alike and alert them to the exciting new world of possibilities for United Airlines.

Implementing the decision, while complex, was not expected to be overly lengthy. That was, however, before the effects of the implementation gap came into play. Communication took place in a period just short of eternity, with confirmation taking slightly longer. The constituencies involved multiplied like rabbits on hormone supplements. By the time the transition of ownership occurred, the flight attendants were still out of the deal and the enthusiasm of the new "owners" had dissipated significantly, according to a multitude of published reports, including a 1995 feature piece in *USA Today*.[3] The delay in the decision-

[3] Judith Valente, "Employee Ownership, One Year Later," *USA Today*, 12 July 1995, p. 1B.

making system sapped the enthusiasm of those who were expected to make the dream a reality. United's buyout may eventually conclude, in the words of T. S. Eliot, "not with a bang but a whimper."

Consequence 5. Data on which the decision is based become invalid or suspect.

It is an accepted principle that decisions are based on a blend of facts and assumptions about a given situation. The better the facts and assumptions, the better the decision. Unfortunately for the decision maker, facts and assumptions are rarely static. Consider the case of computer purchases. The facts and assumptions about notebook computers are examined and a decision is made to purchase a number of them for a company's sales force. A type of notebook is identified, and the implementation gap begins. Purchasing reviews the request; users are canvassed for their views about the machine (having already been canvassed prior to the decision, they now have had more canvassing than van Gogh); the company is alerted to this exciting new development; finance confirms the budget availability in the seventy-nine cost centers into which the purchase will be split to obscure its size. Seven months later the computers arrive. The first sign of trouble occurs when management realizes that nine hundred of the three thousand computers are unassigned. Had people known when they made this decision that they would need to lay off 25 percent of the sales force, they probably would have ordered fewer computers. A second disturbing problem is that the notebook is now a generation old, as new products launched in the last few months have power and capability well beyond these machines. It could be argued that these problems were inevitable and were the result not of decision drag, but of a failure to consider future staffing in the initial decision. While that is certainly true, the implementation gap was also a contributing factor.

When a decision is made, certain assumptions are made about data integrity—in other words, how long the facts on which the decision is based will hold true. When a decision cannot be implemented during that period of data integrity, it is often a disaster waiting to happen. Had the management, in this instance, recognized that its assumptions about employment levels had no more than a few months' life span during a downward drifting economic cycle, the decision to purchase computers would have been delayed until data regarding staffing levels were available with a longer period of integrity. Al Shugart, CEO and chairman of Seagate Technology, has suggested that data integrity—determining whether data are correct—is the single most important element in making successful decisions. In essence, it is possible to make a good decision, implement that choice effectively, and end up with a terrible result because the implementation gap invalidated all or some of the facts and assumptions on which the decision was initially based.

The "Willy Wonka Dilemma" and Its Solutions

In the classic children's story *Willie Wonka and the Chocolate Factory*, executive Willie Wonka often finds himself counseling his group: "So much time, so little to do." He then catches his mistake with a quick, "Stop, reverse that!" The decision-drag paradox suggests that Mr. Wonka's first statement may be closer to the mark for today's business. While decisions, it appears, are being made more rapidly and implementation appears to be more efficient than ever, executives look to the sky, raise their hands in frustration, and ask: "Why does it take so long to get anything done around here?" The implementation gap lengthens the decision-making system so subtly that while decisions appear quicker, the whole system moves more slowly. The effects of the gap go beyond simple frustration and probably contribute much to the difference between the nimble and agile organization and the sluggish and stodgy one. To paraphrase Wonka, the implementation gap takes so much time that little is done.

There are no simple solutions to the decision-drag paradox. In subsequent chapters we will discuss building an organizational proficiency in critical thinking skills, which is an essential component of making and implementing decisions. There a ever, additional actions executives troubled by this pa should consider.

1. Manage the decision-making system.

No one will dispute the importance of making and implementing good decisions. But in today's focus on bottom-line results, often overlooked is the fact that it is a process in which conformation and communication are critical steps that greatly influence both the quality of the decision and the success of its implementation. Consequently, executives and managers in the process of making decisions should ask these questions:

For Confirmation of a Decision

Who can significantly alter or affect the quality of this decision and the success of its implementation?

Which of these individuals or groups involved in making the decision will also be instrumental in the success of its implementation?

Which other groups must be consulted because of a moderate to high likelihood that they will attempt to alter the charted course or that the impact of their involvement could significantly affect the decision and its implementation?

Who can be excluded from confirmation either because of prior involvement in making the decision or low likelihood of having an effect on its implementation?

What is the likelihood that confirmation will "loop back" into the decision system, resulting in a new decision-making process?

For the Communication of a Decision

Who is affected by implementation and must receive general information about the decision?

Who must assist in the implementation and will require more detailed information?

These questions are not the equivalent in management thinking of the discovery of the map of the human genome. They've been asked millions of times. What is less certain is how often they've been asked systematically, how the answers have been constructed into action plans, and how well the importance of confirmation and communication is understood in terms of closing the implementation gap.

2. Manage the implementation gap.

The implementation gap exists for all decisions. By itself it is not a problem—unless left unmanaged. In fact, it can improve the other components of the decision system by exposing weaknesses in a decision or by building enhanced commitment to its subsequent implementation. The price attached to the implementation gap—be it big or small—is time. In our experience, however, an assessment of the time required for confirmation and communication is rarely done. And without such an assessment, it is impossible to know how many of the beneficial consequences will come into play, much less when the beneficial effects of the decision itself will accrue to the organization.

For years the late Orson Welles promised, in a highly visible U.S. television commercial, that the Paul Masson vineyard would "sell no wine before its time." A great sentiment, but it begs the question, "When will we know that its time has come?" The same is true for decisions. By effectively planning the time for confirmation and communication, executives will find the answer.

3. Consider decision drag as part of the decision-making process.

We suggest that when confirmation and communication are added to the list of decision objectives, those alternatives that can be most easily communicated and confirmed may be selected. While that will reduce decision drag, it is important to remember that these elements are always part of the process, regardless of how momentous the decision may be. This was a lesson Moses learned on his descent from Mount Sinai. Down in the marketplace, British Airways' Sir Colin Marshall pointed out that at the end of the Gulf War, "when we developed the promotional campaign, 'the World's Biggest Offer,' one of the biggest reasons for its success was our ability to move it from decision to implementation nearly instantaneously."

4. Consider the decision-making structure of the organization.

Most factors that create or contribute to decision drag are embedded in the organizational structure that legislates patterns for confirmation and communication. For that reason, one of the primary motives for new organizational architecture is the need to increase the speed of the decision-making system. Robert Lutz, president of Chrysler, noted, "When Alex Trotman and I were vice presidents at Ford, our common, number-one beef about working for Ford Motor Company was the slowness in decision making and the insistence on quantification of really meaningless data. I'm convinced that the reason for his reorganization of Ford is to improve the speed of decision making." Hewlett-Packard's legendary bias toward small, highly autonomous business units was driven in large measure, according to HP executives we interviewed, by a need for quick decision making.

A Final Word on Decision Systems

We call the skill of decision making "Decision Analysis" (described in detail in the Appendix). It avoids all the roadblocks and potholes that too often impede the decision-making process. But because decisions always have been and always will be subjective, there is no substitute for human involvement in this process. While artificial intelligence and expert systems will continue to reduce the number of decisions that find their way to executives and managers because they cannot be programmed, the importance and complexity of these decisions will increase. This means the effectiveness of their decision-making systems will become a major determinant of the success of any organization. And they will be required to keep pace with the speed of the business environment. These are difficult challenges indeed and fundamental to business success. We've moved beyond Attila and are well short of R2D2 in the foreseeable future. What is left today are decision makers with a faint wisp of smoke visible at the ears as the human computer overheats.

CHAPTER 5

Rx for Futurephobia

. . . any dollar spent on prevention is probably going to save you $100 to $1,000 in detection and correction downstream.

ROBERT A. LUTZ
President and Chief Operating Officer,
Chrysler Corporation

A popular exhibit at World's Fairs of the past was a depiction of the future some 25 to 30 years hence. Invariably, it was a vision of technological paradise. Cars traveled on rails. We flew between destinations in a Buck Rogers version of the Volkswagen Beetle. Freed by technology from the less ennobling aspects of life and work, we were promised a better life vocationally, avocationally, physically, emotionally, interpersonally, and every other way imaginable. Living in this future was like being adopted by both the Nelsons and the Jetsons. If these exhibits were any indication, the future was to be an unequivocally desirable place.

The time that was portrayed in these visions of the future is now. We all know that the present is decidedly *not* that vision. And the future isn't what it used to be, either. Few people would describe our present day as a technological paradise. The primary impact of technology for many of us has been to greatly extend the work week. Faxes, modems, laptops, and digital personal communicators mean that we can now work anytime, anywhere, all the time. If a person is so unrealistic as to think that vocational, physical, and emotional health is attainable, the key is some Twelve Step program, not technology. If you now view the future as an unequivocally desirable place, you probably need to ease up on your medication. To paraphrase Pogo, "We have met the future and it is our enemy."

The obvious question, then, is: Should the future, which used to be seen as idyllic, now be viewed with the same relish as a sigmoidoscopy, and if so, why?

Futurephobia

When we were discussing a strategy project with Winston Lau, then CEO of Crane Canada, he said rather ominously, "Focusing on the future used to be one of the most enjoyable aspects of my job. Now, looking at the future can be a scary exercise. I used to delude myself that we could affect the future. Given the unpredictability of events in recent years, however, it is very tough to believe that we can. We seem to be victims of the future, and like any victim, we are frightened by what victimizes us."

Lau's introspective comment, though not indicative of his company's approach to the future, reflects an increasingly pervasive view of the future in organizations: It's difficult to predict, beyond our comprehension, and impossible to control. So why should we spend time and effort on the uncontrollable? For many, focusing on the future is seen increasingly as a frustrating, threatening exercise, especially by those who take pride in being in control of themselves and their organizations.

Futurephobia is not an affliction you hear people talking about openly. But you do observe it in the pattern of decision avoidance so common these days in executive suites. C. K. Prahalad points to three widespread "evasive tactics" used by many senior managers. He sums up the first as "Let's get one more study" or "Let's get a consultant to tell us." Second is "Let's put a little bit here." In other words, underinvest in a new initiative. You can always palm that one off as a prudent move by management. Finally, there is the tendency to "overmanage," which entails shackling a decision with countless reports and updates to senior management, almost to the point where no one is paying attention to customers and markets. Such avoidance, unfortunately, prevents senior managers from coming to terms with the future.

In the Yankelovich/Kepner-Tregoe study, 76 percent of the executives polled agreed that the future is less predicable today than in the past. And 87 percent agreed that the consequences of making poor decisions today are more severe than ever before. Big stakes under conditions of uncertainty—that deadly combination leads to fear in both Russian roulette and top executive decision making. Explains Daniel Patterson, vice president and launch site director of the Kennedy Space Center, Lockheed Martin Space Operations, "People today have a tendency not to make decisions. The risk factor is far too great. You make a decision today and you might not be able to recover from it. In earlier times you made a decision and could take the time to monitor the outcome and then adjust accordingly. You don't have that luxury today."

The organizational fear of the future raises several important questions: Why do many companies view the future with a reluctance bordering on hostility? To what degree does the fear of the future inhibit a company's preparation for the future? Finally, how is it that some individuals and companies consistently are better prepared for the same uncertain future than others? Our research and observations help us to at least partially answer these questions.

Alienated from the Future

One effect of viewing the future as unpredictable and uncontrollable is the high anxiety it induces throughout an organization. In the 1960s and 1970s social scientists did a considerable amount of work with the notion of personal alienation, the feeling of being unable to control one's own destiny. Such alienation led to a recession for barbers and Bill Blass, as well as a new meaning to the phrase "Better Living Through Chemistry." The bizarre styles and behaviors of this era reflected a repudiation of the present and a certain anxious fatalism about the future. For us, it is interesting and somewhat alarming to note the similarity between the feelings of powerlessness among many well-coiffed and tailored occupants of corner offices and those of their disheveled and hirsute predecessors.

With the prevalence of downsizing, delayering, and elimination of non-value-added work, some anxiety is expected, understandable, and probably desirable. It could be argued that the recent pressures felt by companies should comfort the disturbed and disturb the comfortable. However, when people feel truly powerless in controlling their own destiny, then dysfunctional anxiety and alienation from the future are the results. Any thinking about the future is avoided, and any preparation for the future is greatly inhibited. Conversely, any company that continuously tries to understand and prepare for the future has an obvious advantage over those companies that are alienated from it.

In his book on the Bechtel Corporation, *Friends in High Places*, Laton McCartney describes the company's response to the predictable demise of nuclear power because of serious concerns about the environment and nuclear proliferation. According to McCartney, the company engaged in a campaign of denial and blame fixing while a cornerstone of its global strategy crumbled. Ironically, Bechtel's alienation from a future world fraught with inevitable environmental and governmental controls on the nuclear industry probably hastened the industry's demise.

The vicious circle created by an alienation from the future is apparent. If an organization feels collective alienation from the future, it will avoid those activities that can prepare for it. Failing to prepare for the future makes it, in fact, more uncontrollable and unpredictable, adding to the feeling of alienation. GM's response to Japanese inroads into the U.S. auto industry may be an overused example, but it is nonetheless relevant. As the market changed from trading up to bigger cars every three or four years to a focus on quality and economy, GM was so alienated from this future market that it not only missed a golden opportunity: it lost its market leadership in several product lines.

The Appeal of Chaos

From the laboratories of science to the corridors of management—often a very long journey—chaos seems to be all the rage. During the past five years a blizzard of articles and books has appeared, trying to bring clarity, if not order, to the concept of chaos. Scientists have been busy writing essays such as "Global Chaotic Mixing on Isentropic Surfaces" and "Seeing and Controlling Chaos in the Brain." And business pundits have waded into chaos with such entries as "Managing in the Midst of Chaos," "Dealing with Chaos—and Learning to Love It," "Thriving on Chaos," and—get this—"Gagging on Chaos." Although chaos from the scientific perspective is seen as ultimately understandable and predictable, the common conception holds it to be unfathomable.

Why has this concept of chaos become at all relevant in our discussion of organizations? For years various gurus attempted to make business and management more scientific, which is to say more controllable and predictable. While the notion of business as a pure science has been out of vogue for some time, the position that chaos has a significant role in business represents a radical swing of the pendulum.

One reason for the popularity of chaos theory relates to the postmodern worldview regarding social change. The ancient Greeks believed in cycles; nineteenth-century and many twentieth-century social thinkers felt history proceeded in "stages"; and today many believe the world is inherently aleatory, or subject to chance. "It's a nonlinear world," explains Tom Peters. "The butterfly effect prevails. Little disturbances at today's pace can blow up on you in a major-league way."

Another reason chaos has become a remotely relevant lens for viewing business has to do with the change in the approach of many businesses to the future. When the future was seen as a projection of the past with minor variations, it was knowable, and it was within an organization's power to determine and orchestrate any significant departure from the past. In recent years events have veered radically from the past with mind-boggling rapidity and unpredictability: The iron curtain folded despite predictions to the contrary; China emerged as the world's fastest-growing economy, although common wisdom held that it would significantly regress after Tiananmen Square, the demise and possible revitalization of companies like IBM and GM occurred with a speed and magnitude that defied expectations. Nobel Laureates sound like palm readers in their discussions of the future behavior of the world's economies. If the past is a less reliable guide to the future than it used to be, then chance, AKA chaos, becomes a relevant alternative explanation. While "The devil made me do it" holds little sway with a board of directors, "How could we possibly predict a chaotic future?" may buy enough time to pack the parachute.

Curiously, there can be some perverse comfort in viewing modern organizations as subject to the whims of chaos. If the future is the convergence of chaotic forces and events, then it is impossible to control and predict. Therefore, why try? *Que será, será*. While this attitude lacks Doris Day's syrupy optimism, it does relieve the pressure to plan meaningfully for the future. And what leader, deep down, would not find some comfort in absolution from responsibility for the unknowable and uncontrollable future of his organization?

The Atrophy of Strategy

The diminishing focus on organizational strategy whenever there is a bump or pothole in the economic road may be an example of leaders' resistance to the preparation of their organizations for what they see as a chaotic future. Much to the chagrin of consultants around the world, including ourselves, the leaders of many organizations shift their focus from the strategic success of their organizations to short-term operational success every time earnings' growth slows. A survey of executives, academics, and consultants, reported in a recent issue of the *Real World Strategist*, found that today the typical strategic horizon is one to two years, as opposed to four to ten years a decade ago. With such a time frame we wonder whether a strategy can be really "strategic." Such a focus is certainly understandable, since strategy is irrelevant if a company does not survive the short term. However, in many companies the chief executive has taken the finger completely off the strategic pulse in an effort to perform operational triage.

For example, a large international pharmaceutical company needed to cut costs and demonstrate some short-term results on its balance sheet. Consequently, it decided to reduce costs significantly in all functions that did not contribute directly to the manufacture and sale of its products. Research and development was deemed to be such a function and was subject to the broad ax. Curiously, the company's strategy, developed only a year prior to the cost cutting, had determined that its R&D capability provided a core competency and contributed significantly to its competitive advantage. By concentrating solely on the company's short-term financial health, its leadership had inadvertently severed its lifeline to the future.

In addition to spastic emphasis on strategy in many companies, we have seen dramatic changes in those companies that do continue to focus on their strategy for the future. In our strategy work with companies, we have seen the average strategic time frame shorten from eight to ten years to three to five years. The rationale for such a shortened time frame is the inability to meaningfully anticipate the future beyond three years. Yet even a three-year strategy rarely includes real visionary thinking. Worse, it is usually predicated on the assumption that the next three years will be some projection of the past.

Xerox's revitalization reportedly has been based on a strategy of reengineering its processes by benchmarking world-class performers. Such a strategy would be based on two assumptions. First, Xerox assumes that its competitors will continue to do what they are currently doing, an obviously invalid assumption that plagues benchmarking. Second, it assumes that Xerox's future lies in the copier market, since it has not created any substantially new businesses. Both assumptions seem to view the future as a projection of the past.

If It Can't Be Measured, It Can't Be Managed

A large number of the initiatives within organizations over the last seventy-five years have had an extremely worthwhile intention: to bring processes and systems under control. A cursory list of examples might cause any red-blooded line manager to break out in a cold sweat and any consultant to drool.

- Standard accounting practices
- Taylorism and its impact on standard labor calculations
- Management by objectives
- Activity-based costing
- The behavioral approach to performance
- Statistical Process Control
- Total Quality Management
- Process reengineering

Unquestionably these initiatives have enabled organizations to improve continuously and to make more responsible decisions. However, they have had a definite downside in their effect on organizations' thinking about the future. Each of these initiatives has a bias toward measurement, and this orientation, while extremely appropriate in addressing issues in the past and present, is inappropriate when applied to the future. The penchant for measurement contributes to the futility felt in dealing with an uncertain future.

From astrology to computer modeling, we humans have been incessant in our attempts to impose measurement on the future. We understand, at a fundamental level, that measurement enables control and predictability, and few notions have been as compelling as predicting the future. Yet the future defies measurement. It would mean accurately assessing the probability that an event will occur and the time when it will occur. Sometimes we can measure one or the other, but rarely can we measure both. To cite some simple examples, the probability of dying can be accurately measured, but uncertainty about its precise timing can lead to all manner of strange behaviors from jogging to eating huge amounts of broccoli. The timing when pregnancy is likely to occur is certainly measurable, but imprecision regarding probability enriches the makers of contraceptive devices and leads to eating copious amounts of oysters.

Therefore, if a predominant view in an organization holds that measurement is a prerequisite to management, then management of the future is likely to be seen as oxymoronic. Such organizations will see any thinking about the future as too imprecise and not worth the rigorous effort that thinking about the measurable warrants.

Recently, we encountered a company that is dominated by engineers. This is a firm that has sanctified process measurement and seems to believe that if a thing cannot be measured, then its value, and possibly its existence, is questionable. We were helping the company's top executives identify the potential problems and opportunities presented in the launch of a certain product. When we began to assess the probability of an opportunity occurring and the impact if it did occur, the result was total frustration. Initially, the team responsible for the product launch tried to use some sophisticated computer models to assess probability and impact, but the models had to be based on certain assumptions that were not measurable and that caused the team to be halfhearted at best in its thinking. Interestingly, the team had identified as a potential opportunity a competitor's technical problem with its product. However, further thinking about this opportunity was thwarted by the inability to measure it. Six months later the competitor did have a technical problem with its product. Since our client had done little thinking about how to take advantage of the opportunity, the problem was corrected and a window of opportunity slammed shut before our client could act. The penchant for measurement had prohibited this company from taking advantage of a golden opportunity to increase market share.

The Cure: Preparation vs. Control

Fear of the future, alienation from the future, the appeal of chaos, the atrophy of strategy, and the obsession with measurement all have their roots in the futile desire to predict and control the future. Rigorous analysis of the future, however, lends itself more to the advice—"Be Prepared"—of Lord Baden-Powell, founder of the Boy Scouts, than to that of well-meaning futurists. The future, obviously, cannot be predicted precisely or controlled. Instead, effective leaders and companies spend a great deal of time preparing. And they see the need to prepare as increasing in proportion to any increase in uncertainty.

Focus is key to being prepared. Let's face it, if you worried about everything that could go wrong, your organization would come to a grinding halt. Pick out what is central to business success and ask what the potential problems are. To make the point, Chrysler's Robert Lutz draws an analogy with a machine: "Even the most perfect machine . . . is going to have random variation. Look at the parts of the machine and ask, 'What are the critical aspects of this part? What must it do? Which change in characteristics of this part could cause a problem?' You have to train people to identify the critical characteristics. And then they have to ask themselves, 'What simple tests can I create [on the line] to test for the presence and the perfection of the critical characteristics of the part? And how do I assure that this process is incapable of producing one single part that doesn't meet those critical characteristics?' "

While preparation as opposed to control has always been the hallmark of those companies that focus effectively on the future, preparation in the face of increasingly rapid and unpredictable change has assumed some interesting wrinkles and heightened importance.

- Twenty years ago a primary focus on potential problems with only a perfunctory look at potential opportunities was sufficient. Now, emphasis on the analysis of upside opportunities has become an integral aspect of viewing the future, particularly in providing a framework for innovation.
- Creativity techniques used to be limited to the development of options and solutions because problems were seen to be obvious and opportunities were believed to be serendipitous. Now creativity is necessary in the identification of future problems and opportunities because these problems and opportunities will be largely unfamiliar.
- In the not too distant past, when the anticipation of future problems was done at all, it was built into organizational procedures. The most frequently encountered examples include emergency procedures or preventive maintenance programs. Disciplined organizations used these processes to

anticipate operational issues as well. In recent years effective preparation for an uncertain future entails the application of what we call Potential Problem and Potential Opportunity Analysis to strategic issues.

- When the future was a projection of the present, there was little need to identify and prepare for a wide range of future events. Since the probability of future events was relatively discernible, preparation was focused on those with the highest probability. Now, the number of possible future events has increased almost geometrically, and the assessment of probability is much more difficult. In response, the techniques of scenario management and Potential Problem and Potential Opportunity Analysis are blended to help organizations anticipate a variety of events, balance experience and measurement in assessing probability, and take action now to assure flexibility and agility for a wide range of possible events.

Obviously, effective and successful executives have taken Baden-Powell's advice to heart and are preparing for an uncertain future, rather than trying with futility to control it.

Upside Focus—or, There's a Pony Here Somewhere

A description of the ultimate in optimism is the little boy who on receiving a box of horse manure for his birthday spends the next hour searching his yard because he knows there is a pony somewhere. Some might argue that the same blind optimism is evident in any focus on the potential upsides available in the future. Given that the future has not been particularly charitable to many individuals and companies, it is not surprising that the tendency is to focus exclusively on the problems that potentially reside in the future. Yet some of the most rewarding thinking about the future comes from analyzing potential opportunities. As the CEO of a leading U.S. computer giant put it, "Fear of complacency is what keeps me awake nights. Senior management's role is to create the environment that encourages business managers to take risks and create new growth opportunities."

The benefits to be derived from preparing for potential opportunities are directly connected with the element of timing. Opportunities generally present themselves for a limited length of time, which is why the "window of opportunity" is such a powerful metaphor. The window opens and then shuts, sometimes with amazing rapidity. If an organization begins to analyze an opportunity only after the window opens, it is likely to slam shut before the organization is ready to act. The opportunity is squandered. If, on the other hand, the organization has identified the potential opportunity before it actually occurs, if it thinks rigorously about how to promote the emergence of the opportunity, and if it has thought through how it will exploit the opportunity once it emerges, then it is ready to leap through the window the minute it opens. Time and energy spent preparing for potential opportunities can have huge payoffs.

An example is the merger of Martin Marietta and Lockheed. With the demise of the Soviet Union, the U.S. defense industry took a huge downturn. Most defense contractors wrung their collective hands and viewed the peace dividend as completely devoid of any upside. Two of the largest defense contractors, however, saw the situation as an opportunity to merge, eliminating redundancies and creating a much more competitive organization.

A Framework for Innovation—or, That Pony Could Be a Racehorse

The capability to be innovative has emerged as extremely critical for any enterprise, not just those in technical industries. For example, even in the realm of megastore retailing, the development of an electronic distribution link between Wal-Mart and its suppliers was a startling innovation in a relatively staid industry. Consequently, the notion of innovation has received a huge amount of attention in the business press in recent years, with more than twenty-eight thousand articles published on the topic since 1990.

The vast majority of these missives, however, deal with two ends of an innovation continuum.

At one end is the mystical school of innovation, which views the creative process as essentially an inspirational, out-of-body experience, warranting the highest possible score on the *woo woo* scale. The mystical school was in vogue in the 1970s, and its influence is still pervasive. Within the past five years we participated in a very reputable innovation seminar that—and you cannot make this stuff up—had us sitting, with our eyes closed, across from a woman whose name was Fatima, trying to envision her creative thoughts. We failed miserably, although we were convinced that Fatima's creative thoughts would have been an innovative breakthrough for both of us.

At the other end of the innovation continuum is the view that it can, in fact, be codified as a multistepped process much like preventive maintenance or becoming an effective salesperson. This is the any-dolt-can-be-a-creative-genius school of thinking. Form triumphs over substance as scores of employees try to bridge their cerebral hemispheres in pursuit of collective innovation.

A problem with the "mystical experience" school of innovation is that the replication and transfer of the approach are extremely difficult. Development of proficiency in innovation throughout a company becomes a daunting task if inspiration is a prerequisite. At the other end of the continuum, the ideas resulting from a "codified process" approach to innovation seem to regress rapidly toward the mean of the group and the average thinking represented in it. But innovation, by definition, requires breaking away from the mean of the group. Therefore, group ideas probably fail in being innovative. As used in most organizations, these techniques—analogies, lateral thinking, challenges of assumptions, alternative points of entry, the six-hat model, brainstorming, and a number of other routes to innovation—while designed to help groups be more creative and innovative, usually fall short of their objective.

Let's take a closer look at the technique or skill that we recommend to prepare for the future: Potential Problem and Potential Opportunity Analysis (described in detail in the Appendix). If one thing is, in fact, predictable about the future of any business, it is that inevitably there will be problems and there will be opportunities. Both will require innovation. Potential Problem and Potential Opportunity Analysis effectively bridges the two ends of the innovation continuum, the intuitive and the intellectual, and is further useful in many other ways.

- It provides a framework for thinking about future problems and opportunities and the innovations that may be necessary, a process that can be replicated and transferred as a proficiency.
- It allows for a great deal of flexibility in its application, lends itself to individual or group use, and can easily be combined with other creative techniques such as brainstorming.
- It is relatively simple. Everything that one needs to know in order to use Potential Problem and Potential Opportunity Analysis could be described in four or five pages. In contrast, explanations of lateral thinking, synectics, and other codified processes consume reams of paper, not to mention the time and expense of finding your way through the morass. Simplicity is a key advantage in any attempt to install the process as an ongoing organizational discipline.
- The most common distinction between creativity and innovation holds that creativity produces the ideas, while it is through innovation that the ideas are implemented. Potential Problem and Potential Opportunity Analysis converts creative ideas into innovative action by focusing on the tasks needed to increase the likelihood of converting an idea to reality. Corning developed the technology for transmitting information via light in optical wave guides. Only by actively promoting every opportunity to convert the idea of optical fiber into reality was Corning able to transform a very creative idea into a highly profitable and beneficial innovation.

Creativity in Identifying Problems

Creativity has an important role in the resolution of tough issues. If a problem is a recurring one, then creativity may be warranted in hypothesizing possible causes. The identification of creative alternatives has always been part of the process of decision making, especially if the normal range of alternatives affords insufficient benefits or unacceptable risks. However, when the past was the best predictor of the future, the issues or problems themselves were relatively obvious. Years ago, if a company wanted to prepare for the future, it would gather its most knowledgeable people in a group and identify potential problems and, rarely, potential opportunities based on the experience of the group. Then, if needed, it would use techniques for creativity to develop methods of dealing with the problems.

How issues or problems are identified changes significantly when the past is a necessary but not sufficient predictor of the future. If some events in the future will likely be outside the collective experience of a company, it has two complementary methods of identifying these events: diversity and creativity. Diversity as a discipline entails drawing upon the collective experiences of a diverse population surrounding an issue. By combining diversity with creativity, an organization can enhance its chances of identifying potential problems and opportunities. The company can accomplish this blend of diversity and creativity through a sequence of activities:

- Identify people with the diverse experiences that have any relevance to the potential problem or opportunity.
- Use the framework of Potential Problem and Potential Opportunity Analysis to structure the thinking of these people.
- Individually or collectively employ creative techniques, like brainstorming or analogies, to use the diversity of the group to help identify potential problems or opportunities within the framework just created.

Johnson & Johnson's response to the tampering with Tylenol was a model of responsible, creative, and effective action. However, in hindsight, McNeil Consumer Products, the Johnson & Johnson subsidiary that manufactures Tylenol, certainly wishes that product tampering had been identified as a potential problem before it occurred. Perhaps the use of diversity and creativity could have been helpful in the identification of product tampering as a potential problem.

Experience and the Future: Another Oxymoron?

We are often amused and a little befuddled by clients who, after vociferously asserting their uniqueness as a company, want to know where we have done similar work before. Likewise, there is irony in trying to assert the role of experience in preparing for an unpredictable and uncertain future. If the future is increasingly unpredictable, then, logically, experience would seem to provide little benefit in preparing for it. In fact, experience plays a critical role in preparing for an uncertain future.

We believe there is an important advantage offered by rigorous, repeatable thinking processes. If the thinking process needed to effectively prepare for the future is Potential Problem and Potential Opportunity Analysis, the inputs to that process are the experience and knowledge of people. Specifically, experience is extremely relevant as input into these four steps of Potential Problem and Potential Opportunity Analysis:

1. Identifying which problems and opportunities might occur
2. Assessing the probability of a problem or opportunity occurring
3. Determining what could possibly cause a problem or opportunity
4. Analyzing the impact if the problem or opportunity did occur

Contrary to the implicit or explicit message in the view of the future as chaos, the past, obviously, is a useful guide to the future. Santayana's familiar observation "Those who cannot remember the past are condemned to repeat it" certainly pertains to the more mundane analysis of a company's potential problems and opportunities. While the future most likely will not be a straight line projection of the past, neither will it be a total departure. The challenge for organizations is to apply experience wisely, without falling into the trap of assuming that the future will replicate the past. Again, diversity is one way to prevent experience from becoming a trap.

Of the two critical variables to be considered in analyzing potential problems and opportunities—namely, the probability that something will occur and its impact if it does, it is in the assessment of probability where wise use of experience is most needed. We have found that most companies can apply their collective experience to the assessment of impact relatively effectively. Probability, though, becomes more elusive simply because the future will not replicate the past. Some companies go to great lengths to try to assess objectively the probability of a problem or opportunity. Others end up with wind-chapped fingers. The companies who effectively use their experience to assess probability determine what level of information is sufficient to make an assessment. They strike a balance between slavery to measurement and soothsaying.

To analyze the potential problems and opportunities associated with a joint venture with an Asian partner, a giant U.S. building-materials company assembled an internal group whose members had extensive knowledge, diversity, and experience in the industry. They quickly identified certain reactions by competitors, such as significant price reductions, as having a negative potential impact. Assessment of the probability of such actions, however, was more difficult because the group was concerned that they did not have sufficient information on how European competitors might react. The company considered two courses of action. The first was to conduct lengthy studies to analyze the probability of various responses by the European competitors. The second was to involve individuals from the Asian partner in the assessment of potential problems and opportunities. They opted for the latter course because it constituted a wise use of available experience. Based on its assessment of probability, the building-products company took several actions with customers and used public relations to decrease the probability of potential problems caused by their competitors. The joint venture was implemented without a hitch.

The Strategic Use of Potential Problem and Potential Opportunity Analysis

In our view there has been less Potential Problem and Potential Opportunity Analysis applied by companies in the past thirty years than any of the other thinking processes addressed here.

Our assumption as to why this is so entails the degree to which the future has been seen as replicating the past. When we knew our competitors, we could predict their response to a new product with a reasonable degree of certainty. However, we have seen some significant changes in the use of Potential Problem and Potential Opportunity Analysis, and these changes seem to have occurred in three stages.

In the first stage, Potential Problem Analysis is used as part of an organizational procedure. The procedures for handling hazardous waste reflect some Potential Problem Analysis in most companies. The preventive maintenance programs in most companies also incorporate Potential Problem Analysis. The potential problems that exist are predictable, and the probability of the problems is relatively certain. Therefore, potential problems can be addressed through the use of a standardized checklist. In preparing its space shuttles for flights, Lockheed Martin Space Operations goes through a checklist consisting of over one million potential problems.

The second stage in the use of Potential Problem Analysis involves the operational use of the process, which is appropriate when three conditions exist.

1. The potential problems that exist are relatively difficult to identify.
2. The probability of potential problems is uncertain.
3. Experience, alone, is the best source of information for identifying potential problems and assessing probability in those cases when the past is still the best indicator of the future.

The operational use of Potential Problem Analysis entails following the process as originally described by Charles H. Kepner and Benjamin B. Tregoe in 1965 in their book *The Rational Manager.* Both potential problems and opportunities are identified for a plan or proposed action. In the case of the former, the likely causes of problems are assessed, and actions to prevent them or mitigate their effects are planned. Examples of the operational use of Potential Problem Analysis are numerous.

- Fiskars, the large Finnish consumer products company, used Potential Problem Analysis when it organized into intact work cells.
- Corning's commercial operations used Potential Problem Analysis to plan actions to reduce low-volume products.
- Procter & Gamble uses Potential Problem Analysis any time machinery downtime is planned.

The third stage of Potential Problem Analysis involves the use of the process to prepare for strategic issues. As uncertainty about the future increases exponentially, the need to extend the search for potential problems into strategic areas becomes more critical. By strategic areas, we mean focusing the analysis of both potential problems and opportunities on, among other things, markets, the competition, emerging technologies, and internal capabilities and competencies. Ironically, as uncertainty increases, the search for potential problems and opportunities needs to broaden rather than, as is the normal tendency, to contract. Examples of the strategic use of Potential Problem and Potential Opportunity Analysis are more difficult to find than those of procedural or operational use. Corning's evaluation of the risks and opportunities associated with its overseas joint venture partners is an example of the strategic use of the process.

Prior to the drafting of the Clean Air Act in the United States, we were working with a small environmental consulting firm in helping it determine the range of services the company should offer. In the process of analyzing potential opportunities, the notion of clean air credits was raised. At the time, assigning credits to a company for clean air was an embryonic idea. Through the analysis, however, the firm determined that if credits became part of the law, a niche would be created for brokering the credits. The firm invested a minimal amount in preparing for the possible existence of credits and quickly exploited the niche when credits became part of the new law.

The three stages in the use of Potential Problem and Potential Opportunity Analysis demonstrate the relationship between certainty and the application of the process. The following chart illustrates this relationship.

Application of Potential Problem and Potential Opportunity Analysis

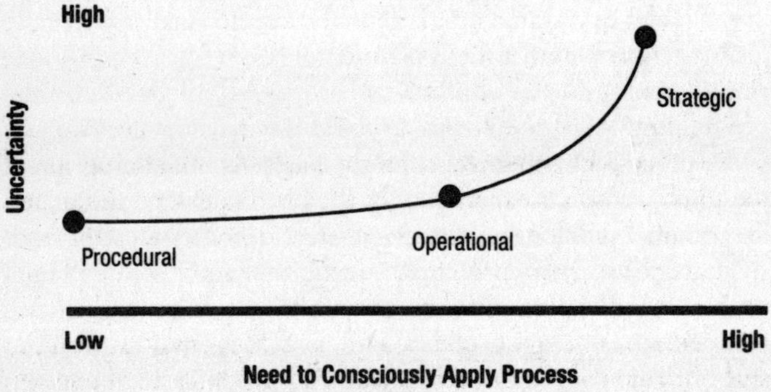

Ready, Ready, Ready, Aim, Fire

More than ten years ago Peters and Waterman popularized the notion of "Ready, fire, aim" in their book *In Search of Excellence.* They were attempting to counter the tendency they had observed to overly analyze, which results in analysis paralysis. Our experience indicates that some managers and leaders have certainly gotten this message, and we see more hip-shooting now than ever before. In fact, the penchant for action as opposed to thought seems to be stronger than ever. We doubt that Intel's initial cavalier response to the problems with the Pentium chip involved much anticipation and preparatory thought. In the rush to introduce health care reform, the Clinton administration failed to anticipate the huge resistance to a large government agency charged with oversight of the health care system.

But there are exceptions. Corning's decision to exploit optical wave technology is a case in point. The decision to move ahead, as James Houghton, Corning's recently retired chairman and chief executive officer, knew, entailed "risks, surrounded by risks, surrounded by further risks." Two potential problems had to be overcome: an uncompetitive cost structure—a big concern, given the production requirements of advanced fiber technology—and being blindsided on the product side by more innovative competitors. Corning's approach to these potential problems was nothing more state-of-the-art than the old Boy Scout motto, "Be prepared." The key was to make heavy front-end investments in the new technology, which Corning did year after year. And it meant gearing up for continual, self-induced, planned obsolescence.

The result? Corning is now in the twelfth generation of products coming from the new technology. It is low-cost producer and also enjoys the lion's share of the market for manufacturing fiber optics. The way to minimize risk, concludes Houghton, is "Don't hold back when you're doing something of some magnitude." And "Keep leapfrogging ahead of your competition. You can't sit still." In other words, be prepared.

Preparation entails an increasing readiness for any number of possible events in the future. Readiness entails problem prevention and opportunity promotion, as well as quick response to problems and opportunities if they do occur. All of which means that in preparing for the future, the heavy emphasis is on ready—not aim or fire.

Creation of Ambiguity

A case could be made that if you think you can control the future, then you obviously do not understand the situation. Based on the recent experiences of any number of companies, the uncertainty of the future can cause the most stalwart to approach tomorrow with fear and trepidation. Yet some companies—like Corning,

British Airways, and Hewlett-Packard—seem to understand that while control of the future is impossible, preparation for the future provides them with a distinct advantage.

An observation that emerges in any discussion of those who are good at preparing for the future is the pervasive ambiguity that accompanies any focus on the future. In some respects, the effective companies and individuals do not just tolerate ambiguity in viewing the future; they create it. They mandate a common framework for thinking about the future but avoid doctrinaire methods that stifle innovation. If asked, "Which is more important, thought or action?" they respond, "Yes." They recognize the value of experience without assuming that the future will replicate the past. They see a structured approach as complementing diversity and creativity, not inhibiting them. They view the uncertainty and chaos attending the future as more reason to prepare, not less. And they see the strategic use of Potential Problem and Potential Opportunity Analysis as more critical in the face of increasing unpredictability, just when many companies are shying away from any remotely visionary focus on strategy.

Arguably, the characteristic that best describes the effective company's view of ambiguity is the value placed on decisiveness. It understands that while decisiveness may be desirable in addressing the present, it is a liability, not a virtue, in preparing for the future. It would find the statement "We're certain that decisiveness is not needed in this situation" to have meaning beyond a somewhat clever bumper sticker.

CHAPTER 6

Taming Data Overload

I worry about techno-freaks who would tell us that if we simply get the right organizational design and apply the right information technology tools, all will be well. There's a wonderful one-liner that I use in my seminars, from the poet Donald Hall, which is, "Information is the enemy of intelligence."

TOM PETERS,
Author; founder of
The Tom Peters Group

For managers at the dawn of a new century the issue of data and information is not so much "How do you keep up with the flood of information?" as it is "How do you keep up with the flood of 'keeping up with the flood of information' books and articles?" It is a frightening fact that each month one major database publisher provides its customers with access to more than seventy thousand articles on information technology.

Unless you've been living in a cave for the past ten or fifteen years, you probably feel as we do about this topic: pretty much fizzed out. We are supposed to welcome the Information Age with joyous abandon as we queue up on the information superhighway. Of course, it is our solemn duty as writers on management to urge our readers to do likewise. Yes, we know that the capability to collect and organize data with mind-boggling speed has had a monumental impact on how we do business. And we know that the ability to access and use information effectively is an absolute necessity for individuals and organizations as we approach the twenty-first century. But enough is often too much.

We're overdosed on all the transportation analogies and metaphors when applied to information.

Nonetheless, we must address the changing role that information plays in core processes like problem solving and decision making. Like all processes, problem solving and decision making require inputs. More specifically, they require data and information. Therefore, the value and the use of these processes are profoundly affected by changes in the nature of their inputs. Let's look at how they have changed, as well as the impact of those changes on decision making and problem solving. Then we'll look at how some companies have accommodated these changes.

Too Much Data—Too Little Information

Data and information tend to be used as synonymous terms. There are departments of data services in some companies and information services in others. Some use the terms "data-driven decisions" and "information-driven decisions" interchangeably. Most would acknowledge, though, that data and information are fundamentally different. Data is the factual input for reasoning and discussion, while information is knowledge gained by investigation. Data by itself has little meaning. Only through reasoning and discussion is meaning, or knowledge, gained from data. As C. K. Prahalad put it, "Data without a point of view can overwhelm you. Throwing raw data at people is like asking them to drink from a fire hose." By contrast, information *is* knowledge; inherent in information is meaning. Data is the raw material of information.

Neither are data and information synonymous in the role they play in organizational decision making. All too often, organizations assume that data is information, thereby overwhelming their ability to make decisions and solve problems effectively. Some organizations collect data as an exercise in ersatz problem solving and decision making. Says Jay Honeycutt, director of the Kennedy Space Center, "Collecting data has almost become a substitute for solving problems and making decisions. There seems to be more fun and joy in collecting data and accessing databases than in using information technology as a tool for analysis."

If an organization fails to make the distinction between how data and information are used, several phenomena are likely to occur. One is that the organization will install all types of systems, computer and otherwise, to generate more data more quickly. These organizations find themselves on the horns of the real dilemma that every organization faces. More and more the ability to use information effectively is critical to sustaining a competitive advantage. If data is a necessary input for information, then the rapid collection of data is a critical organizational capability. However, converting data into information entails reasoning, interpretation, and judgment—still human mental activities that are vastly slower processes than those employed by our fastest computers.

Thus our ability to generate vast amounts of data has far outstripped our ability to convert it into information. The gap between the speed of data collection and the speed of conversion to information is another example—maybe the prime example—of a technological capability exceeding the human capability to use the technology effectively. Yet if an organization assumes that data and information are synonymous, then the technological capability to gather data will drive the data collection activity, and the inevitable outcome is data overkill and overload. Instead, the human capability to convert the data into information should drive the data collection efforts in an organization.

To help Corning better manage costs, we work at getting data—costs, scrap, throughput, inventory levels, etc.—down to the operators in plants. But while we also work to build people's capability to convert data into information, we often find that we have overwhelmed their capacity to make data meaningful. As one shift supervisor said, "Checking my E-mail or my mail slot has become an exercise in guilt. I find all sorts of data that I should use, but don't have the time. The company has invested a lot in helping me understand what the data means and then acting on my analyses. I still can't factor the data into my decisions the way I know that I should because of the sheer volume. I end up not using the data available to me, and obviously I'm concerned that the decisions have overlooked a critical factor."

The Hardware-Software-Humanware Gap

One contributing factor to the gap between the capability to generate data and the capability to convert data to information has to do with technology. The relationship between advances in hardware, software, and human capabilities was best described to us by Winston Lau from Crane Co. The rate of change in hardware has been exponential; software and human capabilities have developed more slowly. The phenomenon is illustrated in the figure that follows.

Relative Rates of Change: Hardware, Software, and Human Capabilities

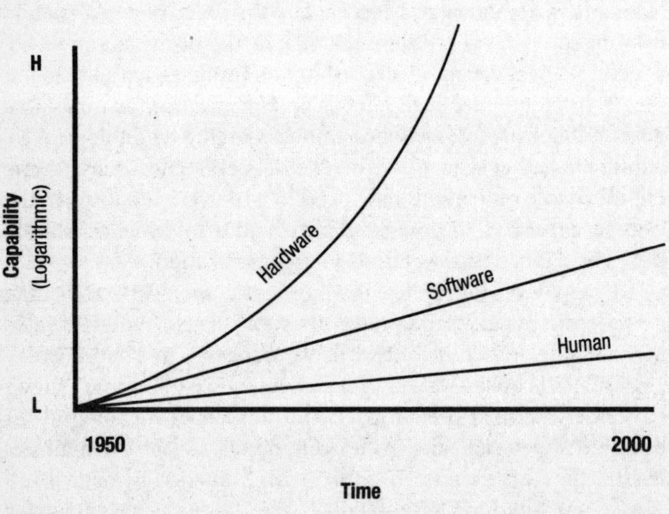

A major computer manufacturer expected to improve the capability of its computer 30 percent per year when it was introduced in 1987. Instead, the capability increased at 60–90 percent

per year. Software development necessarily has lagged behind hardware improvements, since hardware capability drives software applications. Our survey of top managers indicates, however, that the human capability has improved very little over the same period of time. Hardware is the capability to collect and store data. Software is the technological process used to present data so that meaning can be derived from it. Human capability is still required to process data for meaning. The organizational capability to derive meaning from data is limited by the lowest denominator, the human capability.

Modern-Day Luddites

The experience of a senior vice president of a division of a large consumer-products company illustrates the problem of too much data and too little information. The division's senior management was confronted with a decision regarding a new-product introduction. Over the course of several months the group had twelve meetings, some lasting all day. Members of the group had commissioned extensive studies from their marketing people and had hired a consultant to complete a competitor analysis. Manufacturing had analyzed production costs ad nauseam, and R&D had thoroughly assessed the technological problems and risks. When all the studies were completed, each member of the group had three two-inch-thick notebooks filled with the results, and they had endured two-hour dog and pony shows from each functional area, as well as one from the consultant. As they finally wrestled with the decision, they were strongly influenced by impassioned pleas from the VPs of marketing and R&D. The senior VP stated that she could not remember anyone even referring to any of the notebooks during the discussion. She said, "Based on the way this decision was made, the time and money spent on the studies was totally wasted. Now the best use of our time would be weekly prayer breakfasts to implore divine intervention in making sure our decision is a good one."

Like the Luddites who rampaged in Nottingham in the early nineteenth century, smashing new textile technology, the senior managers in the division destroyed the benefit of increased data and information to their decision making. They were overwhelmed by the data on markets, competition, costs, and technologies, so they opted to make a decision based on emotion and persuasion rather than information and knowledge. In fact, the amount of data provided was so daunting that the senior managers consciously spurned it in their decision-making process. Ironically, the staffers who spent countless hours and sacrificed their holidays conducting the studies and preparing impressive presentations thought that they were providing information, not just data. They had tried to provide meaning from the data by offering analyses as well. If, however, intended information does not add useful knowledge, then by definition it is not information. In other words, what is information to one person or group may be treated only as data by another.

We have observed countless examples of decisions relating to such areas as product development, organizational structure, and selection of key people when the decision makers have made a general request for information. Various functions are called on to produce three-ring binders bulging with what they think is information, not just data. Yet due to the sheer volume of the input, it fails to inform and is largely ignored by the decision makers.

Those who try to put data to use often come away frustrated and even paralyzed. "Many people have been put into information overload," observes Joseph Keilty. "It has paralyzed their ability to make decisions. There are too many variables, and they lack the skill to disaggregate data, to establish a hierarchy of importance to make data useful for decision making." Thus, in many companies the sound of a sledgehammer smashing a power loom has been replaced by the silence of dust gathering on binders of data meant to inform.

Data and Information: How Much Is Enough?

Too much data and too little information can be a critical concern. At the Kennedy Space Center it can become a life-and-death issue. Explains Daniel Patterson, "When you have a limited time window in which to make a decision, such as when you must decide whether or not to abort a launch, you keep receiving information the whole time. Updates keep coming and you must keep analyzing them. But at a predetermined time you must stop analyzing, refuse to look at any more information, and make the call."

To address a given issue, what constitutes sufficient information? How do you know when to "make the call?" It has been said that any important concept in life can be expressed on a scale of zero to ten. If we array the information available to us on any given issue on this scale, we can make two statements that are almost always true. First, we never have zero information on an issue. Otherwise we would not even realize that the issue exists. Second, we never achieve a ten on the scale, because we never have all the information relevant to an issue. If we had all the relevant information—and *only* the relevant information—the issue essentially would be resolved and no longer exist. Consequently, the question becomes, where on the zero-to-ten scale of information sufficiency will we be satisfied that we have enough information to address the issue?

A number of factors influence how we answer this question. For lack of a better term, organizational culture is one determinant. The culture of some organizations drives many decision makers to want to achieve an eight or nine on the information scale before they address an issue. Other organizations consistently are content with information in the two-to-four range. Two examples come to mind. One is an organization dominated by engineers, which tries to achieve a very high level of information sufficiency. While that seems commendable, this organization processes the same amount of data and information whether it is making a $1,500 or a $1.5 million capital investment decision. Consequently, decision making is agonizingly slow. By contrast, we once worked with another organization to help executives determine a purpose and structure for a widely dispersed R&D function. After a half day of cursory discussion of markets, competitors, technology, etc., one top manager stood up and said, "Enough contemplation of our navels! Let's get on with making the decisions." The group then proceeded to make significant decisions based largely on opinion; nonetheless, team members felt that they had been particularly rigorous in addressing the issues. Their approach to information sufficiency strongly reflected their founder's penchant to shoot from the hip in making decisions and not to look back. To get these organizations to change their approach to information sufficiency requires that those in command examine—and perhaps confront—some aspects of their organizational cultures.

Two obvious factors that influence information sufficiency are the relative impact of its use in decision making and the amount of time available to use it. The greater the impact of the issue on the organization, the more information is needed to achieve information sufficiency. As the time pressure to address an issue increases, generally the amount of information required to achieve sufficiency decreases. Impact and time seem to push the required level of information sufficiency in opposite directions. Consequently if an issue has high impact and must be resolved quickly, an apparent conflict in the appropriate level of information sufficiency exists.

The question of information sufficiency is situational, as illustrated in the figure on page 115, in which issues are placed in quadrants based on increasing impact and time pressure.

Obviously, issues that fall into the fourth quadrant, high impact and high time pressure, present the greatest quandary about how much information is sufficient to make a decision. Some organizations consistently place issues in the wrong quadrant based on a poor assessment of impact and time pressure. The multibillion-dollar company that invested considerable staff and management time in gathering and assessing information pertaining to a $1,500 savings in supplies behaves as if every issue has high impact. Likewise, the Fortune 500 company that made a decision regarding its R&D function based on very little information about markets, competitors, and technological advances acts as if every decision must be made quickly regardless of its impact. In fact, the decision about a $1,500 savings for a multibillion-dollar company certainly falls in the second quadrant, and the decision regarding the structure of the R&D function belongs in the third. Since the function had existed for several years in its cur-

Relationship of Impact and Time Pressure on Information Sufficiency

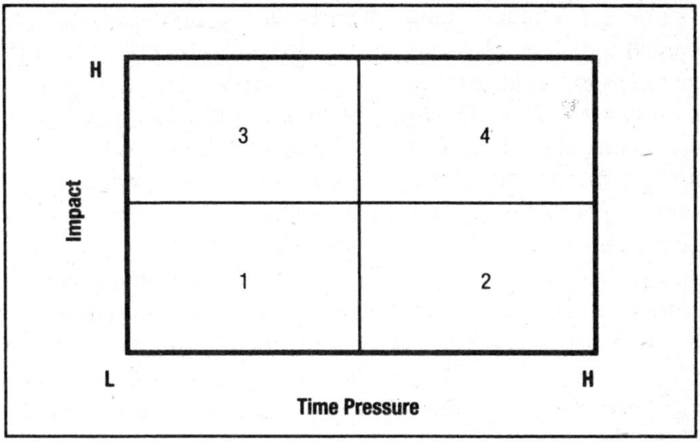

rent structure, and since no crisis loomed on the horizon, the company could have taken the time to gather and analyze sufficient information before making any decisions.

The Functionalization of Information

Recently we were talking with the chief executive of a large company about a wide range of topics. In the discussion of one particular issue, his voice rose in frustration. The issue dealt with the difficulty of getting his company's information system to provide data regarding a potential strategic alliance. His is a widely shared frustration.

Ask the leaders of any public and private sector organization, as we have, "What is needed to gain and maintain some competitive or strategic advantage?" and the answer is nearly unanimous: "Good information." When we ask the same leaders what causes the most headaches, their responses usually include the information systems internal to their organizations. Given these answers, we are continually baffled about why these leaders literally and figuratively functionalize the responsibility for generating and communicating information.

Giving one organizational function the responsibility for specific information has a number of deleterious and unintended effects. For example, information regarding the costs of a business is often seen as the purview of the finance function. Whether we are talking about activity-based costing or the annual budgeting process, finance usually drives these initiatives and, in turn, typically serves as the repository for the information generated by budgeting or ABC accounting. Too often, if finance is given and assumes responsibility for cost information, those who deal with costs on a daily basis abrogate their responsibility for cost reduction to finance. As a result, cost management receives too little focus from the people who can most thoughtfully reduce the cost base of the business. And the finance function is seen as the organizational Grim Reaper.

An egregious example of the functionalization of information is the creation and growth of information services departments in organizations. Even the title of the function is a misnomer. Since the distinction between data and information is a significant one, the old title of data services more accurately reflects the output of the function. Regardless of its title, however, the effects of designating the responsibility for an organization's data or information to one function are insidious.

One effect can be called the tyranny of expertise. As the nature of our businesses becomes increasingly more technical, the role of technical experts in making good decisions has also increased significantly. Because we are so dependent on technology for data, if not information, those with expertise in the technology are given or assume undue importance in using data to analyze issues. We depend on functional and systems analysts to tell us how data should be gathered and communicated. We depend on hardware and software experts to make sure that our companies' revenues do not outstrip our costs by an outrageous margin. Like the typical family in Borneo that consists of 2 parents, 1.8 children, and an anthropologist, the typical business meeting consists of some number of operational managers and an IS person.

This tyranny of expertise plumbs new depths in the designation of someone as a company's chief information officer—the person who presumably has overall responsibility for the information in a company. Just as the chief financial officer is responsible for ensuring the financial integrity of a company, is the chief information officer responsible for ensuring the quality and quantity of a company's information? The absurdity of the notion that one person can or should have overall responsibility for the information critical to a business should be obvious.

A further and particularly insidious effect of this functionalization is the potential abrogation of responsibility for information by those who need information most. An increasingly important expectation of any job is to gather, organize, and analyze the information needed to perform the job well. As data proliferate, the collective acceptance of this responsibility for information throughout an organization becomes imperative. However, the creation and growth of information service functions headed by someone called the chief information officer can counteract the efforts to disseminate responsibility for information.

An example we recently encountered comes to mind. We were working with the senior management group of a sales and distribution company on the control of its inventory. Each member of the group was responsible for a sizable geographic region. During our initial discussion a number of questions were raised, such as: What are the most profitable products sold in each region? Which are the most profitable customers in each region? What is the cost to support the inventory of low-volume products?

While each member of the group had definite opinions about the answers to the questions, none of them, when pushed, were certain of the answers. The group determined that it needed more information than opinion to answer the questions. Consequently, one of the group called the company's chief information officer to find out how to answer the questions. A separate meeting was scheduled with the CIO to discuss the needed data and information. Once the CIO was clear about the needs of the group, he promised that the information would be available in a week. A week later we met with the regional VPs again, but this meeting included the CIO, an information systems analyst, and the company's controller. We were able to answer some of the questions with much help from the IS people and the controller. But in this meeting a decision was reached that more specific information was needed; a project team was formed, comprising people from the regions, IS, and finance, to gather and analyze information in detail. Three months after the initial meeting the regional VPs finally had the necessary information to make the decisions regarding their inventories. Here were nine senior managers, each of whom was responsible for up to $30 million in sales, yet none of them could readily access the information needed to answer basic questions about their business. They had to rely on information services and finance to gather and interpret this information. In effect, they had abrogated their responsibility for information, partly because functions existed that were given that responsibility.

Providing Data with Meaning

Trappist philosopher Thomas Merton once wrote that a thousand failures prove little, while one success proves what is possible. In terms of effectively using data and information, there are countless errors; but then we've witnessed many examples of notable success. If data have to be converted into information to have meaning, and if our technical ability to generate data has far outstripped our human ability to make the conversion, are we doomed to some mythological fate in which we are confronted with more and more data that have less and less meaning? Hewlett-Packard and Procter & Gamble would respond, "Definitely not." They have implemented several initiatives extremely well.

First, Hewlett-Packard and Procter & Gamble have succeeded in putting the responsibility for issue identification and resolution at the appropriate level. Exhortations to push responsibility down an organization have become hackneyed, but very few companies, in our experience, do it well. What Hewlett-Packard, Procter & Gamble, and others that have effectively implemented empowerment have done is to set clear expectations as to which issues are to be addressed at which level. For example, they are clear that production problems are to be solved by the salaried and hourly people on the floor. Capital investment decisions are made at the plant or business level, depending on amounts. Plant management realizes that it is outside its role to get deeply involved in addressing specific production problems. Production teams realize that it is outside their purview to address overall plant issues unless they directly affect their area. Since everyone is relatively clear who has responsibility for addressing an issue, very little undercutting occurs.

Second, these companies have determined that a common process should be used to address issues that are important, because it gives groups charged with resolving an issue a common language and approach. Also, it enables others to understand clearly how a conclusion was reached. If a product manager is recommending a sizable investment in a modification or extension of a product, senior management understands and trusts the process used to reach this conclusion. Questions about the conclusion are driven by the process and therefore elicit less of a defensive reaction. Since everyone is knowledgeable regarding what process was used to reach the conclusion, less second-guessing occurs.

Third, companies who have really pushed down responsibility and authority make certain that their people have the technical knowledge needed to address an issue. They expect their supervisors to have technical knowledge about how a product is made. They expect product managers to have detailed knowledge about markets and competition. The responsibility for knowledge is not functionalized. Instead, these organizations expect those addressing an issue to have a significant amount of the technical knowledge needed as input to the process.

Fourth, these companies make sure that the people responsible for drawing meaning from data have the skills, both process and technical, to perform this task. The emphasis companies like Hewlett-Packard and Procter & Gamble place on training has been amply documented elsewhere. Typically, they specify an organizational standard for training. Corning's standard, for example, is that 5 percent of each employee's time is devoted to training. And it's valuable training; they emphasize both technical and process training for making data meaningful.

There is one other distinction that is a hallmark of companies that are able to convert data to information and knowledge. They work backward. As Joel Kurtzman, former editor of the *Harvard Business Review*, explains, such companies ask: Do we have enough information to know how good we can be? And if so, do we know how to get there? Too many companies proceed from the other end of the telescope. They can tell you exactly where they are but not where they should be headed. Kurtzman cites Nike as an example of a company that knows how to manage the information flow. Nike deliberately limits what it wants to know. It realizes it doesn't have to know much about manufacturing, but it does have to know plenty about design, marketing, and contracting. Says Kurtzman, "Nike has a clear strategy that focuses everyone's attention on the company's core strengths. Nike knows its playing field and asks, 'What do we need to know to compete in this arena?' "

Knowing How Much Information Is Enough

Some companies seem to be able to achieve information sufficiency regularly in addressing critical issues. They are besieged with the inevitable data overloads that plagues us all. Yet they are able to identify quickly the data and information that are pertinent to an issue, and they strike an appropriate balance between whimsy and paralysis in the analysis of the information. Specifically, organizations such as Corning and Harley-Davidson effectively use data and information to improve the management of costs at their plants.

Both Corning and Harley-Davidson understood the need to be better at managing the costs of manufacturing. Both had experienced the roller-coaster ride of cost cutting, costs creeping back in, then cost cutting once again. Key managers in manufacturing had inadequate information on costs, and consequently their understanding about how their decisions affected costs was insufficient. In their analysis of the problem, executives at Corning and Harley-Davidson concluded that they needed a process for identifying the information pertinent to ongoing cost management and for making decisions based on the information.

A key decision both companies needed to make was determining the optimal product mixes for their plants. An inevitable objective for this decision was to maximize profitability. A key piece of information needed to assess various product mixes against this objective was the "true costs" of producing current products. This information is important because we know that the standard allocation of overhead means that low-volume products appear to be more profitable than they actually are. Harley-Davidson and Corning realized that they needed more accurate information on the costs of producing current products. In other words, the process helped them identify what information was needed.

Now the question became, "How much information is sufficient in assessing current product costs?" In answering this question, the companies could have implemented a full-blown activity-based costing system that would have provided extremely accurate information on product costs. It would also have taken huge investments of time and money to install such a system. In the meantime, Corning and Harley-Davidson would be continuing to produce unprofitable products. Therefore, both companies decided that they did not need the information sufficiency provided by an activity-based costing system to make the decision regarding optimal product mix. Instead, they did an analysis of how much overhead was inappropriately allocated to high-volume products. They then knew that this overhead should be allocated to low-volume products, and whether the low-volume product was 100 percent or 1,000 percent underpriced was immaterial in determining the relative profitability of various product mixes. Having directionally correct information was sufficient for a rigorous, fact-based decision.

Thus a viable, repeatable process enabled Corning and Harley-Davidson to identify what information was necessary to better manage manufacturing costs. The process also helped these two companies determine the degree of information sufficient to make decisions. Corning's and Harley-Davidson's experiences with manufacturing costs can be generalized to all types of decision-making and problem-solving opportunities. The right process will determine what information—as well as how much—is required. In other words, the right process will accelerate a company and put it in the passing lane on the information superhighway. Sorry, we couldn't resist.

CHAPTER 7

All Together Now: Critical Thinking in Teams

A few eyes may be sufficient to set a clear vision, but you need many more eyes–and hands–to implement that vision. Teams provide the power for implementation, particularly in complex environments.

KENNETH H. BLANCHARD
Chairman,
Blanchard Training and Development, Inc.

Teams and teamwork have attained an almost sacred status in business today. The focus on teams, from the boardroom to the shop floor, has dominated our view of how work should be done and has provided a significant opportunity for Outward Bound instructors during the off-season. Unquestionably, the impact of the movement toward teams is largely positive. As Van Campbell, vice chairman of Corning, says, "For most decisions the team approach is better because you get broader inputs, and you reduce the chance of missing something important because you have more of the elephant covered." Beyond the argument that there's strength in numbers, as Kenneth Blanchard points out, there's the notion that not all the thinking in an organization is done by the executive elite: "All the brains are not in the top of an organization." Brainpower, experience, and judgment are distributed throughout organizations; the promise of teamwork is that everything can be tapped best by people working together.

Increasingly, however, we have encountered a backlash. Has the teamwork pendulum swung too far? One senior engineer put it to us bluntly: "I'll commit to almost anything as long as I don't have to go to another team meeting to talk about it." Are sentiments such as these—and we have heard many in the workplace environment recently—symptomatic of a larger issue with team-based organizational design, or is it the carping of a few misfits who wax sentimental over the days of Genghis Khan? Most important, does the role of teams effectively aid or hinder successful decision making and problem solving?

Yesterday I Couldn't Spell Empowerment, Now I Am

A central tenet of the team-based organizational structure is empowerment. Few concepts have so captured the attention of business. We have zapped everyone with the wand of empowerment—whether it was wanted or not. And perhaps for good reason. Certainly it makes sense to push down decision making to the levels where the knowledge and experience exist. And now that we have "right sized," a vacuum has been created at the middle-management level, where decisions were most often made in times past. So, rather than be paralyzed by the lack of decision making, we have no choice but to empower everyone in an organization to make and implement decisions.

While individuals certainly can be empowered, most empowerment initiatives focus on teams. The empowerment of teams is a logical blend of these two widespread movements within businesses—teamwork and empowerment. Of course, it is also much more economical to empower multitudes simultaneously. It's like buying the "family-sized" tube of toothpaste. Unfortunately, however, too many attempts at team empowerment seem to be going the way of Quality Circles and T-groups—to the dustbin of failed management fads. It's not that empowerment is a bad idea; it should, theoretically, produce quicker and better decision making and problem solving. But as it is typically implemented, empowerment appears as an end in itself, rather than as a means to an end. Its most common failings are worth closer examination.

The stories of empowered teams failing to make expected and significant contributions to a business are legion. In one company the walls at headquarters and in the plants were festooned with posters extolling the virtues of teamwork and empowerment. Employees spent three months being molded into teams, culminating in a team cookout where everyone had a critical and interdependent role in grilling the burgers. At the end of the three months the teams had fully appreciated each other's Myers-Briggs type, climbed up and down Cogg's Ladder, and amply documented their common objectives and ground rules.

Top management then asked the newly empowered teams to focus on cutting the costs of the business. They floundered. One team was assigned responsibility for reducing the costs of the bidding process on jobs. Top management had set a goal of cutting 15 percent of the costs across the organization. However, this team did not see that as realistic. Furthermore, the team had no information on the cost of the current process, and it found that getting reasonably accurate information on costs was almost impossible. While there were representatives from the current quoting department on the team, these people—though well meaning and conscientious—were not experts at bidding jobs. They did not know what they didn't know. Critically, feedback and consequences to team members remained focused on each employee's performance of his or her regular job. Very little was directed at the team's performance.

The outcome for this team was all too predictable, and it was mirrored by teams throughout the company. Teams spent months spinning wheels, eventually becoming very frustrated. Top management became increasingly impatient, finally despairing about the investment of time and money in the team and empowerment effort. Some top managers from the Conan the Barbarian School of Management felt that their view of team empowerment as nothing more than a radical social experiment was validated.

Norman Blake, chief executive officer of USF&G, observed such a derailment of empowerment as he was turning around his beleaguered company. When he joined the company, USF&G was on the verge of insolvency due to a portfolio of risky, poorly performing investments and a loss of focus on the core business. As Blake recounts the story, "In my early days, we set up teams as a means of embracing the organization and getting high involvement. We discerned that we had a very low level of competency within those teams and not the right set of skills for the jobs at hand. In essence, we were orchestrating the palace revolt. When empowerment is great, however, there are two essential ingredients for it. First, you must provide authority and carefully define the limits. Second, the level of competency within the organization, department, unit, or team must match the capability of the task. Without both these conditions, there can be little or no empowerment."

To these conditions for empowerment success—a basic understanding of the authority and limits of the team, and the competencies to achieve its goals—Robert Lutz, president of Chrysler, adds a third: the need for strong team leadership. He says, "I find that a team that does not have a natural leader who keeps goading and pushing and basically ensuring progress, and who has the moral courage to perhaps lay his popularity with other team members on the line by pushing for a solution or hypothesis he believes to be right—without an individual like that, teams run the risk of becoming institutionalized inaction."

As American Express was confronting a host of organization issues related to its reengineering efforts, teams were employed to make decisions and implement changes. But, as Joseph Keilty, executive vice president, related, where teams were not given task-specific assignments aligned with team members' skills, the results were often characterized by confusion, inaction, and frustration. On the other hand, where leaders were task specific, emphasizing role and goal clarity, teams functioned well and used time more efficiently. These three determinants for successful teamwork and empowerment—authority and defined limits; the competency to achieve the defined goals; and strong, recognized team leadership—may seem elementary. Yet the lack of these factors has created pitfalls for some of the best companies and managers.

The Cows along the Fence

We spend a lot of time driving the rural roads of North America for a couple of reasons. First, many of our clients' sites are located in small towns. Second, we are directionally challenged, and therefore we frequently get lost. Being always in the learning mode, we do not waste these trips listening to motivational tapes or dictating our autobiographies. Instead, we spend our driving time keenly observing the behavior of animals. Whenever we pass a dairy or beef farm, for example, we have noticed that most of the cows are congregated near the fences. Many acres may be fenced in with huge areas for the cows to roam, but invariably cows bunch themselves near the fence. Why does this phenomenon exist, and are there broader lessons to be learned from this bovine behavior? Our hunch is that cows behave just like adolescents and many people in organizations. Given a limit, they will spend a good deal of their time operating up against it. Given no limits, they will roam around until they find one.

Limits on empowerment must be clearly defined. If teams or individuals perceive that few limits exist on their empowerment, there is a tendency to focus on issues beyond their capability or intended authority. If the limits are imposed after the fact—after a team tackles an inappropriate issue or makes an irresponsible recommendation—team members then view leadership as autocratic and team focus as nothing more than a hollow exercise. As Harley-Davidson's Richard Teerlink puts it, "If we are going to have good decisions, we have to have good fences."

We know of one company that made noble attempts to empower union/management teams to address labor relations issues at different manufacturing sites. Unfortunately, the teams were never given a clear idea of the limits on their authority. Even the labor contract was fair game through the mechanism of local agreements. The predictable outcome was chaos and paralysis. In some locations every decision was arrived at through consensus among the teams. Nobody in the management and union leadership had time to focus on the business of the plants because too much time was consumed by meetings designed to forge a consensus among parties who were often at odds on key issues. In other locations all historic protocol was abandoned without much critical evaluation. Consequently, when layoffs became necessary more grievances were filed than at any other time in the company's history.

Finally, corporate leadership stepped in and "disempowered" the teams by greatly restricting the topics appropriate for local discussion. Understandably, the union leadership and most local management felt that the company had reverted to the Dark Ages of antagonistic labor relations, thereby making future union and management cooperation highly unlikely. As one local union leader commented, "We're big people. If there were areas that the company wanted to be off limits, we can accept it. But the way it was handled made us feel as though we were in kindergarten." Not a happy ending to this company's tale of empowerment.

When we reluctantly resort to the wimpy behavior of asking directions during our rural perambulations in search of clients, we occasionally ask farmers if the cows object to being fenced in. After they make sure that all children and livestock are safe from crazed visitors asking stupid questions, we usually get a reply along the lines of "Well, they don't seem to. In fact, when one gets out she usually just stands next to the fence. Seems like there's some comfort in being up against it."

Empowered Ignorance

A second condition for empowerment is that the competency of the team must match the requirements of the task. Yet when it comes to their approach to team empowerment, there are two types of organizations: those that would not empower Einstein for fear that he would blow the budget on hairspray; and those that are so enamored with team empowerment as a concept that they rush to empower ignorance.

For the organizations that resist empowerment, it's viewed as just this side of giving the inmates the keys to the prison. Senior management behaves as if one's IQ rises 20 percent just by walking in the doors of corporate headquarters. As the North American president of a $4 billion company said to us, "I didn't get to this position by sharing power and decision making, and I don't plan to start now." Thankfully, companies like this one are becoming a minority because they squander the resource that is now recognized as the critical resource for any organization—their human capital.

It is the organizations in the other category, those that empower ignorance, that are becoming more prevalent and, possibly, just as troublesome. Team empowerment, when implemented well, is not just a social experiment with the primary objective of providing a warm, fuzzy glow to team members. It is implemented as a means of focusing the collective intelligence of the team on meaningful business issues. In order to employ this collective intelligence, a team needs to have two things: the data necessary to identify and resolve meaningful issues; and the skills to organize and analyze this data. Without the requisite data and skills, any team is little more than a roving coffee klatch. As our colleague George Elliott often says, "Consensus among the ignorant is still ignorance."

Yet we continually work with or read about progressive, well-meaning, and successful companies that focus time and money on forming teams and breaking down barriers to empowerment but that shortchange the teams' need for data and skills. In fact, our experience emphasizes that building the systems to get data to teams and developing their analytical skills are at least as important as a focus on the skills and the environment needed to build teams. Otherwise, the effort expended by teams focusing internally on their own maintenance and growth is never translated into the desired benefit for the organization. The organization rarely realizes a return on its investment in teams because the team does not have the capability to focus externally on meaningful business issues. Empowered ignorance is both pointless and costly.

Working to reduce manufacturing costs at such diverse companies as Harley-Davidson, Corning, and BHP Steel, we were encouraged by the ability and willingness of teams to make hard decisions when they had relevant, user-friendly data, as well as the skills to make that data meaningful. Management teams effectively rationalized which products to offer and which customers to serve when they had proper data on actual costs and value produced by both low-volume and high-volume customers and products. Data—coupled with process skills to organize and challenge those data—produced high-quality decisions that significantly reduced the cost base of the business. When teams of hourly workers got valid information on the cost of scrap and were given a data-driven, problem-solving process, they were effectively empowered to address significant business issues.

All Dressed up with Nowhere to Go

Bill Cosby has a comedy routine in which he talks about some of his experiences playing football at Temple University. He describes the team preparing for the big game, the dressing in game uniforms, the checking of the equipment, and finally, being whipped into a fury by an impassioned speech from the coach. The team rushes to the locker room door to take the field—only to find that the door is locked. This is just how it is in many companies. Work teams have been put through a variety of team-building exercises and they even may have access to the data they need, but they do not have the opportunity to use the data or their skills. They are all dressed and ready to go, but the door is locked.

Two variables are pertinent in considering the obstacles to opportunity—time and fear of failure. The lack of time to use the skills and data as a team can become a particularly significant barrier where cross-functional teams are employed. Intact work groups who are empowered as teams generally can find the time to function as an empowered team because they are constantly working together. The logistics of working as a team are relatively simple for intact work groups. Cross-functional teams, on the other hand, have to make a concerted effort to function as a team. Often the participants' many regular job duties inhibit their efforts. If other job duties are not simplified and if the roles of team members are not given a high priority, then the team will generally devote insufficient time to team tasks. If an organization is committed to meaningful, empowered cross-functional teams, then its leadership has a responsibility to help the team members identify those low-value activities that can be eliminated, redirecting newly available time to high-value tasks.

Fear of failure is often more insidious—and more difficult to address—than insufficient time. If teams see the cost of failure to be exorbitant, they will not take advantage of the opportunity to be empowered. Fear of failure most often stems from the consequences—formal and informal—meted out by the organization for failure. If the history of the organization is to come down harshly on individuals or groups who fail, then teams will be reluctant to exercise the opportunity to be empowered on substantive issues. Instead they are likely to focus on relatively minor issues, such as the location of water coolers or the selection of food in the cafeteria, thereby frustrating themselves and the leadership that empowered them. No organization can tolerate unlimited failure by teams or individuals. The challenge becomes to empower teams to fail early and fail small. Effective limits and oversight by leadership go a long way toward meeting this challenge.

We recently encountered a venerated company that embarked on an initiative to empower teams. Members of management focused on developing both intact work teams and cross-functional teams, investing heavily in providing employees with both the skills and the information to be empowered. However, they made several serious mistakes in implementing their empowerment initiative. First, they allocated an hour and a half on Thursday afternoons for meetings involving cross-functional teams. The consulting firm involved discouraged management from having any input into the issues selected by the teams. Management was also discouraged from any ongoing involvement with the teams; its role was confined to reviewing and approving recommendations from the teams. When, very early in the implementation stage, a team came to management with a suggested improvement in work conditions—really a labor/management issue—the team was harshly criticized by top management and the union.

It's no surprise that the teams ended up planning the company's outings and recommending the decor for the break rooms. They did not have sufficient time to focus on substantive issues. Management was discouraged from putting limits on the issues addressed by the teams or having an ongoing role in the operation of the teams, and an initial failure by a team was dealt with in a discouraging way. As a result, both the team members and the company's enlightened, committed management were totally disenchanted with teams and empowerment. The sound of a locker room door slamming shut resounded throughout the plant.

For Whom the Bell Tolls

The bell curve has fallen into some disrepute lately, as the umbrella for some ill-conceived theories on intelligence. However, it provides a useful model in discussing the limits of teams—regression to the mean. In statistics, regression to the mean refers to the tendency of a group to measure closer to the average for the entire population as that group becomes larger. For example, say the average height for women in the world is 165 cm. If we were to gather a group of women to measure their height, then the larger the group (and therefore the more representative), the closer their average height would be to 165 cm.

In the discussion of teams, regression to the mean refers to the tendency of a team to pull the thinking of any individual back to the average thinking of the team. Regression to the mean in teams is a variation on groupthink. If regression to the mean is a real phenomenon, then teams are not conducive to breakthrough thinking. In talking about teams, Van Campbell of Corning, a company noted for its technological breakthroughs, says, "On the minus side, team-based decisions make it harder to make the unusual choice because you need to forge some kind of consensus. Teams have a tendency to drive the decision more toward the center, which may kill the big idea." When Ralph Larsen, chairman and chief executive officer of Johnson & Johnson, was asked, "What one piece of advice would you give to up-and-coming stars about decision making?" he replied, "Follow your instincts." He elaborated, "Because I think that every time I've been burned it's when I've gone against my instincts. All the facts said that it was the right decision, but I knew that it didn't feel right and I should have stopped it." Team-based decisions can tend to devalue and disregard the role of instinct.

Larsen relates a story about Johnson & Johnson's entry into the contact lens business. The company had bought a small contact lens business but knew that it needed some way to attack the major players in the same business. The technology for a disposable lens seemed to be the best front for the attack. That technology was costly to develop, though, and the development would take years. Top management at Johnson & Johnson makes most critical decisions as a team, and the top team decided to cut off funding for the development of the disposable technology. One member of the team was not present at the meeting when the decision was made, and consequently he was not influenced by any regression to the mean in the team's thinking. When he learned of the decision, he immediately challenged it and browbeat the team into re-funding the technology. Johnson & Johnson, of course, ended up making impressive inroads into the contact lens business through disposables. Had the initial "mean" thinking of the team prevailed, the company would have killed what has become a very profitable business.

Five Golden Rules of Team-Based Decision Making

The difficulties with team-based decisions are substantial. So how can the benefits of team decision making be reaped while minimizing the pitfalls? Our work with a variety of clients has led us to formulate five guidelines that can assure improvement in team decision making:

1. Understand whom to involve in teams and how to involve them.
2. Clarify the limits of teams and the role of the leadership.
3. Know which rational thinking processes lend themselves to teamwork and which do not.
4. Ensure that teams have the information and analytical skills to make substantive contributions.
5. Provide teams with an environment that supports teamwork.

The Who and How of Teams—In Search of the One-Armed Man

Like the protagonist in the popular television show and movie *The Fugitive,* we are always looking for a one-armed man, if for a slightly different reason. Our search is for the purpose of finding someone who cannot say, "On the other hand . . ." Still, the question of who should be involved in teams and what their appropriate role in decision making is deserves a definitive answer. Unfortunately, that answer is, "It depends."

It depends on a number of critical variables specific to each situation:

- The need for a superior solution to the issue being considered
- What information is needed to resolve the issue
- Who has the needed information
- The commitment required from the team to effectively implement a decision
- The likelihood of commitment without the team's active involvement in the decision
- Goal congruence between the team and the organization on the specific issue
- The level of agreement on alternative methods for implementing the decision

While all the variables are important in answering the question "What is the most appropriate role for a team?" three are particularly significant. The first is information. If an organization's leadership does not have sufficient information to make a good decision, then it needs to get that information from the people most likely to have it. Increasingly, the information needed to thoughtfully address an issue does not reside solely in an organization's leadership, and teams are a very effective and relatively efficient way to get it.

The second critical variable is commitment. The relationship between commitment and involvement is axiomatic. If commitment to a decision is a prerequisite to effective implementation of the decision, then those affected need to feel involved in the decision-making process. Involvement of teams is a very effective way to gain needed commitment.

The third critical variable has to do with the notion of goal congruence, and this variable seems to cause the most difficulty in assigning an appropriate role to teams. The difficulty stems from a common phenomenon—the intended or unintended delegation of authority for decision making to teams. By goal congruence, we mean the level of agreement among the personal goals of team members, the collective goals of teams, and the goals of the organization in regard to the issue under consideration. Our views may be near heresy and reveal us to be other than New Age, but we wonder why leadership would delegate decision-making authority to a team whose goals in making the decision differ from the goals of the organization on the issue at hand. If goal incongruence exists, leadership then has a Hobson's choice. It can overturn the decision and thereby undermine the team and its commitment, which the use of a team was designed to engender. Or, as is more likely the case, leadership is loath to overturn a team's decision, especially after public testimony about its commitment to empowerment. Consequently, leadership begrudgingly supports a decision that, at best, is less than optimal and, at worst, is contrary to the best interests of the organization.

As an alternative, when there is a lack of goal congruence in a given situation, teams can serve in an advisory or consultative role to leadership. This role is a very effective one if leadership, from the start, communicates that the team is in an advisory role, with leadership making the final decision. Leadership, however, must give serious consideration to the team's input. The use of teams in an advisory role when no goal congruence exists avoids the pitfalls of delegating decision-making authority while offering two important benefits: 1) the likelihood of having the necessary information available in the decision-making process is high; and 2) leadership gets the benefit of team thinking without being bound by any goal conflict or regression to the mean evident in the deliberations of the team. If the team feels that its views have received serious consideration and if it understands the rationale for the decision, its commitment to the decision can still remain relatively high.

Although many organizations think of team involvement in binary terms, the involvement of teams in decisions is not an all-or-none proposition. These guidelines can help to optimize the effective use of teams based on the specific circumstances of each situation. And the conscientious use of these guidelines provides leaders with a range of roles for themselves, offering alternatives to behaving either like Idi Amin or Mother Teresa.

Good Fences Make Good Teams

In discussing his use of top management at Corning as a team, James Houghton said, "I think that a major liability of teamwork is when the leader doesn't know when to stop conversation. Our favorite phrase here is, 'Tell me when Jamie has his cowboy hat on and when he has his bowler on.' The cowboy hat means that we're all talking and the bowler means that I've made a decision. They say to me, 'Be fair and tell us which hat you have on. Don't lead us to believe that you are a cowboy when in fact you've made a decision.'" With his hat metaphor, Houghton describes a critical role of leadership in the deployment of team decision making—the setting of limits.

Daniel Patterson, launch site director of the Kennedy Space Center for Lockheed Martin, states the need for limits on teams another way. He says, "There must be parameters when giving assignments to teams. In the old Quality Circles, people often just got together for general brainstorming sessions. To be successful, management should ask people to come up with ideas in specific areas, on specific subjects. We have task teams, called 'tiger teams,' as well as natural work teams that receive empowerment with boundaries. They are told they have the authority to go this far, spend this much, talk to these people, work these hours."

The limits needed by teams generally come in two forms. The first is the limit on the team's role in making a decision. Is the team in an advisory/consultative role, or does it have the latitude to make the decision? If the team is in a consultative role, when is it time for the leader to end discussion and make the decision—to replace the cowboy hat with a bowler? Addressing goal congruence can help answer the question of whether a team should be in an advisory or decision-making role. The issue as to when it is time to cut off discussion and make the decision depends on a number of factors, including when information sufficiency has been achieved, when the people who have to be committed to the decision have provided input, and what the real-time constraints are on the decision.

The second form of limit needed by teams has to do with the fences or constraints around their options. Generally these constraints entail resources of some sort—time, money, people, organizational capability, etc. When asked about how he prevented team decision making from consuming too much time, James Houghton said, "You set ground rules. For example, in the beginning of the 1980s we thought that biotechnology was a hot item. As we got further into it, it became apparent that it was a pit with no bottom. We entered the game late, and we were just dabbling. We decided that, other than our deal with Ciba-Geigy, we'd exit the business. It was a difficult decision that could have consumed enormous amounts of time. At the time we didn't have a lot of other opportunities on our plate. We made the decision, though, in no more than six months because we understood the limits on our decision. The limits included money, but more important, they included limits pertaining to our core competencies. We knew up front that if we strayed too far from our core competency in inorganic chemistry, we could get into real trouble." In the team decision described by Houghton, his top management team operated within the fences of time and Corning's core competencies, and the team was clear about the existence of these limits up front. Options falling outside these fences were not relevant.

It is a critical role of leadership to set the limits. Leadership needs to define the role of the team as adviser or decision maker. Leadership needs to determine team composition based on who has the information and whose commitment is essential. Leadership needs to set clear expectations for the team and make sure that the team understands the fences around it. Finally, leadership may need to push and prod a team to act and move away from a regression to the mean. Jay Honeycutt of the Kennedy Space Center states it succinctly: "The key to great teams are leaders who spend their time assuring that the right decisions are getting made."

A common objection to the construction of fences around team decision making is the concern that limits on a team's freedom can inhibit "out of the box" thinking. In other words, if one advantage of team decision making is the diversity of ideas brought to bear on the decision, then limits imposed on the team can neutralize this advantage. Our experience and the research behind the situational approach to the role of teams in decision making indicate that any risk to free thinking imposed by limits placed on a team is worth it. One of the greatest threats to the effective use of teams occurs when a team thinks that it has a blank sheet on which to form a decision when, in fact, real limits on its freedom exist. Teams comprising conscientious, knowledgeable people understand that limits on their freedom usually exist. They appreciate knowing about the limits up front, and they feel more valued if their decision or recommendation is seriously considered because it is within the limits. There is a slight chance that a creative alternative may be stifled, but the usefulness and value of a decision made within real limits justify the risk.

Diogenes Wasn't a Team Player

The Greek philosopher Diogenes was a man who rejected all creature comforts in favor of a futile search for an honest person. Fortunately for him, his self-imposed crusade was not complicated by the condition that he conduct his search as part of a team. By all accounts, Diogenes was not a warm and caring person, and we have trouble imagining him as saying, "Thanks for sharing that with us, Plutarch," as the team meets for the fourth time to agree on a common definition of honesty. The role of teams varies depending on the type of analysis and thinking required, and for some types of analysis, teams may be inappropriate. As was true for Diogenes in his quest for honesty, the search for truth in the cause of a problem does not always require a team effort.

Not too long ago a colleague was observing a group of systems analysts and programmers for a software development company. The group was meeting to determine the cause of a problem in a large program they were writing. Having been steeped in the dynamics of teams, the leader of the team was intent on soliciting and validating everyone's input. On an easel she had posted the question "What do you think is causing the problem with the order entry program?" and the group was busy brainstorming a long list of possible answers—the picture of good problem-solving process in action.

But there were several things wrong with this picture. First, a number of the members of the group had very limited information about the program. Their involvement in the group may have met some team-building objectives, but they certainly were not contributing to the accomplishment of the group's task. Second, and more important, the use of a team to brainstorm the cause of a problem was not appropriate. The theory behind Problem Analysis holds that a problem, as defined properly, is caused by some change in the past. Once the critical facts about the problem are gathered, then Problem Analysis entails a number of logical steps and actions that will lead to identification of the true cause. The determination of the cause for a problem is a search for truth based on fact. Therefore, group or team commitment to the cause is totally irrelevant. The only legitimate rationale for the involvement of a team in solving a problem is that the pertinent facts about a problem reside collectively within the team. The composition of the team to work on the problem is based, then, solely on who has the needed facts. Yet time and again we have seen organizations approach problem solving as if it could best be done by a focus group in which cause is derived from the collective opinion of the group. Instead, effective problem solving as a process is an objective exercise, and it requires a group only when pertinent facts reside with more than one person.

In contrast with problem solving, the use of teams with other types of analyses can be appropriate and beneficial. For example, deciding among a number of options, anticipating and preventing future problems, and determining specific priorities are subjective analyses. The notion of truth is an irrelevant concept in picking an option that balances benefit and risk because there is no right answer. Using the same rational process and considering the same information, different teams and individuals might choose different alternatives because of subjective differences in the importance assigned to the information. We worked with two organizations that were making, almost simultaneously, very similar decisions regarding investments in increased capacity. In one organization costs and return on investment were the most important objectives. In the other organization growth was most critical. It is not surprising that these organizations reached very different conclusions, although they were making essentially the same decision.

When the analysis is subjective, the notion of commitment to conclusions is critical. If no "right" answer exists, then the people responsible for implementation need to buy into the rationale for the conclusions reached. Again, participation by teams in the analysis of issues is an effective way to gain commitment. As George Cobbe of Hewlett-Packard states, "If a team is within the priorities, and then, if it comes to a decision that has all of the team's input, backed up with all of the information that flows around us, chances are that the decision is going to be successful for a longer period of time into the future. It's leveraged across a greater amount of review, a greater amount of organizational stability, a greater amount of employee satisfaction."

The chart below represents the suggested role of teams in the various Kepner-Tregoe analytical processes.

PROCESS	ROLE OF TEAMS
Situation Appraisal	Teams participate in the appraisal to provide data and opinion or with the responsibility to act on the appraisal Team composition is determined by • who has the information • whose commitment is needed to a prioritization of issues

Problem Analysis	Teams have a role only if they have needed facts Team composition is determined by who has the facts and technological expertise
Decision Analysis	Teams participate in the analysis either in an advisory role to leadership or to make the decision as a team Team composition is determined by • who has relevant information • whose commitment is needed for effective implementation of the decision • who is good at focusing on risk
Potential Problem and Potential Opportunity Analysis	Teams participate in the analysis in either an advisory role or with the responsibility to implement Team composition is determined by • who has the information • whose commitment is needed to implement preventive, enabling, promoting, or contingent actions • who has the capability to think well about the future

The indiscriminate use of teams, regardless of the issue at hand and the analysis required, makes little sense. Teams are at their best when the issue requires a subjective conclusion and commitment to the conclusion is critical to effective action.

Empowering Competence

The Total Quality movement has emphasized the value of teams in addressing quality issues; at the same time, it has focused all types of organizations on removing variability from their products, services, and processes. On the surface, the notion of empowered teams and the emphasis on reducing variability seem to be in conflict. People are tremendously variable, and by putting people together in teams to address important business issues, it seems that organizations are encouraging rather than discouraging variability. The solution to any apparent conflict lies in focusing diversity through common processes, requisite skills, and essential knowledge. As Martin Mariner, director of quality at Corning, puts it, "You want to increase the variability of your people in order to make sure that all aspects of a decision are considered. The thing that we are using to maintain consistency is process definition. That means having a process specified and having the roles of teams clear. It means specific training and having measurement systems—all of the things needed to drive variability out of the process. So we have a built-in consistency of process in which we are applying a variability of backgrounds and ideas in order to improve quality."

Similarly, the way to avoid the pitfalls—inaction, frustration, and distrust—of working in teams is the same as resolving the conflict between a team approach and variability reduction: common processes, requisite skills, and essential information. In other words, empowered competence.

We have found meaningful empowerment to be based on the answers to three questions.

1. Who is in the best position to identify and address specific types of issues?
2. For each group, team, or function, what specific information do they need to address the issues within their purview?
3. What analytical and technical skills do they need to act effectively on this information?

The best and simplest definition of empowerment is making sure that the right people have the right information and skills to act on the right issues. Seems elementary, you say. Yet we constantly encounter organizations in the throes of complicated efforts to empower the workforce while ignoring these basic criteria. We have worked with a well-respected company that has embraced empowerment, particularly of its hourly workforce. With a considerable amount of money and time invested in a full-blown empowerment project, the company certainly had reaped some positive benefits. Yet when determining who should be involved in teams to address key issues within each of the businesses of the company, the appropriate teams to be empowered were most often in the salaried, not hourly, ranks because that's where the technical expertise needed to resolve the issues resided. When we assessed whether or not the relevant professional levels within the company had the requisite information and analytical skills to address the issues, we often found significant gaps. Here was a company that was committed to empowering the hourly workforce but that had virtually ignored empowering the people who could best address the significant issues confronting the company—the salaried workforce. This company is not unique. We often find that empowerment efforts are targeted on the hourly workforce based on the invalid assumption that the salaried people in the organization are already empowered.

While empowerment generally results in higher job satisfaction, improved morale is not the primary purpose. Rather, it is to optimize the value and use of the company's human resources in addressing the critical issues confronting the business. Improvement in how people view themselves and their jobs is a positive and intended side effect of enabling the right people to focus meaningfully on the right issues by ensuring that they have the right information and skills. In other words, empowered competency.

Unlocking the Locker Room

The final condition for effective team decision making is providing an environment that supports teams. In short, teams must have the opportunity and motivation to use their information and skills to address key issues. We will address the components of a constructive performance environment in the next chapter. However, a couple of points pertinent to a performance environment for teams are particularly salient.

The first is clarity of expectations. Setting appropriate limits on a team's freedom in making a decision is one aspect of clear expectations. Another is to clarify the role of the team based on the variables for team involvement. Usually the clarity of expectations for teams depends on how well those expectations are communicated. As our colleague James Schlick put it, "With teams you need to state expectations seven times. The first time, people will say, 'That's the dumbest idea we've ever heard.' Around the third time they are saying that the expectations have a modicum of merit. By the seventh time, the team is saying, 'For months, we've been saying that these expectations make sense. We're glad that we were finally heard.' "

The next component of a performance environment that has special relevance in supporting team decision making is the area of rewards and recognition. Striking a balance between individual and team recognition and reward seems to be a constant challenge in many organizations. Ray Marshall, former secretary of labor and current professor at the University of Texas, states it succinctly when he says, "The trick is to identify the performance of individuals in a group or team. Then you can reward individuals and the team for performance. Too much focus on individual performance, though, and you get people in what ought to be a cooperative team working at cross purposes because they are trying to prevent each other from performing."

Since 99 percent of the people in the workplace want to do a good job, and since common wisdom holds that at least a majority of them like to work cooperatively with others, unlocking the locker room door for a team generally does not require complicated organizational contortions. Clear expectations repeatedly communicated and a balance of team and individual rewards often suffice.

So You're Still Enamored with Teams

We have often challenged a seemingly sacred organizational tenet—that teamwork is necessary for top performance. But at the same time we assessed the value of empowerment and the roles of teams in decision making. In our work we have witnessed the struggles of many companies attempting to restructure into an organization based on teamwork. This struggle for most companies will likely be worth it, and it will be made significantly easier if:

- the guidelines for determining the involvement and role of teams are considered;
- the team operates within appropriate limits on its decision making;
- teams are deployed when the issue and type of analysis warrants a team;
- leadership of the organization has empowered competency;
- the team operates in a performance environment that unlocks any doors that obstruct optimal team performance.

If you're still enamored with teams, you're probably both wise and brave. If you're willing to follow these guidelines, you'll also probably be successful.

CHAPTER 8

Systems Thinking: Why You Can't KISS

In any complex environment systems are necessary, but they must serve an organization rather than become its masters.

RALPH S. LARSEN
Chairman and Chief Executive Officer,
Johnson & Johnson

The motto KISS—"Keep it simple, stupid"—has become a well-worn management maxim. But our exceedingly complex business environment makes the quest for simplicity difficult and often ill conceived or unwarranted. The fate of managers who fail to recognize the complexity of their multifaceted operations can be grim. Finding themselves displaced, they are forced to work as consultants and rely on their ability to create and complicate the same systems they once ignored. Systems thinking is invaluable to the success of a company or an individual and a ripe target for original thought in the arena of management theory. Peter Senge's *The Fifth Discipline* has raised our consciousness regarding the importance of a systems view. He writes:

> Today, systems thinking is needed more than ever because we are becoming overwhelmed by complexity. Perhaps for the first time in history, humankind has the capacity to create far more information than anyone can absorb, to foster greater interdependency than anyone can manage, and to accelerate change faster than anyone's ability to keep pace. . . . All around us are examples of "systemic breakdowns"—problems such as global warming,

ozone depletion, the international drug trade, and the U.S. trade and budget deficits—problems that have no simple local cause. Similarly, organizations break down, despite individual brilliance and innovative products, because they are unable to pull their diverse functions and talents into a productive whole.[1]

Universally applicable, systems theory is unexpectedly evident in the usually linear thinking of theology. One of the "Statement of Principles" for Unitarian-Universalists is to respect the interdependent web of all existence, everything of which we are a part. While this statement, in characteristic Unitarian fashion, serves to question the place of humans in the divine hierarchy propounded by other religious thought, it also reflects a biological and ecological fact: Everything is part of a larger system.

The need to see our companies, our jobs, and our lives as parts within a system is a reality to be ignored at great peril. Because the decision-making process occurs within a greater system, all the implications to that greater system must be considered. Decision making and problem solving are ultimately human endeavors, so the complex systems within which people operate must also be considered if the organizational capability for critical thinking is to be improved. But in making decisions, how do we examine, interpret, and align the human side of systems in a way that supports critical thinking?

The Headbone's Connected to the Neckbone: Some Fundamentals of Systems

Before we begin an exploration of the systems that affect decisions and the people who make them, we must discuss the fundamental characteristics of any system. Senge and others have noted some commonalties among all systems, even those as seemingly diverse as our circulatory system and a company's supply chain.

[1] Peter M. Senge, *The Fifth Discipline* (New York: Doubleday Currency, 1990), p. 69.

This discussion of system fundamentals is not intended to be System Theory 101. Instead it will serve as the basis for understanding any system, especially the critical components that involve people and their decisions.

1. You can't do just one thing.

One truism of any system is that since every part is interconnected, one component of a system cannot be changed without affecting every other part. As we have worked with companies to reduce complexity, we have focused on the cost resulting from product proliferation, especially low-volume products. The obvious conclusion—the need to simplify product lines—emerges as a significant opportunity. In one company we found that when costs were adjusted by volume, 25 percent of the products were unprofitable, although standard costing had led the company to believe that all its products were profitable. Stopping the production of unprofitable products seemed like the obvious solution.

But since the company exists as part of a complex system of suppliers, customers, end users, and competitors, the effects of *not* producing certain products would ripple through the industry, potentially causing more harm than good. Before stopping production, company executives had to work with suppliers to determine the effects on raw material and packaging consumption. They had to consult with customers, especially high-volume customers, to determine if their requirements for some low-volume products could be met with high-volume products at a lower price. They had to determine the impact of product consolidation on end users. And they had to weigh the effects on market share and competitor response. Though it seemed the obvious solution, stopping production would not reduce the costs associated with producing low-volume, unprofitable products for this company.

When dealing with human systems, the impossibility of doing one thing without causing potentially damaging shock waves is particularly notable. Improving the capabilities of the workforce is certainly desirable in most companies. When capabilities are increased, the job scopes of the affected individuals must be expanded, or boredom and a lack of commitment might result.

When the scope of jobs is expanded, the rewards for good performance must also be increased. Thus, the result of improving the capability of the workforce isn't always just greater production, it's also greater cost. Focusing only on capability improvement without regard to the impact on other components of the system can result in catastrophe.

2. THE OBVIOUS RESPONSE TO A SYSTEM'S PROBLEM MIGHT BE INEFFECTIVE AND MIGHT DO MORE HARM THAN GOOD.

A related characteristic of a system is that the obvious response is often the wrong response because it overlooks the subtle impact of an action on other components of the system. A classic, simplified example is the reaction of most countries to famine in a specific part of the world. The obvious and well-intended response is to send food. However, the massive influx of food affects in a harmful way the agricultural economics of the area experiencing famine. The decreasing price of food reduces the incentive for local farmers to work. And this decrease in food production heightens the likelihood of future famine. In business as well, the temptation presented by a simple, apparently elegant response is irresistible. But this temptation must be parlayed, especially when addressing systems in which people are a critical component.

When a large restaurant chain analyzed its costs, the company found, predictably, that labor was the largest controllable cost in its business. Top management quickly decided to take an obvious action to reduce labor costs by issuing an edict that limited the number of labor hours per number of customers. Labor costs dropped suddenly and significantly, and top management gleefully puffed on the proverbial cigar. However, it wasn't long before several unintended ripple effects emerged. Because the number of servers and "busers" had been reduced, the average time for table turnover increased 50 percent, drastically reducing throughput. Once people were seated, they had to wait longer to place an order and get their food. Therefore, they tipped less, which caused a good deal of dissension among the staff. Many potential customers simply refused to wait in the longer lines and went elsewhere. In sum, the obvious action to reduce costs was the wrong action when it came to long-term, bottom-line results.

3. A CHAIN IS AS STRONG AS ITS WEAKEST LINK.

In any system of interrelated components, the weakest component determines the overall strength and effectiveness of the system. The sales forecasting system in many companies is a salient example of the impact of the weakest component on a system. In many of the companies we work with, the weakness of their sales forecasting system severely limits the effectiveness of their production efficiency and inventory control. These companies are plagued with emergency runs of products that interrupt longer, more profitable runs, and with wildly fluctuating inventory levels. The weakness of sales forecasting as part of a larger production and inventory planning system dictates the overall strength of the system.

This phenomenon of the weakest component dictating system effectiveness is particularly evident in teams of people. By 1990 the Dallas Cowboys had acquired enough marquee players to win a championship. Superstars Troy Aikman, Michael Irvin, and Emmitt Smith—all first-round draft picks—formed the nucleus of a high-powered offense. However, weak links in the talent chain prevented the team from achieving success. A year earlier the Cowboys had won only one of fifteen games—the worst record in the National Football League. The next year the Cowboys won seven of sixteen games. Hardly the stuff of Super Bowl champions! But the arrival of other first-rate contributors like Charles Haley, Larry Brown, and Erik Williams solidified the team, and the rest is football history. Human systems, whether or not they involve teams, are limited by the strength of their weakest component.

4. A CLOSED SYSTEM CONTAINS THE SEEDS OF ITS OWN DEMISE.

In systems theory, a closed system is self-contained because none of its elements relies on input from external sources. A biological example of a closed system is the community of plants and animals that exist around thermal vents deep in the ocean. Since light cannot reach these communities, they are a self-contained system that produces food in the absence of photosynthesis. Since these systems rely on a delicate balance in the food chain and have little capability to adapt to small changes in this balance, any change can be catastrophic for the community. A closed system has great difficulty in adapting, and therein lies the seed of its own demise.

Until the mid-1970s the auto industry in the United States operated as a closed system. The major carmakers dictated market needs internally through model design that catered to the American habit of purchasing a new automobile every three to four years. While American companies kept close tabs on their domestic rivals, they had little capacity to seek and benefit from external input of customers and Japanese competitors. In addition, the bureaucracy of these companies evolved into a monolithic symphony of discord, extremely resistant to change. When customers demanded smaller, more fuel-efficient cars, the American companies could not adapt. The result of this nearsighted outlook was the near demise of Chrysler and the floundering of Ford and General Motors for the ensuing decade. Operating as a closed system served the American industry well as long as the market dynamics remained stable, but when the market demanded change, this closed system brought the industry to the brink of disaster. The recent focus on the importance of adaptability for all American businesses emphasizes the need to ensure that the people in the organizations operate in an open system. Incorporating input from the external environment is imperative for people at all levels if the organization is to succeed.

The Neckbone's Connected to the Shoulderbone—Why Bother?

While the value of systems thinking in business and life is undeniable, it has subtle drawbacks that must be recognized and managed. Inherent within systems thinking in its broadest application is the realization that if everything is connected to everything else in a gargantuan system, and if most systems tend to self-stabilize, then any effort to affect a system is likely to be insignificant.

Several years ago we attended a seminar conducted by Senge that focused on systems theory and thinking. One exercise during the seminar was to take a fairly mundane example of a specific action, such as taking a vacation, and to demonstrate how that action affected many different systems—in other words, the family system, the work system, the economy of Branson, Missouri, and so on. The exercise was intended to impress on the participants the value of anticipation even with a relatively simple example. At the end of the exercise an entire wall was covered with lines and arrows describing the complexity of the systems affected by a simple vacation. Though unintended, an additional effect of the exercise was to induce a sense of nihilism. If any action has an impact on a multitude of systems, how can anyone anticipate and manage all these effects? If every system is part of increasingly larger systems, then any effort to significantly affect an admittedly tiny sphere of influence can be viewed as ultimately futile. Or as writer Franz Kafka so eloquently queried, "Why in the hell bother?"

Admittedly, allowing nihilism to incapacitate systems thinking is a tad extreme, not to mention esoteric. However, even a modicum of systems thinking can serve to complicate issues tremendously. David Sheffield, Johnson & Johnson's group controller, Worldwide Pharmaceuticals, describes the intertwined systems affecting the commercialization of a drug: "We have to consider the impact that legislative activities and proposals have on our business, and we have to deal with the changing face of our customer. Traditionally, ten years ago, the customer was typically a physician, a health care provider, and we focused almost exclusively on that provider. Today there are many other people in the process of delivering health care whom we have to deal with, including major buyers and purchasers, managed health care organizations, and institutional groups. We also have to deal with patient advocacy groups such as AIDS activists or the National Alliance for the Mentally Ill. In what is already a rather complicated systems change—the introduction of a new product—Janssen

Pharmaceutica[2] now has to consider the impact of other systems on this activity, such as legislative action, the impact of the new product on other systems, managed care. Systems thinking further complicates an already complicated issue."

Just as the need for more data can paralyze a decision, the need to further analyze a decision in the context of an endless chain of systems can also bring things to a halt. Sheffield's example at Janssen Pharmaceutica aptly demonstrates how systems thinking can contribute to decision drag. In the process of making a decision regarding the introduction of a new drug, Janssen Pharmaceutica must consider the impact of the decision on a large number of other systems. To analyze the impact on each variation of managed care systems alone would consume an extraordinary amount of time and effort. Consequently, Janssen Pharmaceutica has to draw a line somewhere, marking the division between prudent analysis of the systems implications of a new drug and analytical overkill. As Robert Ecklin, senior vice president at Corning, says, "The only way to avoid this paralysis is strong leadership and a rational process for considering all the things affected by a decision." The process makes you think about the systems. Strong leadership is able to determine when enough is enough.

The rational process that most encourages systems thinking is Situation Appraisal. In the chapter on Situation Appraisal we emphasized the use of that process to manage the context of business issues and opportunities. Situation Appraisal, when done well, enables an organization to identify and describe the internal and external context in which the business operates. While critical contextual consideration of the systems implications of the issue is essential, Situation Appraisal, like most good things, can be taken to an extreme. As Ecklin points out, strong leadership has to determine when the assessment of systems implications crosses the line between prudence and overkill.

Jay Honeycutt discusses the impact that the shuttle *Challenger* tragedy has had on the assessment of the systems implications of

---

[2] Until recently David Sheffield was vice president of finance for Janssen Pharmaceutica, Inc., a business unit of Johnson & Johnson.

issues and opportunities confronting the space center. "The most dramatic impact [in the center's assessment of issues] was that the tragedy drove us to be ultraconservative. It drove us to fix things that weren't broken and to become extremely inefficient in the number of checks and balances that were imposed on work. The space shuttle program is a huge web of interconnected technical and social systems. It is not surprising that the *Challenger* tragedy caused NASA and the Space Center to self-impose a period of analytical overkill on the system implications of issues." Honeycutt goes on to describe how the center was able to escape the trap of overkill: "It was clear that if we continued to do work the way we were doing it, we couldn't meet flight schedules. I ran around saying that we had to do this and that better. Here's how we can—not why we can't. Some heard it and some didn't. So we did something called the bar czar review. If you look at the schedule for our work, the jobs are laid out on a schedule in bars. One job takes three hours to complete, while another takes a shift. So I got the team together and I said, 'Okay, for each one of these bars I want an owner. I want a person by name assigned as the responsible owner of this job. He is the czar of that bar.' We then got the bar czars together and told them to take 30 percent of the time and effort out of their job."

By asking those closest to the work to determine what constituted analytical overkill on systems, the group found that the time it took to complete various tasks was reduced by 50 percent. Without strong leadership to stop the interminable assessment of the systems implications of everything having to do with the shuttle, the inefficiency imposed by analytical overkill would have continued, and it is unlikely that the shuttle program would exist as we know it today.

For Want of a Horseshoe, a Battle Was Lost—The Decision Chain

Almost no decision, regardless of how mundane, is made in isolation from other decisions. For the sake of an example, imagine a scenario with two people. One is described as a sharp dresser and the other as disheveled. When the sharp one is asked how he decides what to wear in the morning, he replies that he starts with the tie and then decides on his shirt. His decision about a shirt determines his suit for the day, and so on. When asked how he decides on a tie, he answers that his decision is based on the tie he wore yesterday or last week. The disheveled person says that he starts with deciding which pair of shoes to wear; after that, it's pretty much what he wore yesterday, if it's still clean. The point of this commentary on dressing habits is to illustrate the obvious: Each decision is based in some manner on preceding decisions and, to a certain extent, determines the decisions that come after it. In other words, decisions are chained and operate as a system.

An example that is more relevant than our dress scenario relates to Corning's decisions regarding memory disks. Several years ago Corning began developing a new glass ceramic material for the memory disks in computers. The advantage of the new material was its ability to store significantly more information than the material commonly used at the time. As is true for any product development cycle, Corning made a number of decisions, each based on prior decisions, which took the company down a somewhat inadvertent road. Very early in the product development process, Corning conducted a thorough evaluation of a variety of materials that held promise for memory disks. It found that the material eventually chosen for memory disks was vastly superior to any other material in all characteristics except one, its durability. However, durability was not seen as the most important characteristic for a material that was encased in a computer's hard drive.

The next major decision made by Corning related to the need to understand how the material would be finished and put into disk drives. Corning seriously considered purchasing a company that was in the computer media industry. During negotiations, though, Corning recognized the volatility of the industry and quickly pulled the plug on the sale.

The decision to stop negotiations with the media company had several effects. Corning experienced great relief at having dodged a bullet. It also became very suspicious of what it saw as a difficult industry and decided not to pursue purchase of another media company. Significantly, the decision not to investigate the purchase of another company had the unintentional effect of diminishing Corning's ability to understand the downstream use of the material for memory disks. Instead, Corning entered into an agreement with a large computer media company for purchase of the disks made from the new material.

A small aspect of this agreement was the decision to rely on the media company's assurance that the material passed all qualification tests. Based on this, Corning began manufacturing disks from the material in large quantities. Obviously, the company made thousands of other decisions regarding the development of its memory disk product, all of which contributed to the path taken. The regrettable outcome of this chain of decisions was that the material was found by the end user to lose its capability to store information in conditions of high heat and humidity. Since PCs are not used in climate-controlled rooms, this deficiency became the Achilles' heel for Corning's material. Corning executives were forced to lick their wounds and initiate a search for another material.

The point of the example of Corning's experience with memory disks is to demonstrate the decision chain that led to the outcome. The chain can be illustrated as a series or system of decisions, using an admittedly simplified flowchart.

Corning intentionally or unintentionally made decisions that were dependent on previous decisions. The decision to use another company's testing procedures was predicated on the decision not to participate in the media industry directly, which was based on the decision not to purchase a media company in financial difficulty, and so on.

In discussing reengineering, Henry Mintzberg, noted management guru and Bronfman Professor of Management at McGill University, describes reengineering as a form of systems decision making. In our view, reengineering begins with the decision that reengineering is necessary. Based on that decision, the next decision is which process to reengineer, followed by the decision regarding the information needed in the process, followed by the decision on alternative processes, and so on. The results of reengineering are determined by a chain of decisions operating as a system.

Flowchart of Corning's Decisions on Memory Disks

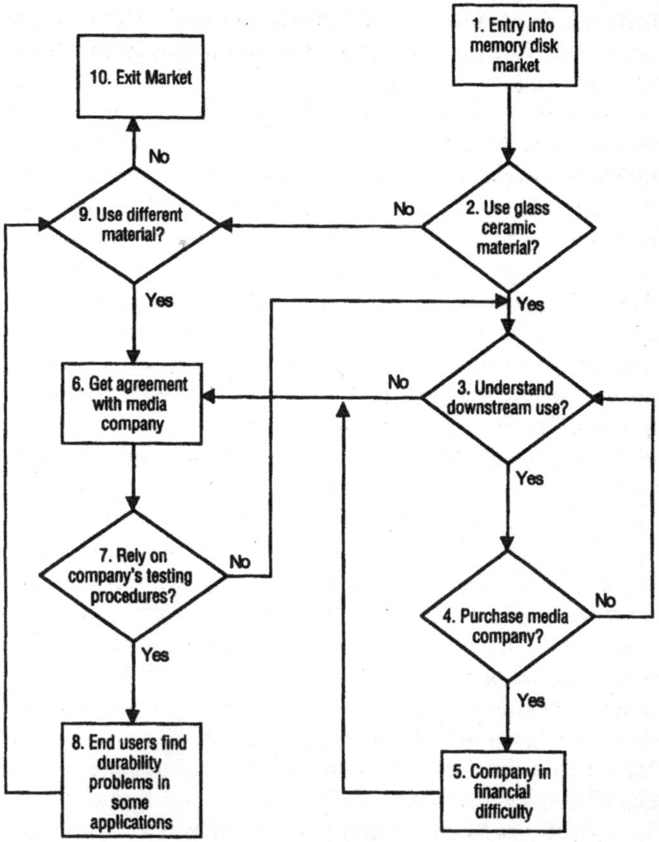

Level of Decision: The Analysis of Painting Floors

At this point a logical question is: Since the interdependence of decisions is fairly obvious, why are we making such a big deal out of it? When making decisions, ignoring the assumptions behind them, including the validity and intentions of previous decisions, can lead one astray. To put it simply, we often paint ourselves into a corner and have no idea how we got there. Inherent in every decision are the decisions that have preceded it, and the decision at hand will determine the scope of future decisions. Consequently, it is critical that decision makers be aware of the impact of past and present decisions on the decision chain. The term Kepner-Tregoe uses to describe this analysis of the decision chain is "Level of Decision."

Recently we were discussing cars with a friend who lives in New York City. Our friend's car had just died, and she was asking us for our opinion on which car to buy. Forgetting our ignorance, we waxed eloquent with our opinions, once again demonstrating that two people who know nothing about a subject know even less than one person who knows nothing. At one point in our discussion, we were struck by the fact that our friend was making a decision without testing some critical and potentially expensive assumptions. She was trying to decide which car to buy without testing the assumption that she needed a car. To own a car in New York is tremendously expensive in terms of insurance, parking, and wear and tear. The decision she should have been making is, How do I best meet my transportation needs? When the issue is framed this way, an entirely different set of objectives becomes relevant, and a broader array of alternatives is open for consideration. By becoming conscious of the assumptions driving her original decision of which car to buy, our friend reframed her decision. She decided not to buy a car, but to rent one for the one or two weekends a month that she needed it.

By raising the Level of Decision from "which car to buy" to "how to meet my transportation needs," our friend became aware of the fact that her initial decision was being driven by a prior, admittedly invalid decision that she needed to own a car. Had she followed through on her decision to buy a car, this decision would have determined many future decisions regarding how she would have spent a large portion of her discretionary income. Only by consciously analyzing the decision chain was she able to create a different system in which this and future decisions would be made and thus expand the scope of available alternatives.

Once a decision is framed, several key questions can be asked to enable decision makers to test the Level of Decision and to determine the links in the decision chain:

- Why is this decision necessary?
- What prompted the need for this decision?
- What need will the outcome of this decision meet?
- Overall, what is the aim of this decision?
- What prior decisions have brought us to this decision? Are these prior decisions still valid?
- If we make this decision, what future decisions will we likely need to make?

By asking these questions, our friend in New York avoided assuming some significant costs. Had Corning asked these questions during the course of its decisions on memory disks, it might have been able to foresee the effects of not thoroughly understanding the downstream use of its product. Whether conscious or not, the system in which decisions operate—the decision chain—exists. Analysis of the Level of Decision enables decision makers to exercise control in the construction of the chain.

The Problem Is Connected to the Decision, and the Decision Is Connected to the Plan

The four critical thinking processes discussed in this book—Situation Appraisal, Problem Analysis, Decision Analysis, and Potential Problem and Potential Opportunity Analysis—operate as a system. The four processes are linked, and the effectiveness of eventual actions is determined by the quality of the least rigorous analytical process—in other words, the weakest link.

The system almost always begins with Situation Appraisal. This process provides the context to elicit those issues confronting an organization and determines which issues merit further critical analysis. If Situation Appraisal reveals that a problem exists that warrants an analysis of its cause, then Problem Analysis—designed to determine the true cause of the problem—is the next component in the system. Once true cause is determined, Decision Analysis will provide the context to decide which corrective actions to take. The final component of this rational system, Potential Problem and Potential Opportunity Analysis, is designed to troubleshoot the implementation plan or take advantage of new opportunities that have arisen because of it.

As we said before, the effectiveness of any action resulting from this critical thinking system is limited by the least rigorous analysis. If Situation Appraisal does not thoroughly assess the range of issues, then an individual or organization may focus on the wrong issue, and subsequent analyses, regardless of their rigor, can be fruitless. Likewise, if Problem Analysis or Decision Analysis is not a disciplined, data-driven exercise in critical thinking, the investment in a thorough Situation Appraisal can yield only a fraction of its potential value.

Occasionally analysis can be conducted sequentially, beginning with Situation Appraisal and progressing through Potential Problem Analysis. While working with a division of a large consumer products company, we were asked to help with the division's quality problems. Situation Appraisal revealed forty-six separate issues relating to quality. Prioritization of the issues led to an initial focus on contamination of a cosmetic product. The true cause of the contamination was unknown until a vigorous Problem Analysis revealed that the most likely cause of the contamination was microbes in the welds of one section of pipe. Decision Analysis focused on how to remove the microbes and keep them from returning. Decision Analysis would have to be thorough, since any action would be costly and result in significant downtime. Executives involved in the decision determined that the action that would constitute the best balance between benefit and risk entailed rewelding the joints where the microbes existed. Due to the potential of significant downtime, the organization engaged in a Potential Problem Analysis to anticipate and avoid any problems. As a result, the rewelds were made in record time.

Parenthetically, the people involved in the Situation Appraisal differed from those in the Problem Analysis, who, in turn, differed from those making the decision. The differences were based on who had the necessary information and where the highest level of commitment would ensure the successful completion of each analysis.

While the example of the consumer products company demonstrates that the system of critical thinking tends to follow a logical progression, more often the initiation point depends on the analysis required. However, entry into the system invariably needs to begin with Situation Appraisal in order to ensure that the right issue is being addressed. The figure below depicts the critical thinking system.

Critical Thinking System

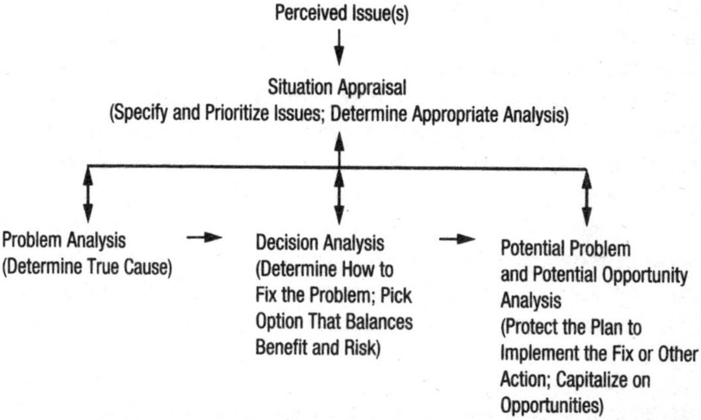

The figure is designed to describe several aspects of the critical thinking system.

- Entry into the system occurs with the perception of an issue or issues.
- Situation Appraisal is always the first process used to ensure that the focus is on the right issue(s), to describe the context for the issue, to indicate the appropriate process for further analysis, and to ensure that the right people are involved in further analysis.

- Depending on the results of the Situation Appraisal, the appropriate process for further analysis may be Problem Analysis, Decision Analysis, or Potential Problem and Potential Opportunity Analysis.
- Occasionally the system can operate in sequence, moving from Situation Appraisal through Potential Problem Analysis.
- After Problem Analysis, Decision Analysis, or Potential Problem and Potential Opportunity Analysis, the system typically should loop back to Situation Appraisal to assess the new context and priorities before progressing with subsequent analyses.
- The looping back to Situation Appraisal on an ongoing basis helps to account for the constant flow of changes affecting any set of organizational issues. This dynamic and flexible system accommodates the complexity of the current business environment.
- The openness of the system is maintained in a number of ways. The involvement of different people in each analytical process, based on information and commitment criteria, brings external input to the system. The information requirements for each analytical process infuse external data into the system. The frequent assessment of issues, including those in the external environment, through recycling to Situation Appraisal, ensures the development of an open system.

If It Weren't for People, This Critical Thinking Stuff Would Be a Snap

An acquaintance of ours recently commented, "This management stuff would be easy if it weren't for people." She was making the tongue-in-cheek observation that when people are a critical component of an endeavor, the complexity of the situation increases exponentially. This inherent complexity has encouraged many futile attempts to design people out of an activity. It is clear from the billions of dollars invested in robotics and artificial intelligence that minimizing the potential for human unpredictability is an objective in certain schools of business thought.

Even so, critical thinking is a fundamentally human process. Given the variability and complexity of people, if an organization wants to develop and sustain critical thinking as a competitive advantage, it must actively support the people doing the critical thinking. To provide the required support, the leadership of the organization must understand how people and their environment constitute a system and engineer this system in a way that removes the potential barriers to critical thinking.

The role of leadership in understanding and engineering the people system is particularly important in effectively managing change. Recently Kepner-Tregoe conducted a study of change efforts in a wide range of organizations. We found that 59 percent of the organizations we studied had engaged in three or more change initiatives in the prior eighteen months. Sixty percent of management thought these efforts were successful, yet only 20 percent of workers concluded that the initiatives accomplished the original objective of the change. The gap was alarming and indicates that disregarding the people system when implementing change is a primary cause for failure.

Over the past ten years a very large consumer products company has spent millions of dollars training people from machine operators to top management in Kepner-Tregoe's critical thinking processes. The company has a well-deserved reputation for disciplined process management and effective implementation of change initiatives. Like any organization intent on getting the maximum return on its investment in training costs, the company periodically evaluated the effectiveness of the training. For the first few years it was yielding significant measurable cost savings. However, in more recent audits the company discovered some disconcerting findings. The use of the skills had decreased at an alarming rate and, not surprisingly, so had the savings attributable to their use. Company executives asked us to help them understand why the change effort had stalled. Our investigation uncovered several obstacles to making critical thinking a core discipline within the company. And they were revealed not only by looking at individual problem areas, but also by viewing the performance of the company as a system.

The Performance System

One way to avoid the usual clichés about people is to look at employees as one part of a larger performance system. The figure below identifies the major elements of an organization's performance system and how they interact:

The Performance System

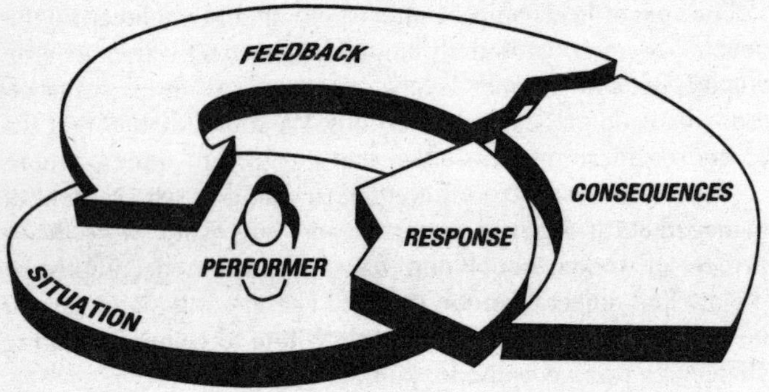

The *Situation* component of the system refers to the work environment in which the individual or group operates. It comprises those precursors to performance that have a significant influence on the performers. Specifically, the *Situation* includes three main elements:

- Performance Expectations: the specific results, measures, and standards desired of the *Performer*. Included in this component is the degree to which the *Performer(s)* views these expectations as reasonable.
- Signals to Perform: the indication to the *Performer(s)* that a certain action is appropriate. The signal, ideally, should be clear and unambiguous.
- Work Environment: how the work is planned, the resources available to complete the work, the physical surroundings, and the existence of competing priorities.

The *Performer* is that component of the system that relates to the individual or group expected to perform. In considering the *Performer* component, the focus is on whether the person or group has the skills, knowledge, and the physical, emotional, and intellectual capabilities to perform.

The *Response* component refers to the specific actions of the *Performer(s)*. It is based on observable behavior and requires some method of measuring the *Response* over time.

Consequences are the events that follow a *Response* and increase or decrease the likelihood of a similar *Response* in the future. This component of the system consists of a complex interaction between the *Consequences* for desired and undesired behavior and the perceptions of the *Performer(s)* regarding the timing and effectiveness of the *Consequences*.

Finally, *Feedback* is the information the *Performer(s)* receives about performance. The key criteria for effective *Feedback* are accuracy, specificity, and timeliness.

The Performance System has all the characteristics of any system. It is only as effective as its weakest component. Even if all the other components of the system are well designed, unclear expectations, insufficient skills, unbalanced consequences, or inaccurate feedback will undermine its effectiveness.

The Performance System is an open system. For the system to operate optimally, every component is dependent on input from the external environment. The *Situation* depends on input from the physical work environment. *Performers* are dependent on the organization outside their immediate Performance System for the development of needed skills and knowledge. *Consequences* and *Feedback* usually originate externally from the *Performer*.

Another characteristic of systems evident in the Performance System is the interdependence of the components, which means that any change in one component has ripple effects in the other components. For example, most companies are intent on developing cross-functionality within their hourly workforces. Cross-functionality requires an obvious change in the *Situation*, specifically in the expectations placed on individuals or groups.

Changes in the *Situation* necessitate changes in the skills needed by the *Performers.* If job responsibilities are expanded, then the *Consequences* component needs to reward cross-functional behavior with some form of compensation. Cross-functional teams require different feedback on their performance from that given to individuals or groups who are focused on a single function.

The Performance System has another important quality. Faults in the system rarely reside in the physical, emotional, or intellectual capabilities of *Performers,* contrary to the frequent focus of many managers and organizations. Our research on a wide variety of organizations reveals that only 3–5 percent of the causes for undesired performance reside in the internal capabilities of the *Performers.* In the preponderance of cases, the problem lies elsewhere, particularly in the *Situation, Consequences,* and *Feedback* components. Yet when performance problems arise we have encountered many individual managers and companies that focus immediately on the *Performers* component. Often their reaction to the problem is the three T's—train, then transfer, and, as a last resort, terminate.

There are two crucial shortcomings to the immediate concentration on the *Performers* as the cause of performance problems. First, efforts to solve the problem will be unsuccessful—the odds of this happening are thirty to one—because of misplaced focus. Second, measures designed to correct the *Performers,* especially training, transfers, and terminations, are very expensive. Far more effective is a thoughtful analysis of the other components of the system, which greatly increases the likelihood of meaningfully addressing performance issues.

Using the Performance System as a framework to understand why critical thinking was stymied in the consumer products company with the stalled change effort, we saw a number of system faults.

- People were receiving mixed messages about the organization's expectations regarding use of the process. Through regular communications by a few true believers within top management about successes resulting from use of the process, people were getting the message that it was expected and supported. However, in response to increased pressures on the business, a significant number of managers and supervisors were now valuing action over thought as the immediate reaction to an issue. In fact, some were actively discouraging any delay to quick action when a problem arose.

- Small meeting rooms that had existed on the floor for impromptu meetings had been removed to accommodate expansion.
- One aspect of our work with this company had been to develop a cadre of internal process facilitators. Attrition had eroded the ranks of these facilitators.
- When we reviewed the process of promoting people from line to supervisory positions, we found that fire fighting was a much more important criterion than fire prevention. In other words, the company seemed to place more value on fixing problems than preventing them.
- This company had successfully embraced the concept of work teams and had delegated much of the responsibility for day-to-day operations to the teams. Information regarding team performance on delivery, throughput, and quality was provided to the teams on a weekly basis. But they did not receive timely feedback in the form of information on key variables affected by the use of critical thinking.

People need clear expectations regarding desired performance, and they need the resources to meet those expectations. They need the collective and individual skills and the critical information in order to perform as expected. The desired behaviors and results need to be specific and measurable. The consequences of performing as expected need to be seen as meaningful and unambiguous. Individuals and groups need accurate, timely feedback regarding their performance.

Given the shortcomings of the various components of the Performance System at this company, it is not surprising that the level to which critical thinking was employed was less than desirable.

Based on our analysis of the Performance System, management at this company encouraged supervisors to become process facilitators, thereby creating the expectation that the use of the critical thinking process would be the immediate response to problems. This improved the organization's problem-solving and decision-making capabilities. Proficiency in the use of the process became an important criterion in promotions, and a system was developed that provided information on key production variables to work groups every four hours. Consequently the frequency and intensity of critical thinking in this company improved dramatically, as did the benefits.

The Power of the Performance System in Implementing Change

An analysis of a company's Performance System is invaluable in any attempt to understand breakdowns in performance. But arguably the most powerful use of Performance System thinking is in designing a system that supports a planned change. In our recent research on change initiatives, 60 percent of the executives surveyed rated their employees' reaction to change as neutral, skeptical, or resistant. And why should employees feel otherwise? Most of the recent change methodologies, including process reengineering, various restructuring approaches, and the increasing dependence on a wide variety of information technologies, are preoccupied with structure and nonpeople systems. In Hammer and Champy's best-seller, *Reengineering the Corporation*, the authors allocate more than four times the space to information technology's role in reengineering than they give to the role of people.

The results of using structure- and system-focused methodologies almost always have a profound impact on people. Yet their role in implementing change is often considered only as an afterthought. Downsizing and delayering are pertinent examples. As organizations attempt to flatten their hierarchies by eliminating management and supervisory levels, the volume of work usually does not change, and therefore the same amount of work must be accomplished with fewer people. Based on our observations, this phenomenon of the same with less is a prevalent result of delayering. But the impact on the people remaining in the organization is rarely addressed directly by change initiatives designed to delayer. Instead these initiatives seem preoccupied with the desired structure and the need to automate work.

We have worked with a few companies that have paid attention to the Performance System in their initiatives to delayer or downsize. They use Performance System thinking after delaying to focus on the remaining people after delayering and to design a system that supports desired performance. They begin with establishing clear expectations around the results and responses required from the remaining jobs. Time-costly, low-value work is identified and eliminated so that expectations can be limited to the critical few. In other words, these companies are not trying to do the same with less but are actively looking to eliminate or reduce low-value work. As a result, the skills and knowledge needed by the remaining people to meet or exceed the fewer critical expectations receive heightened attention. Leadership spends time putting formal and informal consequences in place to support meeting or exceeding expectations. In addition, it focuses on removing the organizational impediments to desired performance.

Companies that focus on the people side of change pay close attention to the type and timing of the information they receive about the company's performance and their own. In an attempt to make feedback less dependent on personal contact by a manager or supervisor, they make dissemination of the appropriate information on performance a requirement of any system. By engineering the Performance System, these companies enable the people who remain after downsizing to both adjust to the change and achieve the results required by the change.

So You Say People and Their Critical Thinking Capabilities Are a Competitive Advantage?

If critical thinking is to be considered a key capability in an organization, then leadership needs to carefully consider the systems implications of the process and the people who are expected to use it.

- Issues exist as part of a larger system, so the impact of one issue on other aspects of the organization must be considered when addressing an issue. The intertwined nature of issues greatly complicates efforts to resolve them, but the frequent use of Situation Appraisal helps to identify and sort out their system implications.
- Decisions cannot be made in isolation but instead are heavily influenced by the decisions that precede them. To avoid venturing down unintended paths, this decision chain needs to be consciously analyzed before proceeding with Decision Analysis. Thus, the validity of prior decisions can be reviewed and the assumptions behind the decision at hand can be evaluated.
- The critical thinking processes are connected in a system. While Problem Analysis can lead to Decision Analysis, which can necessitate Potential Problem and Potential Opportunity Analysis, constant recycling to Situation Appraisal helps ensure that the right issues are receiving sufficient focus. Since the context in which issues exist changes constantly, the use of critical thinking processes needs to be fluid and flexible.
- To effectively implement organizational change, including changes in the core capability to think critically, the Performance System has to be understood and engineered. The recent infatuation with structure and nonpeople systems as the leverage points for organizational change must be heavily supplemented with an intense focus on ensuring that the Performance System supports the change.

KISS is still a useful acronym, but only if it also means "Know it's a system, smarty."

CHAPTER 9

Dr. McCoy, Please Report to the Flight Deck—Intuition and Rationality in Decision Making

Rational decision making is linear and is what you do when you put your facts in order. Intuition is looking at those facts and trying to see a pattern–and the patterns aren't always evident because the patterns aren't always linear. The two together . . . are an extremely powerful combination.

JOEL KURTZMAN
President, Joel Kurtzman Associates
Former Editor, *Harvard Business Review*

The television series *Star Trek* has enjoyed somewhat surprising success and has spawned a cult of Trekkies, who view the series as akin to a passion play. While we have never viewed *Star Trek* as a particularly acute lens on the human condition, the interplay between two of its main characters provides an interesting depiction of the age-old tension between intuition and rationality. Mr. Spock is the personification of reason—so much so, in fact, that he is not even human. In poignant juxtaposition to Mr. Spock is Captain Kirk, who operates from a gut level, making decisions affecting the preservation of the *Enterprise* and its crew with astounding intuitive leaps. Dr. McCoy is the figurative Ego who mediates between the Superego of Spock and the Id of Kirk.

Drawing upon *Star Trek* enables us to delve, however briefly, into the realm of pop psychology—which seems to be a significant asset in selling business books—while illustrating how the opposite approaches and styles of Spock and Kirk demonstrate the apparent conflict between rationality and intuition in human deliberations.

How important is intuition in the decision-making process? Here are the opinions of some experts:

- Scott Davidson, CEO of ICI Acrylics—"Gut feel tells you when you have enough information to make the right decision."
- Ray Marshall, Audre and Bernard Rapoport Centennial Chair in Economics and Public Affairs at the University of Texas; former Secretary, U.S. Department of Labor—"You have to have intuition. You've got to have street smarts, gut feel, however you want to describe it. Any company that doesn't have people with that capability is going to be a sluggard in the marketplace."
- Ralph Larsen, chairman and CEO of Johnson & Johnson—"Every time I have been burned in decision making it is because I have gone against my instincts."
- Richard Teerlink, president and CEO of Harley-Davidson—"You may sometimes choose an alternative that is not the rational alternative, based on gut feel."
- Amy Williams, senior vice president of USF&G—"Even when you have hard facts, intuition is really important. In the area of new products, intuition is what allows you to believe that there actually is a market for your product or service. Intuition is what gives you vision in the first place."
- C. K. Prahalad, Harvey C. Fruehauf Professor of Business Administration at the University of Michigan—"One of the biggest impediments to effective decision making today is that all the literature and all the consultants have recommended that emotion and passion be taken out of management. They think that strategy is a purely analytical exercise."

Yet Decision Analysis, the decision-making process we are advocating, is quintessentially a rational process. But if intuition is as important as these business and government leaders indicate, how do we resolve the apparent conflict between intuition and the rational approach to decision making? Perhaps we need Dr. McCoy to mediate the debate.

Let's Analyze Intuition

Analyzing intuition may seem like an oxymoron, but some discussion of what is meant by intuition is in order. The dictionary defines intuition as "knowledge discerned directly by the mind without reasoning or analysis." Nonetheless, this definition begs some admittedly analytical questions. Where does this inherent knowledge come from? Is it the result of genetic coding? Does it originate in some random firing of neurological synapses? Is it synonymous with knowing something without knowing why we know it—that which we call unconscious competence?

The Myers-Briggs type indicator is a popular measure of the cognitive styles widely used in management circles to foster a modicum of civility in business relationships. One of the eight variables measured by Myers-Briggs is intuition. They define "intuitives" as individuals who "perceive indirectly through the unconscious by making associations with the outside world." People who score high on the intuitive scale tend to focus on the whole as opposed to the parts, and one of their strengths is discerning patterns in seemingly isolated facts. Myers-Briggs, therefore, define intuition as conclusions reached through some sort of inspiration that depends on external stimuli. Interestingly, though, Myers-Briggs use a variable separate from intuition—the "thinking" scale—to measure a penchant for logic and analysis. In contrast with Webster, Myers-Briggs do not view intuition and analysis as antithetical or mutually exclusive.

A number of the people we questioned about intuition defined it as the almost unconscious application of experience and knowledge to the situation at hand. Michael Heron, former chairman of the postal service in the United Kingdom, said, "Intuition is made up of experience, training, learning, and temperament. I suppose it's called judgment." Amy Williams of USF&G equated intuition with experience and judgment when she said, "Intuition is appropriate when the facts and data you have are very subjective and you filter them through your own way of looking at the world." Van Campbell, vice chairman of Corning, said, "Intuition comes from past mistakes."

Because we're intuitives on the Myers-Briggs indicator, we have arrived at our own definition of intuition, based on a combination of the ideas from Myers-Briggs and from the leaders we interviewed. Intuition is the rapid and possibly unconscious employment of experience and knowledge to create patterns from external facts. Both intuition and rationality are valuable cognitive approaches to making decisions. They are not mutually exclusive but instead can complement each other if used appropriately.

Intuition as Unconscious Competence

When Kepner and Tregoe first began their inquiry into decision-making processes, they had three hypotheses:

- Consistently good decision makers use a process that differs from that used by mediocre or poor decision makers.
- Good decision makers could describe the process they use.
- The process could be codified and taught to others.

While subsequent research revealed that the first and third hypotheses are true, Kepner and Tregoe's second hypothesis was revealed to be patently false. Good decision makers could not explain the process they used, and in fact many of them described their decision-making style as intuitive. These individuals were highly competent but largely unconscious of how or why. Consequently, Kepner and Tregoe spent several years studying these individuals in an effort to make their decision-making process conscious or knowable. The result is the Decision Analysis process.

While unconscious competence is preferable to incompetent decision making, it has a number of drawbacks:

- If decision makers cannot explain how they make decisions, they certainly cannot build the capability in others. A process such as "First I determine my gut feel about the issue, then I find some patterns in the data, and last I use a healthy dose of inspiration to pick the best course of action" does not lend itself to easy replication in others.

- People who are unconsciously competent decision makers are often viewed as indispensable by their organizations. While this status may have certain benefits for those seen as indispensable, it certainly places the organization in a vulnerable position. The health and well-being of these individuals would have to be a high-level concern for everyone in the organization. We think that the adage attributed to Harry Truman is wise advice: "Find the indispensable persons and fire the SOBs because they are not doing their jobs."
- With no other way to explain their decisions, people often rely on charisma or other cheerleading attributes to engage others in committing to the decision. "My gut tells me that it is the right thing to do" is not an explanation that makes us want to charge the hill.

Increasingly, decisions have to be sold to a host of stakeholders. If the decision maker is unconsciously competent, then an inability to explain how a decision was made makes selling the decision extremely difficult.

Intuition—or, Critical Thinking at Warp Speed

Our definition posits that intuition is the rapid analysis of facts using knowledge and experience as filters. The definition implies that, in at least some cases, intuition entails the extremely quick and possibly unconscious use of a rational process. In these applications intuition is not only compatible with rationality, but actually employs it—possibly at the speed of light.

Rational process is sometimes evident in what decision makers or observers call intuitive decisions. One corporate leader who might be described as an exemplary intuitive thinker is Richard Teerlink of Harley-Davidson. Harley-Davidson's rise under Teerlink's leadership from the brink of bankruptcy is the fodder for business legends. In 1982 the company had $210 million in revenue and a pretax loss of $30 million. In 1994 it earned revenues of $1.2 billion, with operating profits of $160 million, constituting one of the most noteworthy turnarounds in the annals of business.

Teerlink differentiates between those decisions requiring a rational approach, when some standards need to be met, and those requiring intuition, when no standards exist. As an example of a decision requiring intuition, he cites a situation in which he has data that say there is a market for two hundred thousand motorcycles, but to expand to meet the demand of a market of this size, new products are needed. As he explains it, "I've had someone analyze our product development program, and we came up with the acronym LEWW—late, expensive, and won't work. Now I have a decision to make. Should I risk corporate resources and commit to an aggressive plan of 200,000 to 250,000 units when our product development system is LEWW? There is no rational reason for me to do that. Rationally, the decision is, Don't make the commitment. On a gut level there is the feeling that we are Harley-Davidson, we're going to do it, and we'll make it happen. I decide to go for the larger market, but I try to cover my bets and not overinvest up front. I am willing to be embarrassed later and say that we changed our mind. But I'm not going to allocate tons of resources now."

In making this decision, Teerlink actually employed a very rational process. He had information on market potential, and he factored in Harley-Davidson's recent history of turning opportunities into reality. He realized that the company's product development system might be an obstacle to meeting market demands, so he managed the risk by limiting and staging his investment. He even weighed the risk of public embarrassment over his decision to back off the pursuit of a stated goal, and he decided that the risk was not significant and could be managed. Teerlink drew his conclusions rapidly but, whether totally conscious of it or not, he used a rational balance between benefit and risk in making what he describes as an intuitive decision.

When viewed by others, intuition can often seem to be not

only irrational, but almost psychic. In his book, *Mind Hunter,*[1] John Douglas writes of his work as head of the FBI's Investigative Support Unit. Douglas—who was the model for FBI agent Jack Crawford in the book and movie *The Silence of the Lambs*—describes his role in capturing the perpetrator of a particularly gruesome murder of a woman in the Bronx. After reviewing all the facts, which were lacking any hard evidence, he drew what appeared to be some astounding intuitive conclusions:

- The attacker would be an average-looking white male between the ages of twenty-five and thirty-five.
- He would be disheveled, unemployed, and mainly nocturnal.
- He would live within a half mile of the building in which the murder occurred, with his parents or an older female relative.
- He would be a high school or college dropout, would not have a car or a driver's license, and would be a current or former patient at a mental institution.
- He would have previously attempted suicide by strangulation, and he would have a large collection of bondage pornography.
- This would have been his first serious crime.

The local police and press viewed these pronouncements as inexplicable intuitive leaps, but given Douglas's reputation, the police incorporated his assessment into their investigation. The person arrested and convicted of the crime turned out to be a thirty-year-old white, unemployed actor who lived with his father in the building where the murder occurred. He was a high school dropout with a history of suicide attempts by hanging, and he was currently attending an in-patient program at a local mental hospital.

When queried, Douglas recounted how he had drawn his conclusions. What seemed like intuition was, in reality, the rapid building of patterns of facts using a rational process.

[1] John Douglas and Mark Olshaker, *Mind Hunter: Inside the FBI's Elite Serial Crime Unit* (New York: Scribner, 1994).

- The crime was spontaneous, not planned, because the victim sometimes used the stairs and sometimes the elevator to reach her apartment. The attacker had no way of knowing which one the victim would use on a given day. And everything in the attack belonged to the victim; the attacker had not brought anything to the place of attack.
- If the attacker had not gone to the building to commit the crime, then he must have gone for another reason. For him to be there prior to 7 A.M., the time of the attack, he must have either lived in the building or known someone who did. The victim had not screamed or struggled, so she must have known him, at least by sight.
- Given the sexual nature of the attack, Douglas knew the attacker was in the general age range of the victim. And his experience told him that rarely was this particular type of crime cross-racial, making it likely that the attacker was white.
- This was a high-risk crime with a low-risk victim. Any organized attacker would have picked a less risky place for a sexual attack. This, combined with the spontaneous nature of the crime, led Douglas to conclude that the attacker was disorganized, at least, and probably disheveled.
- The attacker was hanging out in the building when most people were on their way to work. This told Douglas that the attacker was either unemployed or employed part-time. Since the crime demonstrated some very weird fantasies that would be difficult to hide from someone else, and since the attacker did not have enough money to live on his own, he concluded that the attacker must live with family.

As opposed to employing irrational intuition, or lack of analysis, Douglas rapidly sorted the facts into discernible patterns based on his knowledge and experience with similar crimes and then used logic and reason to draw his conclusions from those patterns. And unlike many intuitive decision makers, Douglas was able to describe his thinking process in considerable detail.

In both Teerlink's decision to develop products for an expanding market and John Douglas's crime-solving technique, the process was described as intuitive. However, both reflect a heavy reliance by the decision makers on analysis and logic to draw their conclusions, lending support to the notion that at least some applications of intuition are, in fact, a rapid rational process.

The Cognitive Pas de Deux—Intuition and Rational Process

Even if intuition and rationality are, in some instances, different cognitive approaches, they are not only compatible, but they should complement each other. As Joel Kurtzman says, "Rational process is linear. It's when you are putting your facts in order and looking at them, weighing them, and making a decision based on the importance you assign to each fact. Intuition is looking at the same facts and trying to see a pattern. The patterns aren't always evident because they are not linear. That's where intuition is very valuable. You look at a set of variables, and suddenly it snaps into your mind that there's a pattern. The ability to recognize patterns is intuitive. Rational and intuitive thinking are not mutually exclusive. The combination of the two, when you are lucky enough to have them both, is extremely powerful and useful." The important question, then, is how can the two approaches be melded to take maximum advantage of each?

The effective integration of intuition and rationality entails moving between the two at appropriate times, just as a leader can move from taking quick action in confronting a buzzing mess to taking thoughtful action. In Situation Appraisal, for example, issues rarely present themselves in tidy, specific bundles. Instead, leaders are almost always confronted with a dog's breakfast in which issues seem cosmic and inextricably intertwined. The determination of where to begin to unwind the mess benefits from a healthy dose of intuition. In talking about his role at ICI Acrylics, Scott Davidson discusses the mess he confronted, which included a critical need to expand in Asian markets, opportunities to make investments in technology, and the suck of internal corporate issues that not only tempted him "to go to a funeral," but "to be the corpse as well."

Intuition served Davidson well in unraveling the mess when

he focused on the still general opportunities for acquisitions and joint ventures in Asia and either postponed or delegated the resolution of other issues. In deciding to focus on Asia, Davidson did not employ a traceable analytical process but, instead, used his experience and knowledge to quickly determine which category of issues needed his attention most. Once intuition has determined the sector of the universe where leaders should focus their attention, the use of a rational process like Situation Appraisal enables them to discern specifically which issues or opportunities merit further consideration. When starting to deal with a buzzing mess, intuition first, then rationality, is probably wise.

Let's Do a Hunch Sometime—Intuition and Problem Analysis

In Problem Analysis, the most objectively analytical of Kepner-Tregoe's critical thinking processes, there is a role for intuition as well. After the relevant information has been gathered, using a rigorous analytical approach to describe a problem, intuitive thinking can be very useful in identifying possible causes, whether the problem is new or recurring. Once a list of possible causes has been made, reversion to analysis in evaluating the logical fit between the possible causes and the information is in order. Intuition, again, can be useful in determining how to verify the true cause of a problem.

John Perkins, former chief engineer for British Airways, describes an instance when a pilot on a Concorde's nonpassenger run received information in flight that the aircraft's undercarriage was not locked in. The plane was landed, and it was obvious that one of the undercarriages that contain the wheels and landing gear was not locked in. The implications were very serious, because if the plane were moved and the undercarriage were to fold, a $100 million airplane would be lost. Given the potential impact of the problem and the fact that an unlocked undercarriage had never happened before, Perkins assigned his best troubleshooting engineer to the problem. The data led to a probable cause, which checked out logically, but how to verify that the probable cause was the true cause was much less clear because of the risks associated with some actions. Based on an intuitive leap that he could not explain, the engineer suggested that the aircraft be towed in a circle, which, when done, locked the problematic undercarriage.

Starboard or Port—Intuition and Decision Analysis

Decision making, more than sorting issues or solving problems, is the arena where the tension between intuition and logic is most evident. Decisions are categorized as either intuitive or rational, and the categories are often viewed as dichotomous and mutually exclusive. For example, over the past twenty years much has been made of the distinction between the hemispheres of the brain. People are described as either left-brain thinkers, who rely on logic and rationality, or right-brain thinkers, who tend to employ intuition and creativity in making decisions—the premise being that every person gravitates toward one or the other, not both. Parenthetically, there is obvious irony in the attempt to categorize people according to their dominant brain hemisphere, because, if the theory is valid, only left-brain thinkers would care about such an analysis. Those dominated by the right brain presumably categorize people based on gut feel, first impressions, and pheromones. We believe a balance between the left and right brain is ideal.

In effective decision making the synapses fire on both sides of the brain in a virtual pas de deux of rationality and intuition. As with Situation Appraisal, often it is intuition first, then rational process. The answer to the question "What decision should we be making?" originates with intuition, and very possibly we may think that the best option is intuitively obvious. A rational process, though, serves as a check and balance on hyperactive intuition and keeps us from making some really stupid decisions. As Robert Ecklin of Corning says, "Whenever I am confronted with a situation requiring a decision, I, like many people, form an opinion. But I find that I need to force myself to suspend gut feel and engage in a rational process. Often the process demonstrates that my initial intuition was accurate, but there have been times when the process showed that my initial gut feel would have taken me in a very wrong direction."

Hallucination or Insight?—Intuition and Potential Problem and Potential Opportunity Analysis

Finally, any time the future is the focus of attention, intuition plays a significant role. However, if conjecture about the future is to be more than a purely psychic odyssey, intuition needs to be channeled through a process. A rational process, such as Potential Problem and Potential Opportunity Analysis, helps sort the intuitive insights that have little grounding in reality from those that represent real insights.

For example, during the course of our work with companies on their strategies, actions by competitors inevitably are identified as potential problems or potential opportunities. In order to assess them thoroughly, the strategic team needs to put itself in the place of key competitors and project what they might do in the future. The leadership teams that find this assessment of the competition to be particularly valuable are able to use their knowledge as a springboard into intuitive conjecture about the actions of competitors. These leadership teams use Potential Problem and Potential Opportunity Analysis to combine experience, information, and intuition in a way that produces meaningful insights into the motives and possible moves of competitors.

In the absence of a rational process, a discussion of future threats and opportunities often falls victim to one of two pitfalls. If unbridled intuition reigns, then the group has difficulty separating hallucinations from insights, and rarely is intuition distilled into anything actionable. If the process is so rigid as to thwart intuition, the result will be a perfunctory restatement of common knowledge. Knowing when and how to blend a rational process with intuition enables a consideration of the future that encourages intuitive leaps yet discriminates between the fanciful and the insightful.

The Blend

The following table is designed to indicate how intuition and Kepner-Tregoe rational processes can be integrated.

PROCESS AND STEPS	COGNITIVE APPROACH
Situation Appraisal	
Identify Concerns	Intuition helps in determining which aspect of the "buzzing mess" to focus on. Reason and data should drive the separation of broad concerns into specific issues.
Set Priority	The determination of seriousness should be based on a rational assessment of data. The evaluation of urgency usually can be based on objective data; intuition, however, is often appropriate when assessing growth.
Plan Next Steps	The determination of the next level of analysis required is generally a rational activity.
Plan Involvement	The identification of whom to involve in further analysis is a combination of rational analysis, using the guidelines described in Chapter 7 on teams, and intuition regarding who might be able to think outside the box if needed.
Problem Analysis	
Describe Problem	Rational analysis should definitely rule in determining if a problem actually exists and which information about the problem is relevant.
Identify Possible Causes	Possible causes can emerge from a critical look at the relevant information, or they may be identified through intuition. Both sources

	should be employed, especially if the problem is a recurring one.
Evaluate Possible Causes	Determining the fit between a possible cause and the relevant information is primarily a rational exercise.
Confirm True Cause	Intuition plays a role in identifying how true cause can be verified, especially if verification is difficult or costly.
Decision Analysis	
Clarify Purpose	Intuition is a useful guide in determining what decision should be focused on or the level of the decision. Objectives for a decision are the product of both logic and intuition.
Evaluate Alternatives	Intuition as well as rationality is an appropriate source of alternatives. But the evaluation of alternatives vis-à-vis the objectives should be driven by data and rationality to protect against unduly biasing the decision.
Assess Risks	Identification of salient risks can be a function of rationality and intuition. Risks associated with the fit between an alternative and the objectives are identified, using logic and reason. Intuition is particularly helpful in identifying those risks that originate in the external environment. Rational evaluation of data should drive the assessment of seriousness, while intuition is

	appropriate in the assessment of a risk's probabilty.
Make Decision	Intuition is a useful guide in assessing what is an acceptable balance between benefit and risk.

Potential Problem and Potential Opportunity Analysis

Identify Potential Problems or Potential Opportunities	Much as in the assessment of risks in Decision Analysis, intuition and rationality guide the identification of potential problems or potential opportunities. Again, logic and reason should guide the assessment of seriousness or impact because they can often be quantified using facts. The assessment of probability is usually more intuitive, given that it is a projection into the future.
Identify Likely Causes	Those causes that are identifiable through experience generally emerge by way of rational analysis. Those causes outside the experience or knowledge of the group or individual often emerge through intuition.
Take Preventive or Promoting Actions	In identifying the actions to take to influence the cause of a potential problem or potential opportunity, or in planning to control their effects, intuition and logic come into play.
Plan Contingent or Exploiting Actions	Some actions or plans result from the rational analysis of the cause-and-effect relationship. Others come from intuitive leaps into the future.

The table on the integration of rational process and intuition indicates that in some steps of some processes—for example, the description of a problem—rational process should predominate, because that step is driven by objective facts or data. In process steps such as the assessment of risks in Decision Analysis, both intuition and rationality need to be called upon, because often neither alone is sufficient to identify possible risks. Finally, there are some process steps—the identification of concerns in Situation Appraisal, for example—that lend themselves to intuition almost more than to rational analysis. Overall, however, it is clear that even if rationality and intuition are different cognitive approaches to the resolution of an issue, when the two approaches are used at the appropriate place in a process, they will likely produce a resolution that is superior to that produced when either is used alone.

The long-standing tension between the proponents of the intuitive and the rational approaches will probably continue, even though they can coexist and can be used to complement each other. However, in conclusion, two additional points, while possibly obvious intuitively, merit acknowledgment. First, a dependence on the intuitive approach alone poses several problems, including difficulty in getting buy-in to decisions, the impossibility of transferring the capability to others, and the organizational risk represented by the indispensability of key decision makers. A repeatable process that makes thinking conscious and visible avoids these pitfalls. Such a process also allows us to function effectively in situations in which we lack experience.

Second, at least some thinking that has been described as intuitive is really the rapid use of rational process. In these cases there is no distinction between a rational and an intuitive approach other than the speed and possibly the visibility of the process use. Therefore, in many instances the difference between the two approaches is moot. In those instances when rationality and intuition may be different approaches, the use of a critical thinking process helps determine when each can be of maximum benefit. In fact, any debate about the merits of intuition over rationality or vice versa is usually pointless. Thank you, Dr. McCoy. You can go back to the sick bay.

CHAPTER 10

The Socratic Leader—Asking the Right Questions

What distinguishes crackerjack decision makers is their concern for the decision-making thought process–the kinds of questions you ask–not just the answers.

JOSEPH KEILTY
Executive Vice President, Human Resources,
American Express Co.

On a warm spring day, Albert Einstein, who was then working at the Center for Advanced Studies in Princeton, New Jersey, was pacing in a quadrangle, hands clasped behind his back, mumbling to himself. A bystander observing the great scientist and wondering what he might be saying while talking to himself moved discreetly into hearing range. Lost in thought, Einstein repeated, "If I only had the right question . . . If I only had the right question . . ."

Einstein was trying to develop a theory that would unify the esoteric fields of particle physics and astrophysics. To this great thinker, the journey to understanding began not with solutions, but with questions. As he pursued the answers needed to develop this unified field theory, his focus remained on asking the right question.

We find this story especially instructive because, apocryphal or not, it supports an important but surprisingly elusive point: The focus on finding answers must not obscure the importance of asking the right questions.

Why Question?

In the last twenty years the role of leadership has changed from that of the person with the right answers to that of the person with the right questions. This change has been prompted by myriad altered circumstances. Rapid advances in technology used to process information now dictate that no one person can master all the data needed to address the complex issues that confront today's organizations. Consequently, leadership's role has evolved to a focus on asking the right questions at the right time of the right people and then holding these people accountable for the answers.

In discussing the challenge of making decisions with very technical ramifications, Roger Ackerman, Corning's chairman and chief executive officer, said, "Obviously, our leadership does not and should not necessarily have the technical expertise needed to make some of the decisions we need to make. However, we have people who do have the expertise, and top management needs to ask the right questions of these people in order to ensure that we understand the technical implications of our decisions."

Another change is the new emphasis placed on leadership's role in developing others within an organization. As companies flatten and the span of management increases, leaders become less indispensable themselves. Developing others using the Socratic method of teaching—asking questions as opposed to giving answers—has become a critical skill. Jean Halloran, who, as human resources manager for Hewlett-Packard is responsible for twenty-five thousand Hewlett-Packard employees, says, "In empowering others, we need to agree on what needs to be done, but they need to determine how it is to be done. We have to resist the urge to give them advice and, instead, when they ask for help we need to ask questions so that they come up with their own answers."

Last, as the Yankelovich/Kepner-Tregoe survey indicates, 99 percent of the top management surveyed indicated that critical thinking skills should be a core competency for their companies. Yet recall that, alarmingly, nearly a third of executives, when asked whether Attila the Hun or Socrates would be the more effective decision maker in today's business environment, chose Attila as the preferred model. If critical thinking is to become a core competency, top management and other leaders must become competent in critical thinking. The story about Einstein illustrates that critical thinking begins with the right question. As Tom Peters puts it, "Leaders have to be brilliant questioners. Leaders have to be the askers of the right questions and the stirrers of the right pots."

You Know What Leading Questions Are, Don't You?

Asking questions is critical but insufficient unless, as Peters pointed out, the questions are the right ones. A common affliction we have witnessed among leaders, however, is the propensity to ask leading questions. Leading questions are those that suggest the answer in the question or lead the responder to the questioner's preferred answer. The obvious problem with leading questions is that they thwart the ability of the respondent to think independently.

An example, which doubles as a cocktail-party trick, demonstrates how leading questions limit the options considered in decision making:

- Write the three of hearts on a piece of paper and put it in your pocket.
- Now ask someone to pick two suits from a full deck of cards.
- If hearts is among the two choices, ask him to pick one of those two choices.
- If hearts is not among the two choices, ask him to name the other two suits and pick one of those. If he does not choose hearts, ask which suit remains—obviously hearts.
- Once he has picked hearts, ask him to name six hearts.
- If the three is among the six, ask him to pick four of the six. If he does not pick the three, ask him to list the hearts that are left, and continue to have the person either pick one of the hearts he has mentioned or the hearts he has not mentioned until he says the three.

Then show him the piece of paper.

If the people you try that trick on are as impressionable as we are, they will immediately assume that you have powers akin to David Copperfield's. In fact, through a series of six to eight leading questions, you have led them to an answer that you have already picked, rather then encouraging them to consider all fifty-two possibilities. Obviously, asking leading questions quickly limits options and alternatives that might otherwise be considered.

While our trick *consciously* uses questions to lead a person to a preferred option, it is the *unconscious* use of leading questions that incapacitates organizational decision making. In one company management asked questions of a project team making a recommendation for a greenfield siting of a plant that focused on the favorable features of management's preferred alternative. Not surprisingly, management's pet alternative was selected. Nonetheless, the organization touted the impartial way in which the decision was made.

Which Questions?

If we accept that questioning is an important role for leaders, and asking the wrong question debilitates rather than encourages thought, then which questions should leaders ask? The best way to approach this question is through a case example. Read the material that follows, in which a fictitious entity, the Montgomery County Park Board, has been asked to decide on the location of a new recreation area. After reading the case, select the one site that you believe would be most appropriate for the new park.

The Case of the Montgomery County Park Board

Background Information on the Decision Facing the Board

Montgomery County is located eighty miles from a large metropolitan area. Ten years ago the county was a rural area of small lakes, rolling hills, woods, and farms. The two major communities were Danville, population 8,800, and the county seat, Hightstown, population 16,200. Over the past decade significant growth has occurred throughout the county, particularly around the two towns. Danville's population is now 20,200; Hightstown's has risen to 24,300; and the rest of the county is home to 7,700 residents. Much of the once open land has been turned into subdivisions. However, the county is justifiably proud of the way it has managed its sudden growth. Generally, schools, sewage and water systems, and highways have more than kept pace with the change. While there is some concern about a lower quality of life, most residents agree that the county is in good shape.

However, there have been a few complaints from some of the residents. Historically, the citizens of Danville have felt that Hightstown had always been treated more favorably because it was the county seat. For example, the newly constructed countywide high school was located in Hightstown. Recently the complaints from Danville have become more bitter, since its population has grown so much faster than the rest of the county. There is also growing discontent throughout the county regarding several recent tax increases.

Harvey Forbes was one of the pillars of the Hightstown community. He was a lifelong resident of Montgomery County and served as president of several countywide community organizations. When he died early this year, he left a sum of $500,000 to be used to purchase land and build a park for his fellow county residents. His only stipulations were that the park should, as soon as possible, serve as a place where entire families could recreate together while enjoying nature, and that it should satisfy unmet community recreational needs. Money not used for the purchase of the park would, according to the terms of Harvey's will, be used for improvements in the Hightstown Youth Center.

The board has been informed that there are no additional county funds available to purchase or build a park. However, in future years a maximum of $40,000 per year could be set aside each year for maintenance and improvements to the park.

THE PRESENT SITUATION

You are a recently elected member of the Montgomery County Park Board. Four sites have been proposed for the new park, and you must now vote on the one you believe will be most suitable.

1. *Oakwood Estate*

An executive's country retreat, this 110-acre area already includes a log cabin that could be used as a community center, a twenty-foot-by-forty-foot swimming pool, and a tennis court. Several paths have been constructed through its beautiful woods and streams. Although the estate is well developed, there is an open area that could be converted to six tennis courts, an archery range, or a baseball field. The cost of the conversion would be $20,000, and the park could open by May 31. Access to the estate is very convenient, since it is one mile off a state highway on an asphalt driveway. Power lines, water, and plumbing are already operative.

Purchase price: $470,000
Estimated cost of annual maintenance: $90,000
Driving time from Hightstown: 5 minutes
Driving time from Danville: 35 minutes

2. *Campbell's Lake*

This parcel consists of 175 acres of lake and farmland. The lake covers 90 percent of the acreage and provides some of the best fishing in the county. It would be easy to convert the shore to a swimming area, small playground, and picnic area. No land would be available for baseball, tennis, etc. During February the children from a nearby subdivision already use the lake for ice skating, although it is illegal. The site would be ready by early June and would cost only $60,000 for park preparation. Although the area is somewhat remote, a graded highway surrounds the lake and is accessible from a state highway eight miles away. Power lines are convenient, but wells would have to be drilled.

Purchase price: $420,000
Estimated cost of annual maintenance: $20,000
Driving time from Hightstown: 30 minutes
Driving time from Danville: 20 minutes

3. *Smith's Woods*

A total of 130 acres of rolling, wooded terrain with several small streams. Construction would be difficult because of the terrain; however, several flat areas are available for eight tennis courts and two playgrounds. Much of the wooded area could be used for picnic grounds, as a few paths through the wilderness already exist. Conversion costs would be $120,000, and the park would be ready by July 4. Although the woods are two miles from a state highway, it would be necessary to repair the access road. It would be necessary to construct new power lines as well as provide for water and sanitation facilities.

Purchase price: $360,000
Estimated cost of annual maintenance: $30,000
Driving time from Hightstown: 20 minutes
Driving time from Danville: 20 minutes

Note: During some springs, one of the streams floods a small area of bottomland and covers some of the picnic area.

4. *Korn's Bluff*

Consists of 120 acres of breathtaking beauty above and along the river. The wilderness and view of the river would make an ideal picnic area. The terrain is such that baseball diamonds, tennis courts, etc., are out of the question, although a small playground could be built next to the picnic area on a beautiful cliff high above the water. The park could be ready by May 31. Power is readily available. Conversion costs, including water and sanitation facilities, the upgrading of roads, and the construction of parking lots, would be $50,000. An older state highway runs next to Korn's Bluff.

Purchase price: $350,000
Estimated cost of annual maintenance: $10,000
Driving time from Hightstown: 40 minutes
Driving time from Danville: 40 minutes

Note: The state has plans for building a new highway through this area, but if it becomes a park, the highway would probably be rerouted. The bluffs are currently somewhat inaccessible because of poor roads. Approximately 40 acres are located in the flood plain next to the river.

Our reason for presenting this case is not to evaluate the quality of your choice, but to make certain points regarding questions. Assume for a moment that you are the chair of the Montgomery County Park Board, and you have assigned us the responsibility of evaluating the options and making a recommendation. After a careful analysis, we come back to you with the recommendation that the park should be located at Smith's Woods.

Write down three or four questions you would want to ask us to evaluate our recommendation, then put the questions to the side.

The types of questions you would ask us can be sorted into one of two categories.

Examples of Category A Questions	Examples of Category B Questions
• What will we do if conversion costs are more than $120,000?	• What were the objectives for your decision?
• How much will it cost to repair the access road?	• What other alternatives did you consider?
• How much will it cost to drill wells?	• How well did the alternatives meet your objectives?
• What will we do in the event of heavy spring rains?	• What are the risks associated with putting the park in Smith's Woods?

Now we want to pose some questions about the two categories.

- Which category requires you, the questioner, to have more specific information about the proposed park and the potential sites? The answer is Category A, because to ask these questions, you have to understand some of the engineering involved in building a park and some of the characteristics of the different types of land.
- Which category allows us, as the recommenders, to try to snow you with technical information or details? Again, the answer is Category A. Because you are asking for specific information, the fact that we spent considerable time analyzing the data means that we are likely to have more command of the details and technology than you do.

- Which category allows you to test the quality of the rationale behind our recommendation? This time the answer is Category B, because you are asking us to describe the process we used to arrive at our recommendation.
- Which category enables us to learn and, possibly, improve our future decision-making capabilities? Once again, the answer is Category B, because these questions are appropriate when reviewing any decision, not just the decision regarding the new park in Montgomery County.

We label Category A questions as *Content* questions and Category B questions as *Process* questions. Both are essential to good decision making. However, in our extensive work with companies and leaders, we have found that in decision-making situations the questions asked by leaders are preponderantly based on content. In other words, for most leaders, Content questions come naturally, while Process questions require conscious attention.

Now look at the questions we asked you to write down regarding our recommendations to the Montgomery County Park Board. Into which category do your questions fall? Using a case to describe a situation that is unfamiliar means that you do not have much detail or technical knowledge about the decision. In such situations Process questions generally are best because they force us, as the recommenders, to examine how we made our decision. Also, they allow you, as the decision maker, to determine the degree of confidence you have in our conclusion, based on the soundness of our process.

Which Process Questions Should Be Asked?

Obviously, we think that the Kepner-Tregoe critical thinking processes are a good source of Process questions. The key is knowing which Process questions should be asked in a given situation.

Situation: **The Need to Focus and Prioritize**

Questions: What specific issues and opportunities confront us?
Which are most critical?

Which analysis is needed to address the high-priority issues or opportunities?
Who should be involved in any further analysis of the issue or opportunity?

Situation: The Need to Determine Whom to Involve in Addressing an Issue

Questions: Who has the information needed to address the issue?
Whose commitment is needed to effectively implement a resolution to the issue?

Situation: The Need to Find True Cause of a Problem

Questions: What is the relevant information regarding the problem?
What, possibly, could be causing the problem?
How do the possible causes explain the relevant information?
How can the true cause be verified?

Situation: The Need to Decide among a Number of Alternatives

Questions: What are the assumptions that lead us to making this decision?
What are our objectives in making the decision?
What are the alternatives we should consider?
How well do the various alternatives meet the objectives?
What are the risks if we go with the alternative that best meets the objectives?

Situation: The Need to Protect a Plan or Capitalize on an Opportunity

Questions: What are the potential problems or opportunities that may confront us as we go forward?
Which are most critical?

How can we prevent the problems and promote the opportunities?
If a problem occurs, how can we minimize the damage?
If an opportunity occurs, how can we maximize the benefit?

Situation: The Need to Determine Why People Are Not Performing as Desired

Questions: What do they view as the expectations?
What, if any, mixed messages are they receiving?
What skills, knowledge, and information do they need, and do they have them?
What happens if they perform as desired, and what happens if they do not?
What feedback do they receive about their performance?

Starting with the appropriate Process questions gives respondents access to questions that help them formulate and explain their thinking. In comparison, by starting with Content questions the reviewer runs the risk of leading respondents and limiting the range of their response. If the reviewer has position power, the risk that Content questions will limit responses is particularly high. In general, the preferred sequence is to start with Process questions and then proceed to Content questions.

Socrates as Maestro

Daniel Patterson explains the role of the mission control manager in space shuttle flights, using a mixed metaphor. "He's an orchestrator. I envision him as someone standing up there conducting this whole complicated process. He's a conductor, but unlike a conductor, he has not predetermined what he wants and is not giving the beat to get there. Instead, he does not know the right answer and is questioning his mission team to get maximum benefit from its expertise and thinking."

This image of a mission control manager can be generalized as a model for leaders in any organization—a conductor and integrator using questions to access the expertise of the people in the organization. The open and nonleading questions asked to probe the specifics start with Process questions and are followed by Content questions. In other words, the effective leader is Socrates—with a baton.

CHAPTER 11

Campfire of the Vanities—Values in Decision Making

My firm belief is that values are the buoys in the channel of commerce. During the course of your career you've got to make thousands of decisions. You've got to react to what happens every day. But if you can't tie your decisions back to your core values, you get lost. Totally lost.

JAMES R. HOUGHTON
Former Chairman and Chief Executive Officer,
Corning Incorporated

Twelve-year-old boys are, for the most part, a danger both to themselves and to society. As hormones rage, they can demonstrate an awe-inspiring creativity in making mischief. We suspect it is for that reason that Baden-Powell founded the Boy Scouts, an organization dedicated to placing twelve-year-olds in remote areas and thus minimizing their potential for mayhem.

As twelve-year-old Tenderfeet (the highest scouting rank either of us achieved), we busied ourselves around the campfire dreaming up wonderful, devious ploys. The decision-making process was simple and straightforward: How could we make this a memorable trip for our Scout leader? The Scout leader was then subjected to clandestine applications of shaving cream, warm-water hand baths while sleeping, and various other types of juvenilia. And the outcome was predictable. By the end of the trip we would be informed that we should not invest heavily in camping equipment as we would not be doing much more of it.

Today many of those mischievous twelve-year-olds have moved on to other endeavors. A few who "orienteered" their way to Wall Street have found different pranks to play. They sometimes involve the disappearance of hundreds of millions of dollars in a financial snipe hunt called derivatives. But then again, boys will be boys.

Aren't There Any Boy Scouts in Business?

Scouting's true aim is to inculcate young men and women with a set of values that will make them better citizens. Hence the phrase "He's a Boy Scout" came to mean the individual possessed high ethical and moral standards. Yet whether they were once Scouts or not, a disturbing number of business executives seem to have made decisions totally devoid of traditional societal values. Nick Leeson, for example, lived in luxury while bringing about the 1994 collapse of Barings Plc. Eighteen months later a Japanese manager, Toshihide Iguchi, at Daiwa Bank Ltd. in New York, duplicated Leeson's feat. Executives in a Japanese car company developed a kickback scheme from dealers, an idea they may have learned by following the example set by executives in a United States aerospace company in Japan a number of years earlier. Robert Maxwell pillaged his employees' retirement fund, then took an ill-advised midnight stroll. Juergen Schneider left German banks with hundreds of millions of D-marks in worthless paper. Remarkably, these examples are only the most recent in our memory. And we haven't even mentioned the savings and loan debacle.

While all these incidents have criminal implications, if we consider decisions that merely transgress ethical or moral standards, the litany of unsavory decisions might prove to be endless. Which begs an important question: Is decision making increasingly devoid of ethical and moral considerations? Aren't there any Boy Scouts in the business world today?

Decisions predicated on questionable values are more than simply fodder for investigative journalists or sanctimonious speeches by business ethicists. They also destroy companies—such as Barings, Polly Peck International Plc., and Maxwell Communication Corporation Plc. They cost employees jobs at places like American Honda; Kidder Peabody Group, Inc.; and Daiwa Bank. They lose millions for company shareholders, often in out-of-court settlements kept secret through nondisclosure clauses. As is the case with most social phenomena, these breaches of trust cannot be laid at the door of a single, willful miscreant. Instead, these "morally doubtful" decisions are rooted in the decision-making components of a corporate culture.

The phenomenon of sleazy decision making is not new. It may, however, be on the rise because of shifts in the way decisions are made within companies. In order to understand these shifts, we will need to do a little detective work. We'll pull out our pipes and put on our "deerstalkers." As Sherlock Holmes would say, "The game is afoot," and we're in search of the three components in any investigation—the motive, the means, and the opportunity.

The Motive—Golden Parachute or Golden Rule?

When *The Rational Manager* was published in 1965, Kepner and Tregoe made a compelling argument for viewing a decision less in terms of the final choice and more from the perspective of the decision objectives that shaped that choice. The logic behind this thinking was that the decision objectives of any decision maker reflect the rationale supporting his or her final choice. Thus the motives of the decision maker are, indeed, at the nexus of our discussion about values in decision making.

Kepner and Tregoe believed that values should be incorporated into a decision maker's objectives, thereby putting them "out there," where they could be discussed, agreed upon, and committed to. In a recent article written by two professors from the Northwestern University J. L. Kellogg Graduate School of Management, the authors shore up Kepner and Tregoe's insight. Ethical flaws and biases, they contend, "are likely to influence decision making more when decisions are intuitive, impulsive, or subjective rather than concrete, systematic, and objective."[1]

[1] David M. Messick and Max H. Bazerman, "Ethical Leadership and the Psychology of Decision Making," *Sloan Management Review*, Winter 1996, pp. 9–22.

For most decision makers, values occupy a significant place in the listing of decision criteria. For example, Edward Snider has consistently managed his decision process by placing values above economic considerations. His decision to build the CoreStates sports arena was seriously limited from the outset by his unwillingness to pit New Jersey against Philadelphia, an unheard-of practice in his industry. Economically driven sports owners are notorious for playing one city or state against the other in order to secure tax concessions, rent-free city property, and interest-free loans. The result over the last five years has been a movement of sports franchises that makes Bedouin nomads look like Trappist monks:

NFL Oilers	Houston to Nashville
NFL Browns	Cleveland to Baltimore
NFL Raiders	Oakland to Los Angeles to Oakland
NFL Cardinals	St. Louis to Phoenix
NFL Colts	Baltimore to Indianapolis
NFL Rams	Los Angeles to St. Louis
NHL Stars	Minnesota to Dallas
NHL Jets	Winnipeg to Phoenix
NHL Avalanche	Quebec to Colorado

Says Snider, "I have one of the worst new building deals in North America because everyone knew I was emotionally committed to Philadelphia. My hometown means more to me than making a financial killing. But we'll make it work anyway because while I may have the worst deal, I also have the best people." Incidentally, in 1996 Snider was able to correct the deal problem in a brilliantly designed merger with Comcast Corp. that allowed him to keep the Flyers in Philadelphia and continue to manage his business with the same outstanding people. In addition, in September 1966 he opened what many people consider to be the best new sports and entertainment venue in the world, the

CoreStates Center. Like many of the best business leaders, Snider has a clear sense of values that guides his decision making.

It is not surprising to us that the most celebrated companies are also those that place the most emphasis on the moral and ethical components of decision making. Robert Wayman, executive vice president at Hewlett-Packard, was asked why the company has one of the most talented workforces in the world. "We have a clear sense of our values and culture," he noted. "And those are critical factors in all of our hiring decisions. As a result, we rarely hire people who don't fit."

Ralph Larsen, chairman and chief executive officer of Johnson & Johnson, mirrors Wayman's remarks while putting them into personal perspective: "My job first and foremost is to set the moral and ethical tone for our organization. You must start with an ethical and moral base for your business. That way you can hire the right people, train them, and when I'm ready to turn over the company to these people, they will be better able to run J&J than I am." Hewlett-Packard, Corning, and Johnson & Johnson are just a few of the many leading companies that place a premium on ethics in decision making.

Unfortunately, there are also an alarming number of companies where ethics and outcomes seem to have diverged in the decision-making process. We believe there are several important reasons why values are not part of the motivation for decision makers at these organizations.

1. ABSENT OR UNARTICULATED VALUES.

For many managers, values are like baby powder: you don't need them until you start to chafe. When all the rational explanations for poor results or bizarre initiatives have been exhausted, it's comforting to talk about "building for long-term growth," or "investing in people," or even "operating on a basis of trust." What makes these otherwise valid assertions somewhat disingenuous is that it is often the first time such values have been discussed, or at least resurrected, after years of consignment to annual reports and a pocket card used as a coaster. We were in a Fortune 100 telecommunications company several years ago when an employee offered this observation: "We go through a lot of change around here. Every time there is a major change announced, the values return like the swallows to Capistrano. In the interim, the only real value is the bottom line."

More troublesome are the executives who have a clearly defined set of personal values that are treated like the numbers of Swiss bank accounts—so important that they can't be shared with anyone. One chief executive officer of a midwestern consumer products company, in a shocking display of arrogance or ignorance—your choice—offered that his values were a basis for his corporation's competitive advantage and, therefore, couldn't be divulged for reasons of confidentiality. Other executives believe that values are "soft," that it's up to each employee to find his or her own ethic. While this may be true in part, such a philosophy leaves people who are acting on behalf of their companies, in Houghton's words, foundering in the currents of commerce without anything by which to navigate.

The best companies not only have clearly articulated statements of values like the Johnson & Johnson credo, they go to great lengths to communicate them. Harley-Davidson's Richard Teerlink notes, "Everyone in our company goes to a course called 'Putting Values into Action.' Our Leadership Institute has also added extensive courses on values issues." When Whitney McMillan was chairman of Cargill Incorporated, a discussion with him was virtually impossible without some reference to Cargill's values. For McMillan, values weren't paraded out for ceremonial occasions, they were part of every conversation.

Robert Eaton and Robert Lutz of Chrysler invested huge amounts of time spelling out a set of values to guide Chrysler into the future. They conducted annual sessions to demonstrate their commitment to these values and to plan specific actions to make them come alive in Chrysler. They said they wanted to invest in people and did so with an eighteen-month effort to build core thinking skills in twenty-five thousand workers. They said they were committed to safety as part of their obligation as a manufacturer to the public. As a result, they led the charge to meet federal standards for trucks and vans years before they were required to do so—in stark contrast to Chevrolet, for example, which is only now installing driver's side air bags in its Suburbans. Chrysler stated that it wanted to manage the business for the long term so that investors, suppliers, and employees would gain some measure of protection against the vagaries of automotive industry cycles. So it worked to build a cash reserve to give this value some meaning. Most important, people in the business community began to notice. Chrysler's prestige as a manufacturer, partner, and employer began to skyrocket.

2. FOCUS ON A SINGLE VALUE.

In interviews with maximum security inmates in the Arizona Correctional System, we learned something that to more astute people was obvious. Felons have difficulty establishing sound priorities. The thought process of the armed robber is clearly focused on the payoff—the cash. It is doubtful that he is overly concerned with the occupational health and safety of the people in the store he is robbing. He is probably not considering the possible damage to his reputation in the community that might result from a state-sponsored tour of duty in a five-by-nine-foot jail cell. And he's probably overlooked the slight decline in his employability and long-term earning potential if he builds a nine-year résumé as a metal worker specializing in punching out "Arizona, the Grand Canyon State."

Businesspeople, however, are not like that at all. They are not just into profit and financial measures. First and foremost, they consider the well-being of employees, the community, and the long term. Or do they? Regrettably, many do not. A 1995 Kepner-Tregoe workplace survey suggests that employees do not feel they are factored into the decision-making process.[2] In fact, only 16 percent of the employees polled believed that company initiatives were undertaken with their objectives in mind—a truly startling response and surely one of the reasons for the increasing activism of interest groups who apparently believe they can influence decisions only by forcing themselves on the process. In fact, the

[2] Kepner-Tregoe, *People and Their Jobs: What's Real, What's Rhetoric?* (Princeton, N. J.: Kepner-Tregoe, Inc., 1995), p. 11.

common response from John Jett of Kidder-Peabody, Nick Leeson of Barings, and Toshihide Iguchi of Daiwa Bank was that their companies placed nearly obsessive emphasis on profits at all costs. Whether their views were self-serving or not, it is hard to deny that many businesses, particularly those that are foundering, have placed economic values so far ahead of other less tangible considerations as to create a single omnipotent objective—profit.

Executives are not alone in this dangerous single-mindedness. However values-driven Eaton and Lutz of Chrysler may be, the company has a values problem in the form of one major shareholder. Kirk Kerkorian has focused on one value—returning cash to the shareholder. (We suspect it is just a coincidence that he holds so much Chrysler stock.) This fixation on a single value, with its exclusion of others, is evident in a variety of corporate relationships. And when it happens, it is not surprising to find bond traders, plant managers, and salespeople "cutting corners" with ethical concerns to ensure the delivery of the profit. But don't blame them; that's what they've been told—maybe not in so many words, but certainly in the actions of management. As one worker in our 1995 workplace survey commented, "There's a big difference between what management says and what it does."

Values do not become a realistic component in the motivation behind the broader array of corporate decisions until they are well articulated in the workplace, allowing them to be considered as part of the decision-making process. Walk into the lobby of Johnson & Johnson in New Brunswick, New Jersey, and you will find its credo etched in stone in bold lettering. Walk into any Hewlett-Packard facility—whether it's Helsinki or Boise—and you will see Hewlett-Packard's values prominently displayed. Visit Teerlink's office in Milwaukee. Harley-Davidson values occupy a place of prominence on walls that less enlightened executives might reserve for corporate artwork. Profit is not the first value mentioned by any of these companies (though their performance clearly shows that financial values have not been forgotten). In short, if the values are comprehensive and if there is parity among the economic values and those that are less tangible—both in thought and in action—then an organization's values will be more recognizable in the outcome of the decision deliberations.

The Means—"Power Corrupts; Absolute Power Corrupts Absolutely"

Businesses around the world are in a paroxysm of generosity. They are handing out one of their most important assets as if it were holiday candy. To a certain degree, almost every employee can benefit. What companies are distributing is power! This power is delegated in the authority to make decisions. But it's how people respond to this power that makes the difference. Some hand it back. Some use it on appropriate occasions, while others grab the ring and accept what they view as a new anointing.

Regardless of their response, people are being asked to make decisions where they were never asked before. This creates a problem in corporate values that is fundamentally mathematical. There is a percentage in every segment of society that will take liberties with rules. Prisons are full of bandits, thugs, rapists, doctors, lawyers, business executives, and engineers—criminality is not simply relegated to those at the bottom of the socioeconomic ladder. While the percentages of people who are willing to violate social or organizational norms is one mathematical variable, there is another critical variable to consider. That is: how often these violations occur.

The frequency of transgressions operates on a different mathematical model. As societal approbation for the "questionable" practice increases, so does the practice. Speeding and cheating on tax returns, for example, are unlawful but more broadly extant in society than murder and rape because they are generally accepted as less despicable. In the case of business, the empowerment process creates values problems in decision making in geometric proportions because of these phenomena. If a certain percentage of any segment is likely to take liberties with the rules, broadening the power to make decisions increases statistically the likelihood of ethical problems within the organization. When combined with the less salacious nature of white-collar malfeasance—cheating on taxes or financial reports, lying about late product shipments, or inventing customer stories to mislead prospects—the rise in the number of incidents of unacceptable behavior can become alarming. In one Fortune 500 company of extremely high repute, three of the executive staff reporting to the chairman were fired in one twelve-month period—one for sexual harassment, one for embezzlement, and one for theft of company property. The chairman, a man of the highest personal and professional standards, must have had more than a few sleepless nights that year.

There are, of course, principled people making improper decisions and being pilloried for them because they do not know they are illegal or improper. A midlevel manager in a company specializing in temporary employment charges a customer for "phantom workers" because he has heard it is the standard industry practice used to recover nonassigned overhead. A shipping supervisor at an auto supplier lies to a customer about a key delivery date because she does not want to embarrass her company and she is hopeful they might be able to come close. An attorney "pads" billable hours because his billing rate has been increased and the client expects an invoice reflecting the old billing rate. He does not want to hassle the client, who is sensitive about these rates, so he adds the imaginary hours, figuring it results in the same total in the end.

These stories, and dozens more like them, reflect the ethical dilemmas faced by honest or at least well-intentioned people in their daily business decision-making routines. The confusion over ethical gray areas can confound even the most principled among us. Robert Potamkin, the highly ethical chief executive officer of Potamkin Inc., one of the top one hundred privately held companies in the United States, described the confusion in ethical decision making this way: "I can't believe the number of businesspeople who are making the front pages for being indicted for things I didn't even know were crimes!" Given that Potamkin is a graduate of the University of Pennsylvania Law School and is a member of the Pennsylvania Bar, his comment is, indeed, sobering.

Knowing that more and more people are making decisions that will require ethical clarity, a corporation cannot relinquish its responsibility with the complacent, negligent view that if you hire good people, their actions will always be honest and ethical. Organizations must translate their statements of values into clear and unambiguous codes of conduct. Companies like USF&G, Lockheed Martin Corporation, American Express, and dozens of other top organizations invest heavily in detailed, written descriptions of the behavior they expect to see as well as that which will not be tolerated. They ensure that every employee reads and understands actions that best reflect how their values should affect day-to-day decision making.

Firms like Prudential Bache Securities are part of another growing trend. Recognizing that no document can describe all of the confusing situations an employee may encounter, the company has appointed an ethics officer, Jim Settel, who reports to the chairman. Settel's role is not to act as corporate saint, but rather to ensure that ethical decision making is discussed in the firm and not simply "read" by a trader or broker and promptly forgotten. He also serves as a resource to people who find themselves in tricky situations and are not sure of the proper response. Perhaps most important, Settel acts as an ombudsman so that people who must make ethically sound decisions with the potential for adverse financial consequences can do so without the fear of reproach.

At holiday time some organizations like Chrysler take a proactive step by notifying suppliers to refrain from gift giving or other acts that might improperly influence their employees. This does not mean Chrysler or companies with similar policies believe their employees are dishonest. Instead, they are shielding their employees from situations where they are required to make decisions in morally ambiguous circumstances.

Communicating the basis for ethical decision making or appointing an ethics officer may appear to be overreacting, but unfortunately it is not. The chief executive officer of a major packaging company offered this arcane view: "I'm not adding another expensive bureaucracy just to tell my people not to steal from me." In a time when ethical dimensions are clearly growing more complex, that view is based on the absurd notion that the decisions people face today are black and white. Brushing aside this concern may ultimately prove to be bad business when, for example, a simple misstep in ethical decision making might require this executive to spend hundreds of thousands of dollars on public relations counsel and damage control specialists. As the old Bendix Fram oil filter commercial advised, "You can pay me now or pay me later." Those chief executives concerned about the potential that unethical decisions have for dealing damaging blows to their corporate reputations are playing it smart and paying now.

Opportunity—"Just Because You're Paranoid Doesn't Mean They're Not Out to Get You"

The observant reader will have noted that concern and active involvement with ethical decision making may work for the majority of honest and decent people but still offer limited protection from those with more questionable behavior. Certainly no amount of communication by handbook or corporate ethics officer will insulate an organization from deviant behavior.

In the past, the dangers to which a business was exposed by the rogue decision maker were fairly well controlled for a few simple reasons. Businesses were populated by a cadre of middle managers, whose jobs included ensuring that decisions remained "within the box." Spans of control—the number of people supervised by a manager—were typically five to eight, allowing managers adequate opportunity to review decisions. Business used to be run with extensive approval processes—a single financial decision required several levels of sign-off. The manager and employees worked in the same physical space, and periodic observation provided its own measure of security. Managers were more likely to have a working knowledge of the activities of their employees as a result of having recently participated themselves.

Today the situation is quite different. The middle managers of today no longer dine in the corporate cafeteria, which, when all is said and done, is the only good news for them from the massive corporate layoffs. They have disappeared in a blight of corporate anorexia. These flattened organizations no longer provide for direct supervision of work at every turn. Managers who have survived the cutbacks are often responsible for twenty or more people. Since approvals of certain lower-level decisions have been abbreviated in order to bring faster service to the customer, these less visible decisions are not often subject to multiple authorizations. This lack of sign-off is just as well, since the employee needing approval is based in Johore Bahru, Malaysia, and what executive wants his or her dream of the Cubs winning the pennant interrupted by a 3:00 A.M. phone call requesting approval for a $3,000 price deviation? Typically, managers—acting in their roles as coaches—are of little help in many decisions anyway because they do not fully understand the nuances of each employee's area of expertise.

Make no mistake about it, we are witnessing two dramatically different business worlds only five to seven years apart. Within the first was a certain amount of oppression and clandestine villainy as managers stood over the shoulders of workers, inspecting their every move. The pendulum has now swung to an environment where decisions abound for every worker, and the inherent danger in the swing from corporate villainy to corporate anarchy is obvious. Decisions cannot be properly made in either realm. No one will dispute that problems occur when the person with the most knowledge is prevented from making appropriate decisions because of oppressive oversight. Yet the problems with abandoning decision controls are colossal. Czar Nicholas II once remarked, "I don't run Russia, ten thousand clerks do." History quickly proved that those clerks did not do Nicholas any favors. Clearly, decision making should not be an activity subject to rigid controls. Yet the current trend of minimizing control provides an equally disturbing final effect.

The bifurcation of structure and anarchy may stem from giving power in decision making without providing accountability. As John Kay wrote in a recent article in the *Financial Times,* "Constructive accountability gives people freedom to make decisions but holds them fully responsible for the consequences."[3] This means not only the financial consequences, but the tarnishing of a corporate image by a less than acceptable practice. Holding an individual fully responsible is easier said than done, of course. Responsibility begins with clarity. One must ask if the worker knows what is expected. Clear, simple, and specific ethical guidelines are critical to providing a decision maker a fair chance to act responsibly.

[3] *Financial Times* (London), 17 November 1995, p. 13.

But is unethical and improper behavior thus eliminated? Of course not. Once the ground rules are clear, what happens when an individual acts improperly? In the 1980s a U.S. company was contracted to provide services at a U.S. naval shipyard in the Philippines. In order to provide these services, the company's managers would need to work in concert with a group of twelve civilian Filipino maintenance workers, and it quickly became apparent that the project could not be accomplished within traditional hours. The civilian hourly workers insisted on differential pay in order to participate in the project. However, the commanding navy captain made it clear that the request for differential pay would set a shipyard precedent that was unsustainable, and he denied the request.

The contractor was now faced with a dilemma. Without the differential pay the company would be unable to get the cooperation of the civilian workers, and without their participation it would be unable to take the contract. Despite impassioned appeals, the navy captain was intransigent—no-pay status changes. It was at this point that the company's vice president for international operations and local managing director developed a "creative solution." They instructed an employee from their Australian operation to fly in with an amount of cash equal to the civilian workers' demands for differential pay. The money was given to the workers in plain brown bags without comment. The navy was never informed of this largesse, and in short order the project began with the full cooperation of the twelve civilian workers. Was this action illegal? Maybe. Was it improper? Almost certainly. The failure to notify the navy and the need to bring in an Australian "bagman" tell a lot about how "aboveboard" the company felt about its action.

This subterfuge became broadly known to the company's employees. The president brushed it off as simply an unusual business arrangement. When pushed, he responded angrily that any concerns only reflected a naiveté about the necessity of adjusting business practice to meet local practice. Lower-level employees mentioned that such practices, if known, might jeopardize the company's domestic business with the U.S. Navy. They were brusquely notified to keep their opinions to themselves. The incident was subsequently forgotten, and the president continued with his regular declarations of the company's basic belief to "act honestly and ethically in all business dealing worldwide."

The failure here is obvious. When a value is trodden underfoot and decision makers act in contravention of written ethical standards, the company has a chance to demonstrate the true importance of these values. In this case the company demonstrated by its actions that it gives decision-making authority but does not demand ethical accountability. The message to the rest of the organization is clear: Basic beliefs do not govern performance. In this type of company, ethical problems in the future were almost certain. Over the next seven years the firm lost millions in Canada, Sweden, the United Kingdom, Japan, and the United States in a series of both illegal and unethical practices. Was this trend coincidental? We doubt it! When companies fail to take action in clear-cut matters, the implications for more ethically ambiguous situations become significant. The decision maker no longer sees the need to take advice and follows the most expedient course. In short, failure to link decision-making authority and ethical accountability leads to the likelihood of a values-flawed organization.

Born-Again Decision Making?

Discussions about values often produce slight waves of nausea in the listener, due to the cloying scent of sanctimony. We have not, to date, encountered a canonized decision maker whose choices are so morally pure as to be above reproach. Decision makers inevitably face values considerations that can direct the decision along a variety of different paths. Does Rupert Murdoch's News International in the United Kingdom demonstrate a moral callousness when it reportedly pays only slightly more than a 1 percent tax on over £1 billion in earnings despite its extensive use of tax-supported public services?[4] Is its contribution to U.K. employment and the wealth of its taxable shareholders sufficient to

[4] Mathew Horsman and Jeremy Warner, "Fresh Tax Revelations at News," *The Independent* (London), 4 December 1995, p. 18.

offset this anomaly? These are questions for the executives of the News Corporation to answer within their own corporate value construct. Yet, while it is impossible for us to pass reasonable judgment on the individual decisions of corporate leaders, it is fair to comment on the way a company factors values considerations into its decision-making culture.

Six Rules for Effective Decision Making Based on Organizational Values

We submit that the secret of sound decision making, based on clear communication of corporate values, can be summarized in these six rules:

1. **Values Are Good Business.** Values do not mean altruism, nor should they present a way to parade leadership righteousness. They have financial implications. Companies with a strong moral and ethical basis perform well. The financial consequences of questionable ethical actions can be enormous, even catastrophic.
2. **Write Them Up.** Even God put the Ten Commandments in writing. Written statements of basic beliefs or core values help communicate their importance and insure understanding.
3. **Put Filthy Lucre in Its Place.** There is nothing wrong with financial values, but there is something wrong when they're the only operating ones. Make the values comprehensive and versatile. Put money in its proper place.
4. **Test for Understanding.** With more and more decision makers requiring buoys in the murky channel of commerce, we need to be sure employees know company values and fully understand them. The implication of any value on any individual decision is difficult to ascertain without some discussion.
5. **Provide a "Father Who Knows Best."** Bud Anderson could always count on his dad for ethical guidance in the popular television series of the 1960s, *Father Knows Best:* "Dad, I

have two dates to the prom. I'm going to tell Bobby Sue I broke my leg." "Bud, remember, honesty is always the best policy." Because today's business decisions are slightly more complex than Bud's prom dilemma, the moral and ethical options are not always as clear cut. By having a person who can advise on decisions from solely an ethical perspective, an organization demonstrates a commitment to matching decisions to its values.

6. **Publicize Your Hangings.** Despite all of our most noble efforts, there will be unsavory or improper decisions and actions in any organization. Decisions that fall outside the moral boundaries of the business but are made without malevolence or blatant self-interest require counseling and education to ensure there is no recurrence. When, however, the decision traces back to a more nefarious motivation, it is important that the organization react swiftly and forcefully to convey to others that such decisions will not be tolerated, regardless of the positive benefits the company may derive from it. No one in the organization who was aware of the decision should be left in doubt about how important values in decision making are to the company. A brief corollary should be added to this rule. While the focus of rule six is on malefactors, organizations are populated with a greater number of people whose values and attendant behavior are exemplary. Therefore, remember to erect an award dais next to the organization's scaffold.

Talk about values should never imply that all organizations are populated with miscreants ready to have their awful way with the organization's moral code. While there is always a small minority in any grouping that fits that bill, people are fundamentally honest and ethical. The problem is the ease with which they can be led astray in today's complex business world when making decisions that they have never made before. Attention to the ethical dimension of decision making is not really akin to prisoner rehabilitation. It's more like "born-again decision making"—a renewed commitment to consider seriously the role of ethics in the business choices we make. Amen!

CHAPTER 12

Deployment: Putting It into Play

Technological progress and value added are really the substitution of ideas, skills, and knowledge for physical work and physical resources. That means creating the right work environment, one in which a premium is put on continual learning and improvement.

Ray Marshall
Audre and Bernard Rapoport Centennial Chair
in Economics and Public Affairs, University of Texas
Former Secretary, U.S. Department of Labor

Several years ago we were playing golf at McCormick Ranch in Scottsdale, Arizona, with colleague Sho Suzawa from our Tokyo office. On the back nine we found ourselves in a perilous position. Between us and the green was a cavernous sand trap about the size of Rhode Island. We weren't intimidated by the sand trap; we were terrified of it. We knew that if we hit our golf balls into it, we would probably never see our families again. Suzawa hit his ball safely onto the green, then turned to us and in a soft, measured tone requested that we drop our clubs on the fairway, look carefully at the green, and imagine our golf balls resting there. He then asked us to close our eyes and softly repeat the phrase, "There is no sand, there is no sand." We did as Suzawa suggested, feeling slightly stupid and worrying just a little about the harsh words coming from the foursome waiting behind us.

After a moment or two we opened our eyes, picked up our clubs, and addressed our golf balls. One of us hit the ball squarely into the middle of the sand trap. The other, in a breathtaking display of solidarity and incompetence, followed with a shot that landed only inches away. Glaring, we turned to our Zen golf instructor, Suzawa. "Now there is sand," he remarked.

Five collective shots later we finally landed on the green, and it looked just as we had envisioned it. While we learned nothing about golf from this episode, we did acquire an important lesson in life: No amount of vision will overcome shoddy implementation.

We have a vision of how critical thinking skills can be used effectively to address important business issues. We have noted that the manner in which they are used today is very different from that of the past. We have seen that they must be viewed within the changing context of other cultural and organizational factors, such as how data is used, the role of intuition, systems thinking, and the growing importance of teams and of corporate values and beliefs. We are acutely aware that there are difficulties with our vision. Organizations attempting to assess complex situations and build proficiency in how they make decisions, solve problems, and manage potential threats and opportunities face a daunting implementation challenge. And all too often they are finding themselves stuck in sand traps.

Fortunately, there are also organizations that have demonstrated an uncanny knack for implementing changes that other organizations simply envision. For these organizations, the deployment of the core thinking skills of Situation Appraisal, Problem Analysis, Decision Analysis, and Potential Problem and Potential Opportunity Analysis offers a series of success stories worth close examination. In a poor imitation of Aesop, we'll tell these stories in seven lessons.

Lesson One—Horses for Courses: Choosing the Right Skill-Building Approach

A few years back we decided to put the decision-making process outlined in the Appendix to the ultimate test. We bought a copy of the *Daily Racing Form*, developed our criteria, and scored the horses accordingly. Speed was an objective that had a weighted value of "10," because *Washington Post* racing editor Andrew Beyer said it was most important. Then came "9," "8," and "6" weighted objectives for jockey, prior race performance, and distance respectively. Confident in our analysis, we set off for Bowie Raceway in suburban Washington, D.C. After a midday monsoon drenched the racecourse, our system began to fall apart because we had not given enough weight to track conditions.

While we salvaged a break-even for the day, we talked to a man for whom racetrack gambling appeared to be more than a once-a-year event, as it was for us. He had won a huge bet that day on a 17–1 long shot named Zelda's Gift. He explained that on a wet day there were certain horses that were not only good on a muddy course but actually trained for it. Most horses were trained on relatively firm tracks, but Zelda's Gift was trained on "soft" courses and was specifically stabled as a "mudder." With that information, a $20 wager on Zelda's Gift to win did not seem that big a gamble. Later, as we made our way home from the track, we reflected on this unusual training regimen, and it occurred to us that horse trainers might know something that we did not.

Business trainers use the classroom as their firm track, where important skills are learned and job knowledge acquired. It is undisputed that such training has had an impact. But is the standard classroom the best approach for all employees and all organizations seeking to teach business skills? Is it the best way to build proficiency in the critical thinking skills involved in problem solving and decision making? Or do we have some "mudders" who need a different approach to training?

Recalling the Learning Ladder we described in Chapter 1, we recognize that proficiency begins by providing knowledge and understanding rungs on the Learning Ladder that are easily established with written text. Top-notch businesses like Siemens AG invest substantial energy in making available to employees around the world written material describing the critical thinking process. Certain Hewlett-Packard businesses have put a similar written description on a database so that it is accessible to all employees, from the incoming recruit to the seasoned contributor.

But companies like Siemens and Hewlett-Packard do not want simply to remain at the knowledge and understanding levels of the Learning Ladder. They aggressively climb the rungs of higher understanding and application.

Classroom learning can play an important role in climbing the ladder to organizational proficiency in critical thinking, especially in deepening the intellectual understanding of its concepts and in improving the ability to apply them. Classroom programs designed to build skills in effective problem solving and decision making have been broadly accepted, especially if the programs offer sufficient opportunity to apply these skills to work-related issues during the learning experience. But because classroom training does not fit all work environments, executives who rarely get involved in specific skill-development activities in their organizations must play a role in helping to select the best approach.

At American Honda Motors, Vice President Thomas Dean realized that a classroom experience of several days would not be fully effective in developing the critical thinking skills of employees. The people who most needed the skills were unlikely to be easily available in three- or four-day blocks, and they would be distracted by the ongoing pressures of work compounded by a three-day absence. Dean decided that Honda would develop these critical thinking skills by offering a four-day program that would be held each Monday for one month so employees could return to work, practice the skills they had learned, and return the next week to refine their usage.

Sony used a different variation. Like Corning and British Airways, the company felt that problem-solving and decision-making skills were at the core of a successful quality-education program and made them a component of its superb QMEDI quality program worldwide. Then Sony decided that classroom training was needed to reflect the world in which its employees would be working in the late 1990s and twenty-first century. The company has now embarked on transferring the critical thinking skills to its employees in a *paperless*, group-based classroom environment.

In NASA's Kennedy Space Center, team-based learning is critical. Launching the space shuttle requires the efforts of teams comprising NASA employees, Lockheed Martin employees, and those of many subcontractors. Often these teams are from many different functions and disciplines, and for them, a team-based learning approach supports the classroom experience. The same is true for organizations like Chrysler, General Mills, and Harley-Davidson, where team-based work environments are becoming the preferred approach to running the business. In other organizations or divisions, employees work individually or in teams only intermittently, and these entities have found that climbing the understanding and application rungs of the Learning Ladder requires less conventional methods. Federal Express and Hewlett-Packard have both used interactive computer-based learning to fill the needs of their people in these types of units.

Whether paper based or computer based, group directed or individually directed, the movement of skills from application to competence and proficiency requires a practicum—an opportunity to apply the skills over time in the workplace. During the practicum, the use of facilitators to coach and refine the understanding of these skills is crucial. At Chrysler, facilitators ensure that skills gained in the classroom are immediately supported on the plant floor. Because these analytical skills are put in a prominent position in the workplace, the manufacturing problems that confront other businesses are less likely to get out the factory door at Chrysler. That's how competence and proficiency are built.

Perhaps the ideal model for developing critical thinking competence and proficiency is Procter & Gamble. At its Mehoopany, Pennsylvania, site, where the company manufactures a variety of consumer paper products, a significant number of employees are becoming the plant's experts in problem solving and decision making. Procter & Gamble expects that managers and high-level technicians, in particular, will fill this role. They receive four weeks of additional training beyond the three-day experience given to all employees, which enables them to take a leadership role in applying these thinking processes in the workplace. The results are seen in exceptional performance in equipment uptime, scrap reduction, safety, throughput, and product quality.

The flexibility to choose the right learning method and then support that method in the workplace is a sine qua non for any organization committed to making critical thinking standard operating procedure. When the results come in, investments in the right kind of training will pay off even more handsomely than Zelda's Gift.

Lesson Two—Decisions Wellington: Leading from the Front

In his landmark military history, *The Mask of Command,* John Keegan contrasts the styles of two great military commanders: the duke of Wellington and Ulysses S. Grant. He observes that during the nineteenth century the style of command began to shift from the commander leading from the front lines, as Wellington did, to the commander operating from the rear, as did Grant. In the business battles of today, some Western managers are now so far in the rear that they are nearly invisible. While we are not prepared to enter the debate on either side of these competing leadership styles in the military, we do have a strong bias about which style is best when it comes to building organizational proficiency in the core critical thinking skills. We're voting for Wellington!

Leading from the front in skill building necessitates the suspension of the executive hubris that has afflicted so many businesses in recent years: the belief that top managers achieve their positions by virtue of a rare omniscience—a notion that would be amusing were it not so pervasive. At the worker and middle-management levels, the typical response when we talk about our concepts of problem solving and decision making is, "These are good ideas, but you're talking to the wrong people. The people who really need these skills are in senior management." But when senior management is delicately asked whether there might be truth in these admonitions from the "minions," the reply is often, incredibly, "It really wouldn't be of any value for me," or, "I've had all the development I need," or, "I don't have enough time." Such responses speak volumes about the real weight senior managers put on the acquisition of critical thinking skills in their organizations.

There are, however, a few Wellingtons in business today. We noted earlier that Chrysler president Robert Lutz has made a commitment to ensuring that problem solving remains an organizational proficiency in his company. The "Root Cause Analysis" program, as it has come to be known at Chrysler, was targeted initially at twenty-five thousand salaried Chrysler employees. Lutz told the members of his staff that he hoped they would actively support this initiative and find the time to attend the programs. In short, he did what dozens of other executives have done in launching initiatives about which they had both strong feelings and some degree of ownership.

But then Lutz went a step further. He made sure that he, too, attended one of the programs as a group member. It was not a token appearance, and he missed only one hour of the program for a meeting with Ambassador Walter Mondale and trade representative Mickey Kantor. As the program's instructors quickly learned, Lutz, who has been proficient in problem solving throughout his thirty-odd years in the auto industry, could easily have taught Root Cause Analysis himself. His point in attending was a more powerful one than simply refreshing already well-honed skills. Lutz has always felt that gaining commitment means leading from the front and by example. It wasn't a surprise, therefore, that Chrysler executives did not say they didn't have time or didn't see the need to acquire these crucial skills. Lutz and Chrysler are serious about producing the best vehicles in the world and are building the skills to continue to fulfill that commitment.

When the executives do not lead the campaign to build critical thinking skills, their organizations will limit their rewards to the pockets of people who gravitate to these concepts on their own. In the dozens of companies we've worked with over the last twenty years, we have yet to find a commitment to excellence in problem solving and decision making without visible leadership from the top executives. In his leadership role, Seagate Technology's chairman, Alan Shugart, assumed an interesting 1990s variation on the role of king's taster. Shugart and his executives wanted to validate the approach they had selected to building the company's problem-solving and decision-making capabilities. Their theory was that until they could be certain of the approach, they would be unable to generate the enthusiasm they needed to guide the organization through what would be a significant undertaking.

Shugart and his top team became the first group to begin developing critical thinking skills.

Leadership by example is not, however, relegated to a classroom experience. It requires doing something with the concepts after they are acquired. An executive in a major chemical company once commented, "We spend millions on building skills, but when you walk into one of our plants, you'd be hard pressed to see any evidence of it." Executives are equally guilty. In the same way that rings in the trunk reveal the age of the tree, some argue that an executive's age can be determined by the number of three-ring course binders on his or her bookshelf.

This was a situation the top executives at Corning were determined to overcome. In 1993 Corning made the decision to build an organizational proficiency in problem solving and decision making to further support its celebrated quality program. The top seven executives kicked off the project by participating in a problem-solving and decision-making workshop. When the program concluded, discussion began in earnest on the best methods to build this proficiency in the organization. Corning's Roger Ackerman asked the group's view on making the program mandatory for all Corning employees, an option favored by some in the company.

Corning's vice chairman, Van Campbell, offered a powerful alternative, noting that the real key to building proficiency was usage in the workplace. He argued that the seven executives in the room held the key to building organizational proficiency in critical thinking skills. "If we use the processes ourselves," he said, "and we ask others to present their work to us using these critical thinking skills, there will be no need to mandate this program." Campbell's viewpoint was immediately endorsed, and over the next year the executives rigorously and visibly applied critical thinking skills toward the major operational issues facing Corning. The message took hold, and today Corning can claim a proficiency in solving problems and making decisions that will make a significant difference for years to come.

Organizations seeking to move from the competence gained from a flexible and well-supported skill-development program to a proficiency that can make critical thinking a source of competitive advantage will find the task nearly impossible without forceful, committed, and "up-front" leadership such as that demonstrated at Chrysler, Seagate, and Corning.

Lesson Three—Systems Serenade: Building Process Alignment

We were recently treated to a fourth-grade orchestra concert featuring one of the most often performed works in the classical repertoire—"Twinkle, Twinkle, Little Star." Knowing that Itzhak Perlman and Isaac Stern had undoubtedly played this same piece, we waited in eager anticipation for the virtuosity of the children. The first twelve measures were more reminiscent of Miles Davis on amphetamines than Sir George Solti and the Chicago Symphony. The players raced to see who would finish first. The winning viola had reached "star" while most of the violins were just approaching the second "twinkle." The audience, of course, roundly applauded their efforts and properly ignored the cacophony.

We are frequently reminded that businesses operate with a cacophony all their own—one component playing at its own tempo and working against another, often without anyone being aware of the friction. This is particularly true where the business systems operate in conflict with efforts to build core thinking skills. When such companies find they are not gaining the proficiency they desire, they do not understand why their efforts are falling short.

A situation we encountered in the early 1980s brought the point forcefully home to us. We were working with the Naval Sea Systems Command to help build a proficiency in problem solving within a group of six naval shipyards. We had completed some training activities at the Norfolk Naval Shipyard and begun the process of reinforcing the skills back on the job. Our first task was to see the effects of the training, so we conducted a series of interviews with class participants. We began in Shop 17—the sheet metal shop. We were, to say the least, surprised by the result.

Q: Did you like the course?
A: Yes! One of the best we've had.

Q: Were the ideas relevant to the work you do?
A: Yes, these skills could really help on the job.

Q: Do you understand these processes well enough to be able to use them at work?
A: Yes, they are very clear and understandable. I certainly know how to use them.

By this point we were very pleased with ourselves. Obviously, we were successful at helping to build these critical thinking skills in this organization. Unfortunately, not leaving well enough alone, we asked the crowning question.

Q: How have you used these skills on the job?
A: We don't use them at all.

When we probed this response to find out why we had failed on the only true measure of success, the group explained the shipyard's troubleshooting system to us. If a machine broke, or there was a mechanical failure, they could not fix it themselves. Instead, they were required to call Shop 06. The Shop 06 personnel rarely asked them for their views or attempted to involve them in the repair process. The system in place in the shipyard had made the troubleshooting skills of the workers in Shop 17 valueless. The problem was compounded because the personnel in Shop 06 had never received the training provided to the other shops in analytic troubleshooting.

While this problem was subsequently corrected in the Norfolk naval shipyard, it served as a source of continual embarrassment to us. We had failed to recognize the obvious. There were extant systems for troubleshooting problems and fixing breakdowns, and without bringing these systems into harmony with the thinking skills being developed, we had no chance of increasing the proficiency of the organization.

British Airways, with its total commitment to passenger safety, has as many problem-prevention, troubleshooting, and corrective-action systems and procedures as any organization operating today. Not content to rely on what were already superior critical thinking skills by industry standards, the company embarked on a program to ensure that problem-solving and decision-making capabilities in their aircraft engineering and maintenance operation were the best in the industry. To accomplish this task, British Airways conducted well-designed training workshops and developed a cadre of talented facilitators. The "up-front" leadership of chief engineer John Perkins and director of engineering Alistair Cumming advanced the initiative further. The program would have been stillborn, nonetheless, without strong commitment to reconcile the British Airways systems with the new skills. Immediately, trouble reports were changed to a format consistent with the critical thinking processes. Trouble boards, work requests, and the morning status meeting were organized around these concepts and their implementation. Thus, technical systems complemented the new skills rather than competing against them.

Organizations that have had the most success in achieving proficiency in the critical thinking skills put significant effort into charting or mapping their current systems for problem solving, decision making, problem prevention, and issue resolution. Often this effort reveals that there are several competing systems, or the system is poorly articulated, or the system is missing some key components. We have found, for example, that issues are often brought to the surface effectively, but the systems for ensuring follow-up action are rarely linked to the system that encourages the articulation of such issues.

Once the systems are mapped, they can be modified to fit the critical thinking processes, or the critical thinking processes can be used to fill holes in the system. In the case of the Norfolk Naval Shipyard, both situations applied. First, the data hole between Shop 06, which fixed the equipment, and Shop 17, which ran the equipment, needed immediate attention. Not taking advantage of the real-time knowledge of the Shop 17 operators would severely impair the efficiency and effectiveness of the troubleshooting effort. By designing a "trouble report" to be completed by the Shop 17 operators that was consistent with the skills they had learned, good problem-solving information was gathered quickly. Often the maintenance personnel in Shop 06 could troubleshoot the problem over the phone, leading to a return to production without a time-consuming trip across the yard.

Ultimately this type of proficiency begins to create a momentum for broader systems changes. In British Airways the age-old barriers prohibiting one trade from working in another area began to come down as it became apparent that only by working cross-functionally could problem solving and productivity reach the benchmark levels British Airways strove to achieve. When this happens—a perfect blending of skills and systems—it is harmonious music indeed.

Lesson Four—The Industrial Inferno: Harmonizing Skills and Social Systems

It is unlikely that Nobel Prize winner Jean-Paul Sartre was the sort of guy with whom you'd want to go have a couple of beers. The writing even in his most optimistic works can only be characterized as somber. *Huis-Clos (No Exit)* is more accurately described as morbid. In this work Sartre gives us his own existential view of hell. This place is full of constant haranguing; each action or comment results in a punishing, negative response from one of the three protagonists—a circumstance that will last through eternity, with literally no exit. A colleague from our French office tried to help us unravel the many layers of meaning in this classic. He explained that after years of study by dozens of literary critics around the world, there remained only one great mystery in *Huis-Clos*: which French business Sartre was describing.

Many people have written about, commented on, or experienced a workplace reminiscent of Sartre's hell. In this organizational environment people are not quite sure what they are supposed to do. If they know, they are usually unclear about why they are doing it. The only comments employees receive are negative ones. Feedback is vague, nonspecific, and punitive. In a 1995 survey of 1,516 managers and workers conducted by Kepner-Tregoe, one employee described the feelings engendered by such a workplace: "The only thing that motivates me is knowing that one day I won't have to work here anymore." It's possible Sartre interviewed him before we did.

This type of workplace is one in which the performance system is dysfunctional—a business inferno of the first order. Rather than encouraging superior performance, the system discourages it. As we noted in our discussion of the Performance System in Chapter 8, a seriously flawed performance environment is an unhappy circumstance for any employee in any business and leads to a structural misunderstanding of performance problems, their causes, and their solutions. In the context of deploying critical thinking skills, a poorly engineered performance system is a "stake in the heart" for any effort to build these skills on a broad organizational basis.

A large midwestern consumer food company experienced this problem firsthand. The organization trained several hundred employees at five sites in the critical thinking skills of problem solving and decision making. As in the case of the naval shipyard, we surveyed these employees to determine whether the training had achieved its desired effect. As with the shipyard, the results were discouraging. We were told that after the training took place, they were never asked by anyone in a supervisory position about the skills or their use. When they attempted to troubleshoot problems using the concepts, they were told to "patch" the situation and get production going again. They explained that these patches were never removed, and there was no attempt at subsequent troubleshooting. One operator suggested that the supervisors were simply afraid of these concepts because they didn't understand them. The workers were nearly unanimous in their view that it really wasn't worth the "hassle" to use these processes when it was obvious that management was wedded to business as usual. This situation was particularly disturbing to us because we recognized that providing these employees with critical thinking skills left them worse off than if they had never received them. They now faced the frustration of understanding how to work more effectively, while barred by a flawed performance system from doing just that.

Engineering a performance system that supports the use of crucial thinking skills is not as challenging as putting a man on the moon or locating an honest politician. It does, however, require some attention to the role that the five elements of the performance system play in reinforcing these skills. The following questions and answers can serve as guides.

Response—Do we know what we want employees to do on the job with the new critical thinking skills? How do we expect them to behave differently?

Situation—Have we explained what response we're expecting? Have we described how we'll know or measure if they're using the skills successfully? Do they know when to use them? Have we provided adequate time and resources to use these new concepts?

Performer—Are we providing the skills to people whose job is suited to those skills and their use? Are we providing critical thinking skills to people whose job requires critical thinking?

Consequences—Do employees perceive that something good will happen when they use these concepts? Conversely, do they perceive a risk or threat in attempting to behave in a new and different way when making decisions and solving problems?

Feedback—Do we communicate to employees our perception of their performance in applying these critical thinking skills? Is the feedback specific, timely, and balanced between good and bad observations? Have we described the benefit to the organization derived from the employees' efforts in this area?

The best organizations have found that they must have good answers to these questions or their efforts to build proficiency in critical thinking will stagnate.

Hewlett-Packard's Analytical Instruments Division in Newark, Delaware, builds extremely sophisticated scientific equipment, including mass spectrometers and gas chromatographs. As with any Hewlett-Packard business, employee commitment to defect-free products is total. For that reason executives in the division expected their highly educated workforce to be experts in problem prevention, problem solving, and decision making.

One week before the classroom experience designed to enhance these skills was to begin, Hewlett-Packard's leadership assembled each class group for a two-hour meeting. The meeting, led by a member of the plant leadership group, was held specifically to ensure that answers were provided to the questions we just mentioned. The groups could ask questions, raise concerns, and participate in modifications to make the classroom exercise more appropriate to their work. Not content to rely on a single two-hour orientation meeting, Hewlett-Packard assembled the class groups one month after their classroom training to address again the same set of questions. This meeting led to further refinements of the learning experience, as well as to modifications of some Hewlett-Packard work practices in an effort to gain even more leverage from the new skills.

Hewlett-Packard is not the only excellent business that recognizes the importance of aligning the social systems of the organization with the effort to build problem-solving and decision-making proficiency. BHP Steel, Sony, and Reuters Holdings Plc. are among a long list of businesses that place a premium on providing answers to the Performance System questions as part of their critical thinking deployment efforts. These companies are not building work environments with "exits." They are building workplaces where no exit is necessary.

Lesson Five—Evolution or Revolution: Attainment of Critical Mass

In 1996 residents of the northeastern United States added another four-letter word to their vocabulary of curses—SNOW. One of us lives in Harrisburg, Pennsylvania, and as he labored with a snow shovel, he noted that the most likely result of his effort to clear his driveway would be a coronary. He was prepared to abandon the effort in favor of a glass of Scotch next to a roaring fire when four neighbors arrived, shovels in hand, to help with the work. An hour later the driveway had been cleared, and brimming with satisfaction, he could nearly taste that glass of Scotch. Then it dawned on him that there were four more driveways to be shoveled, and by the time that job was done he arrived home too exhausted to drink anything. He learned two important lessons from that experience. First, hiring a snowplow for $25 is an excellent investment. Second, difficult undertakings, such as clearing three feet of snow from five long driveways, require a certain critical mass to be accomplished—in this case a group of willing and neighborly people.

Becoming proficient in critical thinking is, similarly, a difficult undertaking and, likewise, not one to be undertaken individually. While competence can be acquired person by person, proficiency requires an organizational commitment—a critical mass. Our experience suggests there are two roads to building this critical mass—one revolutionary and the other evolutionary.

The *revolutionary* approach entails the identification of those individuals in the organization whose jobs require critical thinking. That's usually a lot of people, and these employees are then rapidly exposed to problem-solving and decision-making methodologies. This approach has much to recommend it. It is quicker, allowing the organization to take rapid advantage of its proficiency in problem solving and decision making. It has high visibility because of the numbers of people involved. People are able to communicate in problem-solving and decision-making terms quickly, particularly cross-functionally. Business operations can be adapted to these practices more rapidly, since the large numbers of employees involved create a strong momentum for change. The size of the commitment made by the business reflects the importance of the effort. And the direction is clear, since there is less time for course changes, modifications, or equivocating.

There are, of course, disadvantages to being revolutionary. It is expensive to commit so many dollars and human resources to this type of initiative. The change is directive, and as a consequence, ownership rests, at least initially, with the initiative's sponsor rather than throughout the organization. A broad-scope approach to building critical thinking proficiency could dilute other important initiatives. And often businesses find the momentum is difficult to sustain after the initial development is completed. Nonetheless, the revolutionary road to critical thinking skills has been taken recently by Chrysler, Corning, British Airways, Seagate Technology, and others with great success.

The *evolutionary* approach involves more targeting. As in the revolutionary approach, the people whose jobs require critical thinking are identified. These employees are then put into a priority queue, which is typically done by function, job category, or job site rather than on an individual-capability basis. For example, the application engineers of a company may be first to acquire the critical thinking skills, followed by those in manufacturing supervision. Alternatively, Southeast Asian plants may lead, followed by European operations. The targeting of the evolutionary approach allows those individuals and areas that can most benefit from enhanced critical thinking skills to be accessed quickly. The phased nature of the initiative allows for ongoing modification and refinement of the skills for better on-job usage. The costs associated with the initiative are spread over time, making it easier financially. And as the new problem-solving and decision-making abilities are acquired, they are often woven into the fabric of the company culture.

There are drawbacks, however, to the evolutionary approach. It is slower, so payback is less immediate. Frequently one unit cannot effectively support another because one of them has yet to develop these critical thinking processes. Over time, new concerns, programs, and initiatives will arise, and without strong ongoing support the critical thinking initiative can be relegated to the dustbin of management fads. However, as in the revolutionary approach, this approach can be effective. Hewlett-Packard, Sony, Reuters, Honda, and others have found this approach more suitable for their needs than revolutionary efforts, and they have had equivalent success in building organizational proficiency.

But which approach is best? The answer depends on the organization, its objectives, and its culture. Four factors most significantly influence this choice:

1. *Organizational Size*

Smaller	Larger
Revolutionary	Evolutionary

2. *Success in Radical Change Efforts*

Successful	Unsuccessful
Revolutionary	Evolutionary

3. *Driving Current Business Issue Requiring Critical Thinking Proficiency*

Major Issue	No Driving Issue
Revolutionary	Evolutionary

4. *Variability (Product, Market, Geography, Workforce)*

Low Variability	High Variability
Revolutionary	Evolutionary

Beyond these four factors, others undoubtedly must also be taken into account. For that reason, each organization should give careful consideration to how it should proceed. Either way, businesses should remember that sending people out alone with shovels in hand is the hardest and slowest way to get the driveway cleared. They should also note that, whether their approach is revolutionary or evolutionary, new employees will need to be included in the initiative as they enter the organization. After all, the snowplows are never far off, clearing snow from the roads and blocking the driveway again.

Lesson Six—Creating the True Believers

Decades ago American philosopher Eric Hoffer's classic, *The True Believer,* alerted readers to the uneasy relationship between total commitment and fanaticism. In either case, a fervency of belief, coupled with the drive achievable only through a certain single-mindedness, can produce astounding results. These results can be good or evil, ranging from Live Aid to the bombing of Pan Am Flight 107 over Lockerbie, Scotland.

Hoffer's notion that powerful ideas invariably produce a cadre of "true believers" is as valid for business today as it is for broader society. The business "true believers" are not to be found in airports in white robes selling copies of books by Jack Welch. Rather, they are the people who gravitate to new initiatives, volunteer time for their implementation, become expert in their ideas and concepts, and invariably become identified with the program. In the 1980s such people associated with Total Quality initiatives were often disparagingly labeled "Quality Cultists." Whether they are labeled cultists, zealots, true believers, or simply adherents, it is a rare initiative that can be deployed successfully without their enthusiasm and energy.

Assembling the true believers in today's businesses is a bit more difficult than producing banners and buttons and holding a street rally. The prevailing initiative frenzy has engendered a healthy dose of cynicism in the workforce for new initiatives regardless of their apparent merits. There is too much risk and too little reward in being associated with the program du jour or this year's management fad. Further downsizing in many companies has intensified workloads so that even interested workers find the trade-offs required from their current job assignments to be too great to warrant commitment to some new program. More important, people who have committed fully to an initiative, joining a program team as a temporary assignment, have found that when the program winds down, the reentry points have disappeared. With these barriers in place, the option of finding true believers by asking for volunteers is an increasingly ineffective one.

The organizations that are most successful in implementing initiatives in critical thinking take a different tack for most of their important programs. It involves four key steps.

First, opinion leaders are identified, gathered together, and exposed to the new program or idea. When Red Lobster Restaurants sought to use critical thinking skills to help drive a "Guest First" initiative, they identified sixty such people. This was an arduous undertaking given that Red Lobster is one of America's largest employers, with over fifty thousand employees. The Red Lobster group spent several weeks ensuring that the candidates for the program were balanced in geography, tenure, job duties, level, and restaurant profile. These sixty were then interviewed, and a smaller group was assembled. This smaller group, which came to be known as the "Terrific Twenty," included servers, chefs, restaurant managers, and hostesses. They were a true cross section of the employees of this seven-hundred-facility restaurant chain, and they were all very talented. Red Lobster then made the considerable investment of flying them to Orlando, Florida, for three weeks. During that time they were exposed to a set of critical thinking skills and an array of data about guest satisfaction. Using the skills and the data, they returned to their jobs and were able to produce a voluminous menu of valuable ideas, enabling the company to make its "Guest First" initiative a reality.

Second, during the introductory experience, the opinion leaders who show particular skill and enthusiasm for the initiative are identified. These people are engaged individually to determine their underlying interest in the concepts they are being taught and their importance in the organization. At the Kennedy Space Center, director Jay Honeycutt and Lockheed Martin vice president Daniel Patterson made it clear that they would release their most talented people to the task of making the Kennedy Space Center the premier governmental facility in its proficiency in problem solving, decision making, and project management.

Third, this select group of supporters of the initiative are provided with the opportunity to become experts. They are given in-depth training, on-job coaching, practicums, and consulting and facilitation experience. Superior companies like Procter & Gamble will commit a number of weeks to this effort. The people emerge with a foundation in critical thinking skills that becomes a knowledge asset for the business.

Fourth and finally, the organization provides these experts with the chance to strut their stuff. Chrysler has experts in the organization to lead Root Cause Analysis teams tackling thorny production problems. British Airways has created an ongoing internal newsletter, alerting management and staff to the names and workplaces of its internal experts. Siemens has developed an entire entity—PD-41—to which the organization can turn when expertise is required. Common among all of these great companies is the mechanism they provide to channel newly developed consulting talent in problem solving and decision making to the organization's key issues.

The best businesses we have encountered realize that proficiency in critical thinking skills requires internal expertise in lieu of a stream of outside consultants. They have mastered an important business equation:

RELEVANT IDEA + INTERNAL SUPPORTERS +
EXPERTISE DEVELOPMENT +
OPPORTUNITY TO CONTRIBUTE =
THE TRUE BELIEVERS

Lesson Seven—Analytical Ambiance: Creating Venues for Solid Thinking

Return trips from France to the United States invariably lead to discussions about wine. After one such trip, the argument about the relative merits of French and American wines surfaced among our international colleagues for what seemed to be the fiftieth time. We decided that the only way to settle the argument once and for all was to host a comparative tasting. The date was set, and an acquaintance with more money and sophistication than either of us offered his lovely Princeton, New Jersey, home as the venue. We selected our wine carefully, choosing a 1970 Château Latour, a 1970 Château Lascombes, a 1970 Robert Mondavi Reserve, and a 1970 Heitz Martha's Vineyard. At this point the assembled wine had a value slightly higher than the car in which we transported it (although the car had more sediment). At the last minute we also added a rare 1953 Château Latour and a $2.95 Bulgarian red to round out the lot.

The tasting was a lovely affair that, like many tastings, proved only that once enough wine has been tasted, people quickly cease to care who produced it. Still, we had not resolved the question of the moment, so our friend and colleague Peter Tobia volunteered to demonstrate how a cultured palate such as his could discern a great French grape from one that was merely an American pretender. He was blindfolded, six glasses of wine were placed before him, and he began to sip from each. He then removed the blindfold and in a stentorian voice announced that while he could not identify each wine, it was obvious which was the celebrated, old Latour. He picked up and held aloft the glass of Bulgarian red. The august group of wine tasters promptly fell into paroxysms of laughter. Tobia was in wine disgrace, but, ever nimble, he quickly turned to our gracious host and hostess and declared, "When consumed in a setting as elegant as your home, any wine is easy to mistake for a Latour." Check and mate!

Peter's comment was a good reminder to all that the venue is often more important to the outcome than what transpires within. This is certainly true in business, where millions are spent annually to select just the right location for that important meeting. Why golf course venues produce better business meetings remains a worthy question, but there is little argument that people perform better in certain work environments than in others. Critical thinking skills such as problem solving and decision making permeate the entire corporate workplace. Because decisions are made and problems are solved daily in virtually every nook and cranny of the business, this may suggest that deployment of these skills, if not environmentally neutral, is not affected in a significant way by venue. Our experience suggests just the opposite. The best businesses create the venue for critical thinking.

It has been estimated that each day the average person will make over one hundred decisions. These can range from a business decision such as selecting the best candidate for the vacant controller position to a more important decision such as whether to order sweetened or unsweetened iced tea with barbecue for lunch. (The correct decision is, of course, sweetened iced tea.) The sheer number of analytic events—problems to resolve, decisions to make, situations to assess, priorities to set—can create a crisis in real time. By this we mean that real-time issues are so overwhelming in number that broader, overarching analytic issues can be tabled in perpetuity. The old poster motto—"When you're up to your rear end in alligators, it's hard to remember to drain the swamp"—is a euphemistic tribute to this phenomenon. However, organizations that strive to build proficiency in critical thinking skills are not satisfied with the their superb response to real-time issues using critical thinking skills. They require that these skills be applied to broader business concerns as well.

In order to provide an escape from the alligators, proficient businesses create issues forums so that the important issues benefit from the use of analytic processes. Perhaps the best-known business forum of this type is General Electric's legendary workout process. A team, using solid analytic processes and removed from the minute-by-minute distractions of workday decision making, can produce breakthrough solutions to seemingly intractable business problems and structure the actions required to ensure that the solution is implemented. General Electric is not, however, the only business that creates such a venue for the application of analytic problem-solving and decision-making tools. Nearly all of the proficient organizations we studied have some type of venue or structure that they use for this purpose.

One such structure that we found particularly interesting was the Johnson & Johnson's FrameworkS, a process by which groups of twenty company managers are assembled for a concentrated period off-site. They are deputized to act as members of the Executive Committee, and in fact, some members of the Executive Committee usually participate. These multinational, multidisciplinary groups raise issues, debate them fiercely, and emerge with ideas that continue to energize Johnson & Johnson.

Ralph Larsen, Johnson & Johnson chairman and the driving force behind FrameworkS, noted that "FrameworkS turned out to be a whole lot more important that I ever thought it would be. At first, we thought of it as a relatively narrow process way of looking at an issue. We didn't understand its power, which has been accelerating ever since it began." What Johnson & Johnson has done is to create a high-energy venue to consider what Larsen calls "the profound strategic issues that will determine the future of this company." Whether the venue is labeled a "workout process" or a FrameworkS session, great companies recognize that the big issues require a venue within which critical thinking can comfortably take place. It is out of such venues that big decisions emerge with a refinement and elegance worthy of a 1953 Château Latour.

"That's All We Have to Do?"

When considered one by one, the seven lessons just outlined do not seem especially earthshaking. In their totality, however, they require an effort of Herculean proportions. Businesses must change social and technical systems, find a committed leader and true believers, transfer skills to large numbers of people over varying time frames with varying learning approaches, and develop new discussion venues. On reviewing these requirements, one colleague offered that if that's all businesses have to do, then while these efforts are under way perhaps they should bring about world peace, cure cancer, and end global hunger. Our reply was that unlike ensuring world peace and curing cancer, the building of organizational proficiency in critical thinking was something more than a hope and a dream. These seven lessons define how companies like Johnson & Johnson, Hewlett-Packard, Corning, Honda, Chrysler, British Airways, Siemens, Sony, and BHP Steel have actually climbed to that last rung on the Learning Ladder.

To be sure, there are other ingredients in the successful implementation of analytical problem-solving and decision-making skills in organizations. They include all the things required for management of any major change initiative. Perseverance is essential. The businesses we have observed up close have worked for years to reach the level of proficiency they now enjoy. Hewlett-Packard, for example, has had critical thinking as a priority since the early 1960s. Because such efforts take time, it is important to recognize and, in the words of Tom Peters, "celebrate" successes along the way. Both Corning and British Airways are particularly skilled at gathering and giving prominence to examples of how these critical thinking skills have saved a major project or recovered a million pounds in costs.

Melding the critical thinking initiative into other important programs is essential to avoid leaving the organization with the notion that the enterprise is being run like a cafeteria. ("Well, George, are you going to work on making sure our products have total quality or are you going to improve how you make decisions?" "I think I'm going to allocate April for quality and then see what time I have in May.") In businesses like Sony and Harley-Davidson, the critical thinking initiative and the Total Quality initiative are virtually indistinguishable.

Finally, proficient companies recognize that "P" stands for proficiency, not perfection. Even as celebrated as these businesses are, they continue to have their share of unsolved problems and regrettable decisions. But unlike their lesser competitors, they invest time in problem-solving and decision-making autopsies. Why did we make this poor decision? How did our problem-solving approach lead us to the incorrect cause? They then begin the process of fine-tuning their critical thinking approaches. Some Johnson & Johnson companies introduce tales of their failures into the learning experience so all employees can benefit from them. Corning has begun to reemphasize critical thinking skills when a business unit is struggling. In the case of all the companies we have studied, they have achieved prominence in critical thinking, at least in some measure, because they treated the effort as dynamic, requiring strong, ongoing change-management initiatives.

Beyond Proficiency

The companies that we have studied, while well deserving of their prestigious rank among world businesses, are also the organizations least likely to rest on that prestige. Hewlett-Packard vice president George Cobbe attributes his company's legendary lack of complacency to "a kind of controlled terror. We arrive at work each morning in dread fear that someone has moved ahead of us." Companies like Hewlett-Packard are unlikely to rest comfortably when others may be preparing to go beyond proficiency. This, of course, raises an intriguing question: Is there a next level of success in critical thinking? We believe there is.

As we examined the companies that seemed to have a particular strength in problem solving and decision making, we were struck by the fact that they were often organized with a different architecture from that of their competitors. Hewlett-Packard, for example, was organized into relatively small, highly autonomous divisions. This approach was based largely on founders William Hewlett and David Packard's desire to preserve an entrepreneurial spirit by ensuring that business units remained relatively small, self-contained enterprises. We noted that Alistair Cumming, British Airways' deputy director of engineering—and currently chief operating officer—and John Perkins, chief engineer, ran engineering literally as a separate business. Our conversations with Johnson & Johnson chairman Ralph Larsen invariably brought us to a consideration of Johnson & Johnson's 150-plus company structure. These and many other examples suggested to us that the processes of problem solving and decision making may have a lot to say about how an enterprise is organized.

There is little argument with the notion that the seminal organizational structures of the past were directly related to how decisions were made and communicated. In the Western world Roman armies and the Roman Catholic Church were organized so that decision making rested at the top and effectively flowed to the bottom. Since those halcyon days, more modern structural considerations have shaped business architecture, such as business process flows, distribution channels, quality parameters, or customer service requirements. We have, in recent times, encountered matrices, functional silos, cells, and clusters. While these and other structural devices may not have measurably advanced the enterprise, they have produced wonderfully complicated organization charts that bring to mind a Jackson Pollock painting. By contrast, the companies we examined seemed a great deal more resistant to structural fads or the frequent practice of restructuring the business, known colloquially as rearranging the deck chairs on the *Titanic*. Among these companies there seemed to be a recognition that decision making and problem solving remain among the primary factors shaping organizational structure.

That is why the structure these organizations prefer appears most often to be a loosely held collection of smaller businesses. The smaller businesses, they believe, offer several decision-making and problem-solving advantages. First, they allow decisions to be made and problems to be solved by people closer to the product and the customer. Second, they shield risk. As Larsen noted, "To make the point, I will exaggerate, but you know it would be hard to inflict lasting damage on Johnson & Johnson even if you wanted to because of our decentralization. In a highly centralized company, it is possible for either the CEO or a small group of executives to make one or a series of profound decisions that will affect the corporation for the next twenty years. It's terrific if they are right, and it's catastrophic if they are wrong."

Finally, the smaller business-unit structure produces greater accountability for decisions, since its effects are felt directly at the source of the decision. There are many other benefits and certain drawbacks to this type of structure, but what is apparent is the structure's clear correlation to organizational decision making. In the future, businesses that have achieved proficiency in critical thinking will be typified by emerging, innovative structures. Some have characterized these structures as the frameworks for the new knowledge-creating company. We believe they will be more closely aligned to how that knowledge is deployed by the organization in the decisions it makes and the problems it solves.

Gray Matters

It is no longer necessary to make the case for the better use of the intellectual asset of the business—its employees. There is an emerging consensus that in the world of business, knowledge is the currency of the future. People are no longer simply mouthing the words. Gray matter does matter.

The thinking that occurs in today's organization is creative, strategic, linear, out of the box, innovative, tactical, intuitive, logical, noble, and elementary. Translating thought into action is, therefore, a substantial challenge, if only because it comes in so many forms. We believe that critical thinking is the translation vehicle. Businesses that are proficient in assessing complex situations, solving problems, making decisions, avoiding potential problems, and seizing potential opportunities are those that can mold thought into results. It is hard to envision a more powerful platform for competitive advantage. In the world of business, heads always win.

APPENDIX

The Kepner-Tregoe Rational Processes: An Overview

Throughout this book we have stressed that effective managers excel in the art of questioning; they cut through the clutter to bring clarity and order to confusion. They go straight to the heart of the problem and uncover its underlying cause. When they take action, they have an uncanny ability to home in on the relevant data and choose the best alternative. And they reach beyond the fixed boundaries of the present to identify the threats and opportunities that lie ahead.

The primal managers of yesterday and today's effective executives share an important trait. They not only ask insightful questions, but they also question the world around them in an organized, systematic way. Their inquiries proceed in a certain sequence, using a certain discipline or logic. They also seem to know, instinctively, how to touch all the bases as they gather information and make judgments on the central problem-solving and decision-making issues confronting them.

How do they do it? And how can effective managers pass on their superlative instincts to their colleagues? Kepner-Tregoe's contribution has been to document carefully the thought patterns of good problem solvers and decision makers, bring them into the open, and convert them into systematic thinking processes that can be shared with others. With these processes in hand, it becomes possible to improve the critical thinking capabilities of managers and workers as they go about their most vital tasks.

There is no single thought pattern that a person can apply universally to all his or her job tasks. In practice, the most effective managers we have observed have used variations of four distinct patterns of thinking to handle the issues that come across their desks:

1. **Situation Appraisal:** Bringing order and clarity to a complex situation, setting priorities, and planning actions to resolve each concern.
2. **Problem Analysis:** Investigating the cause or causes of failure. When something goes wrong, the question is, why? Effective managers tackle this question differently from those who fumble.
3. **Decision Analysis:** Making choices when confronted with different courses of action. Whereas Problem Analysis looks to the past to discover why something has gone wrong, Decision Analysis is concerned with making the choice that best meets the needs or objectives in the present.
4. **Potential Problem and Potential Opportunity Analysis:** Future oriented, this fourth thought pattern involves anticipating trouble or opportunities and planning appropriate action before they become reality.

Since 1958 we have seen dramatic results from improving organizational brainpower through the use of these four rational processes. These results have been achieved across the industrial landscape, in private organizations and government agencies, at every level from the plant floor to the boardroom, and in forty-four countries around the world.

Since every job is now a *thinking* job, proficiency in these four processes is pivotal to the success of any organization. Each process has its own set of questions to guide thinking and organize information and judgment. When organizations master these fundamental process skills, they achieve an advantage over competitors that will never be duplicated or become obsolete.

What is truly remarkable about these thought processes is their universality and durability. As you read these words, chances are that somewhere in the world, from Brazil to Brisbane, from New

York City to Tokyo, from Bangkok to the center of Paris, they are being employed to solve problems, make decisions, and plan for the future.

This book has focused on the radical changes that have already taken place—and many that are still under way—in today's business organizations. We have seen how these changes suggest new ways to apply the four fundamental processes and new ways for organizations to integrate them into their business practices. But the processes themselves remain as valid today as when they were first developed almost forty years ago.

In order to give you an overview of the four fundamental thinking processes, we have created a fictitious company: Smoothco, Inc. Smoothco manufactures a variety of consumer oils—bath oil, baby oil, suntan oil, etc.—that are shipped to retailers throughout the country. In the following pages we will join Smoothco's managers as they use the four thinking processes to deal with a variety of critical issues facing their company.

As we review each process, pay special attention to the questions. And remember, simplicity can be deceptive! Having taught these processes to thousands of managers and workers, we have come to respect their subtlety and richness, especially as one makes the climb from knowledge and understanding to proficient application.

Situation Appraisal

Today is May 31, and Smoothco's general manager is meeting with receiving, production, and shipping team leaders to share information on the company's current status.

Since a new management team has headed up Smoothco, things have been going pretty well. Line efficiencies, product quality, and shipments have, for the most part, maintained their high levels. Production cost targets have been reached. Although there was some early grumbling from a few of the longtime employees about outsiders taking over the company, it quickly died down, and cooperation between employees and management has been good.

Several improvements have been made in operations. About two months ago corrugated pallets for storing inventory replaced the old wooden ones. On May 14 a new method of sealing the dispensing spout to the container on all plastic containers was adopted in order to improve quality. The reject rate suddenly increased, with all of the rejects due to imperfect seals between the spout and the container neck, resulting in leakage under a pressure test. However, since May 23 production has maintained its normal efficiency and is producing units that meet its rigid quality standards. A modified pressure test went into effect on May 24. Production is now looking for a way to salvage the product that was rejected prior to May 23.

During the first week in May, a series of meetings with the team leaders was conducted to explain the reasons for some of the improvements. Management hoped the meetings would forestall any trouble, but there are reports that there is still some muttering among employees. Recent headlines about employee turnover in other local companies have raised concerns. Smoothco depends on a skilled workforce to remain competitive.

Unfortunately there have been some serious complaints in the past week. Dealer and customer complaints on leakage of Baby Oil-8 containers are mounting daily, and the sales manager is furious that bad product has been sent out from the plant and demands appropriate action before Smoothco loses out to Baby Products Company, its main competitor in the baby oil line. One of the largest retailers has been guaranteed a replacement rush order of five hundred cases of BO-8s.

One of the salespeople has passed on to the shipping team leader some complaints that a few dealers have about the new 48-Pak. They are unhappy because it requires that they change their method of handling the BO-8 cases.

With the peak season for suntan oil approaching, Line 1 will be fully scheduled for June, including Saturdays. Line 2 will also be working at full capacity. The schedule will be tight, but if production hits its usual 90 percent on Line 1 and 95 percent on Line 2, there won't be any sales order delay.

On May 29 the production team leader learned that Amos Huxhold, head of quality assurance, has had a recurrence of the back trouble that kept him out of work the week of May 14. He expects to be out another week, but his assistant indicates that he will be able to hold down the fort until Amos returns.

Smoothco is obviously facing a complex situation requiring action. But how should its managers go about getting a clear understanding of the issues? And in what order of priority should they plan their attack?

All of us, Smoothco executives included, need a Situation Appraisal process to:

1. identify concerns or issues that require action,
2. set priorities,
3. determine the next steps needed for resolution,
4. plan the involvement of key people.

1. IDENTIFY CONCERNS.

It's easy enough to recognize concerns that arrive at our desks: a phone call about a late delivery, a memo about decreasing productivity in a particular work unit, the need to replace an employee who has resigned. But it takes a conscious effort to seek out opportunities to improve the effectiveness of the entire organization or of our specific area of responsibility. Identifying concerns involves systematically surveying the work environment for threats and opportunities and then separating and clarifying those that need our attention now and in the future. Here is where having good questioning skills is crucial.

Listing Threats and Opportunities: Key Questions to Ask

- Where are standards not being met, and where are they being exceeded?
- What changes are anticipated that will create threats or opportunities?
- What areas should be improved?
- What decisions need to be made?
- What plans should be implemented?
- What actions do we need to take?

If Smoothco's management team had asked the foregoing questions during their monthly meeting, they might have ended up with a list of concerns similar to this one:

- Muttering among employees
- Possible excessive employee turnover
- Customer and dealer complaints
- Get five hundred *guaranteed* cases to retailer immediately
- Tight schedule for peak season
- Head of QA out for the next week
- Salvage rejected product

As concerns are listed, we may know exactly what we mean by each concern. But often the lists we generate include broad or general concerns ("complaints," "muttering") or indicate an area of concern about which we don't have many facts. We can make little progress toward resolving these issues until we know specifically what is meant by the concern.

To help separate a general concern into its components, we ask a set of questions designed to clarify the situation by focusing on specific, hard data.

Separating and Clarifying Concerns: Key Questions to Ask

- What do you mean by . . . ?
- What evidence do you have?
- What exactly is . . . ?
- How can this concern be broken apart?
- What are the actions we must take to address this concern?
- What else concerns you about . . . ?

These questions would have helped the Smoothco managers move from discussion to action. One of their concerns was "muttering among employees." By asking, "What exactly are they muttering about?" they might have learned that the muttering was only about the container sealing change, not other improvements. Then, by asking, "What exactly is bothering them about the change?" they might have learned that the workers were uncomfortable because they were not completely familiar with the new equipment. It would then have been a simple matter to schedule a few training sessions, which would answer the employees' questions and, as a result, stop the "muttering."

As you can see, through the use of systematic questioning, Smoothco's general concerns, which would have been impossible to resolve in one step, could have been broken down into manageable issues and resolved one by one.

2. SET PRIORITIES.

To effectively determine which concerns should be handled first, a priority-setting system must be based on the available information about each concern. Such a system should be easy to use and flexible enough to accommodate changes. It should also be based on information about the concerns that can be readily determined and compared. Three areas are highly relevant when we are attempting to set priorities: seriousness, urgency, and growth.

Considering Seriousness, Urgency, and Growth: Key Questions to Ask

Seriousness:

- What is the current impact on people, safety, money, production, reputation, and so on?
- What tells me this concern is important?
- Which concern is most serious?

Urgency:

- When would resolution become difficult, expensive, or impossible?
- When should resolution begin? end?
- Which concern is most urgent?

Growth:

- What evidence is there that the seriousness will change?
- Which concern will become most serious?

The answers to these questions provide specific information that can be used to judge the relative priority of the concerns. First, the seriousness of each concern is assessed. The most serious concern, based on the data, is used as the benchmark for asessing the rest of the list. High, medium, and low indicators can be used. Once the assessment for seriousness is complete, the same can be done for urgency and growth. Scanning the scores in all three categories will indicate the highest-priority concerns.

An example of priority setting, using some of Smoothco's concerns, illustrates how this technique works.

Identify Concerns		Set Priority		
List Threats and Opportunities	Separate and Clarify	Seriousness	Urgency	Growth
Muttering among employees	"Outsiders taking over"	Limited to a few longtime employees (L)	No action being threatened (L)	Seems to have died down (L)
	Recent improvements • Container sealing change	Employees unhappy but are able to operate new equipment (L)	Training should be done soon (M)	Not spreading to other workers (L)
Customer and dealer complaints	Customers • Leaking BO-8s	Customer satisfaction is our # 1 priority (H)	Need to give customers good product right away (H)	Complaints mounting daily (H)
	Dealers • Leaking BO-8s	Dealers are our link to customers (H)	Dealers "screaming" for replacements (H)	Complaints mounting daily (H)
	• 48-Pak handling complaints	Not hurting sales (L)	Can be addressed during next sales call (M)	No new complaints (L)
Get 500 replacement cases out		One of our largest retailers is involved (H)	Rush order promised (H)	If we don't make good on our promise, our relationship with dealer will deteriorate more (H)

The assessments indicate highest priority for the concern about getting promised replacements of BO-8 to the retailer. That won't solve the problem of the leaking BO-8s, which is also of the utmost concern, but it will buy Smoothco some time.

Because priority setting assesses three separate factors, it is easy to adjust priorities as situations change. Ascertaining the seriousness, urgency, and growth of a new concern, then judging it against the existing list, will make it easy to determine its relative importance.

3. DETERMINE THE NEXT STEPS.

Different concerns require different analytical approaches. Each approach has its own intent: to gather facts to understand what has happened and why; to define our needs and values in order to choose what should happen in the future; and to plan ahead to ensure that what we want to happen will actually happen. Also, some things already may be understood about the situation. A partial analysis may be sufficient to guide effective action.

Determining Analysis Needed: Key Questions to Ask

- Is there a deviation between what is actually happening and what should be happening?
- Is the cause of this deviation unknown?
- Must cause be determined in order to take action?

If the answer to each of the above questions is "yes," the concern should be located in **Problem Analysis,** which is the thought process used to search for the cause of deviations.

If the answer to one or more of these above questions is "no," continue with the following questions:

- Does a choice from among alternatives need to be made?
- Is there a single alternative to be evaluated?

If one of these questions can be answered positively, then the concern calls for **Decision Analysis,** the thought process used to evaluate choices. If not, continue asking:

- Is there an action to be taken?
- Is there a plan to implement?
- Is there a need to monitor an existing plan?

Positive answers to any of these questions indicate the need for **Potential Problem and Potential Opportunity Analysis.**

An inability to answer these questions with confidence indicates a need to return to Situation Appraisal to separate and further clarify the concern.

Let's return once again to Smoothco and see how the table opposite illustrates the result of using the pertinent questions to determine which process is appropriate.

4. Plan the involvement of key people.

The final step in Situation Appraisal is the assignment of concerns for analysis. Help is usually needed to gather necessary information and to ensure successful resolution. Answering these additional questions will ensure that we are prepared to resolve the concerns effectively.

Determining Help Needed: Key Questions to Ask

- Who should be involved to provide information, to contribute to the analysis, or to take responsibility for conclusions reached?
- Who should be involved in order to ensure commitment to the action determined?
- Who should be included as part of their own training?
- What help will they provide? When?
- How will the information be collected, documented, and presented?

We can use Situation Appraisal to plan our workday or workweek, to set direction in departmental or cross-functional meetings, to manage a rapidly changing environment, or to appraise a major change in systems or procedures.

Situation Appraisal is the only one of the four thinking processes that does not resolve a specific concern. Rather, it provides tools and techniques to help us clarify and assess the concerns we face. Once this is done, we can move on to resolving those concerns using one or more of the remaining three critical

Identify Concerns		Set Priority			
List Threats and Opportunities	Separate and Clarify	Seriousness	Urgency	Growth	Process Needed
Muttering among employees	"Outsiders taking over"	Limited to a few longtime employees (L)	No action being threatened (L)	Seems to have died down (L)	Situation Appraisal . . . Understand more about uneasiness with outsiders
	Recent improvements • Container sealing change	Employees unhappy but are able to operate new equipment (L)	Training should be done soon (M)	Not spreading to other workers (L)	Decision Analysis . . . Choose training method
Customer and dealer complaints	Customers • Leaking BO-8s	Customer satisfaction is our #1 priority (H)	Need to give customers good product right away (H)	Complaints mounting daily (H)	Problem Analysis . . . Find cause of leaks
	Dealers • Leaking BO-8s	Dealers are our link to customers (H)	Dealers "screaming" for replacements (H)	Complaints mounting daily (H)	Problem Analysis . . . Find cause of leaks
	• 48-Pak handling complaints	A few dealers, not hurting sales (L)	Can be addressed during next sales call (M)	No new complaints (L)	Decision Analysis . . . Select response to dealers
Get 500 replacement cases out		One of our largest retailers is involved (H)	Rush order promised (H)	If we don't make good on our promise, our relationship with dealer will deteriorate more (H)	Decision Analysis . . . Select way to make delivery Potential Problem Analysis . . . Protect shipment

thinking processes: Problem Analysis, Decision Analysis, and Potential Problem and Potential Opportunity Analysis.

Problem Analysis

Problem Analysis techniques are used when

- the performance of the system, individual, or machine is below, exceeds, or has never reached an expected standard—that is, the actual deviates from the should;
- the cause of that deviation is unknown; and
- the cause needs to be known so that corrective action can be taken.

The case of the leaking BO-8s at Smoothco is an excellent example of a deviation where it was of paramount importance to find cause and take corrective action. Here are some additional facts about the problem, which were in the possession of the Smoothco team as they set about solving the problem.

> In mid-April Smoothco introduced throughout the country a new 48-Pak display case for BO-8 containers in response to dealer requests for a lighter, smaller, more attractive shipping case with built-in display features. This replaced the old 96-Pak. The changeover to the 48-Pak had been scheduled for September. However, marketing and sales felt that introduction of the new BO-8 48-Pak display case at the beginning of the peak sales period would help build sales and extend the peak period. The sudden decision to introduce the new display case in mid-April did not permit full testing of the case, method of handling and shipping, and so on.
>
> Shortly after the introduction of the BO-8 48-Pak case, the shipping loaders found that if all cases in one-product full-truck loads were side stacked on pallets, they could load an additional seventy-six cases per truck. This resulted in an average saving to the customer of seven cents per case and in neater, tighter loads. The side-stacking suggestion appeared feasible and was promptly adopted.
>
> During the third week in May, dealers and their customers in Dis-

Smoothco Sales Districts

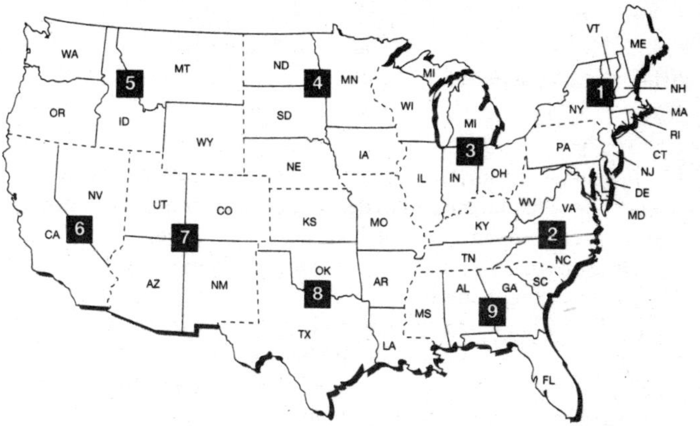

tricts 1, 3, and 8 began complaining that BO-8 containers were leaking from a small crack at the neck. The problem grew to the point where, by the end of May, thirty-two thousand containers were being returned as damaged. Sales immediately began replacing containers while the Smoothco management team attempted to find the cause of the problem.

The product is palletized, either bottom down or side stacked at the end of each line. Pallets are forklifted to the warehouse as filled. Pallets of product are loaded directly into trucks. Materials management provides shipping with a daily order set for each day's shipments. Appropriate carriers are scheduled as required.

A clerk handles the bookwork required for storing and shipping product. Shipping works closely with division materials management, which provides shipping instructions to distribution points and handles the coordination among production, sales, and inventory.

Working daily with division materials management, shipping maintains a three- to five-day inventory of finished product. Because of the frequency of large orders, this inventory buffer stock is constantly rotated and first-in-first-out followed. Loading is directly from production whenever possible to maintain handling costs. The average peak period inventory (five days) and low period inventory (three days) for each product is as follows:

	Average Daily—Peak		Average Daily—Other	
	Month	*Inventory Cases*	*Month*	*Inventory Cases*
ST-16	M,J,J,A	1,500	S through A	900
ST-4	M,J,J,A	2,900	S through A	1,700
HH-4	O,N,D,J,F,M	1,200	A through S	700
BO-8	A,M,J	1,500	J through M	900

In general, the inventory policy has been to maintain this inventory in line with meeting sales demands. This is critical to all items because of seasonality and product and price changes.

Division materials management provides shipping with a daily order set for shipments to a central distribution point in each sales district. Distribution to customers is handled by sales except in District 6, where direct sales orders are filled and shipped only in partial truck-load (PTL) quantities. The percent of sales by product for each product for the last three months has been as follows:

Sales District	*ST-16*	*ST-4*	*HH-4*	*BO-8*
1	18	12	18	18
2	6	9	8	6
3	19	11	19	19
4	5	4	10	2
5	7	5	5	7
6	19	23	19	17
7	6	5	2	7
8	10	10	11	18
9	10	21	8	6
	100 %	100 %	100 %	100 %

During its peak period, a product is shipped to those districts with over 15 percent of total sales in straight, one-product truckloads to take advantage of handling savings, except in District 6 as stated previously. During a peak period, districts with less than 15 percent of total sales and all districts during the rest of the year are shipped by mixed-product full truckloads or in partial truck-load (PTL) quantities. Shipping charges are normally paid by the dealer.

The central distribution point in all sales districts typically receives a shipment every three days. During peak periods, shipping time to the East Coast is eight days; about six to areas east of the Mississippi; and one to five days to the rest of the country. During nonpeak periods, shipping time runs one to ten days, depending on type of load and distance.

The receiving team leader, in response to an order from division materials management, began to diversify suppliers on all products, as of May 1.

It began with new suppliers on plastic containers for ST and BO-8 products. Bids were obtained from the Thin Plastic, No Seam, and XYZ Companies, on a one- and one-half-day order size per product, as requested by marketing. As XYZ could supply immediately, he used their stock for both ST and BO-8 products through midshift on May 25. Since then they have been alternating between XYZ and Thin Plastic. Teams say the No Seam Company loads are better loaded and the cases holding the containers are roughened, making for better palletizing and movement. Since receiving ran out of its supply of No Seam containers on May 23, No Seam is rush shipping additional containers for use during June.

The sales manager is frantic. The complaints on BO-8 have just been compiled. To date: District 1—200; District 3—300; District 8—150. The complaints are from both dealers and their customers. About 800–1,000 cases will need to be replaced, although the loss of goodwill is always difficult to make up by replacement. The salespeople in the other districts report no complaints.

In every instance the complaint is the same: The container leaks around the neck. The complaints appear random. Three cases of product returned to dealers by customers in the New York area were gathered up and are being returned to division quality assurance by AAA Transfer. This may give the problem solvers more information. So far there have been no complaints on ST or HH-4 products.

The receiving team leader wants to go back to the old, reliable supplier of plastic. Shipping has one hundred of the old 96-Paks in storage and wants to use them while waiting for more. Production insists it can solve the problem by raising the heat when sealing the containers. The sales manager wants to do all of the above—and whatever else Smoothco can think of—to get good product out of the plant right away.

If you were Smoothco's general manager, which of these proposed actions would you take? If you answered "None," then you are well ahead of most people in your understanding of the use of the critical thinking process. Taking action without knowing the cause of a deviation is the quickest way to compound the problem and waste both valuable time and money. Instead, how about stopping to ask a few critical questions?

Problem Analysis includes the following steps:

1. Describe the problem.
2. Identify possible causes.
3. Evaluate possible causes.
4. Confirm true cause.

At each step, asking specific questions will ensure that we get the pertinent facts—and only those that are pertinent—to help us find true cause.

1. Describe the problem.

In order to obtain a useful description of the problem, we need to ask questions about its nature, location, timing, and extent.

Describing the Problem: Key Questions to Ask

- How can you state, as specifically as possible, the deviation between what should be happening and what is happening?
- What exactly is wrong? What could be wrong but isn't?
- Where is the problem occurring? Where is it not occurring?
- When have you had the problem? When has it been absent?
- How large or widespread is the problem? How large could it be?

In the Smoothco case, a clear, specific statement of the deviation would have been "BO-8s leaking." You might want to get even more specific in your statement, adding "in the field, or at dealers and customers," to make sure there is no confusion between this problem and the one that was experienced earlier in the plant. Asking these five questions would have resulted in a description of the problem similar to the one that follows.

Describe Problem

State problem (object/defect) BO-8s leaking (in the field)

Specify problem

	Is	Is Not
WHAT	BO-8 containers	ST or HH-4 containers
	Leaking, cracked	Misshaped, mislabeled
WHERE	Around the neck	Cap, body of bottle
	In the field	In plant
	Districts 1, 3, and 8	Districts 2, 4, 5, 6, 7, and 9
	Random within districts	Specific dealers
WHEN	Third week in May	Before
EXTENT	District 1—200 complaints	
	District 2— 300 complaints	More or less
	District 3—150 complaints	
	800–1,000 cases	Fewer; all
	"Small" crack	Large crack
	Increasing trend	Decreasing or staying level

2. IDENTIFY POSSIBLE CAUSES.

Once you have a clear, specific description of the problem, you can actually use it to develop possible causes. How is this done? Once again, the answer lies in systematic questioning.

Logic tells us that whatever caused the problem affected only the Is side of the specification, since it is there that we observe the problem. Therefore, the cause of the problem must be acting on something unique about the Is when compared with the Is

Not. For example, there must be something unique or distinct about BO-8s as compared to ST or HH-4 products; otherwise all would be leaking. In fact, there are several distinctions between the types of oil Smoothco markets, and focusing on these distinctions can help us develop possible causes for the leaking of the BO-8s.

The second factor that can help us identify possible causes is change. After all, if BO-8s have been around for years and they have just begun to leak, then something must have changed and, in doing so, caused the problem. If we can find the *relevant* changes that have occurred, we can develop possible causes around those changes.

Distinctions can help us focus on relevant changes by directing our attention to areas of uniqueness in the Is compared with the Is Not. Changes in, around, or about these distinctions may have caused the problem, since they would have acted only on the Is and not on the Is Not.

Developing Possible Causes: Key Questions to Ask

- What is unique, peculiar, special, or different about the Is data as compared with the corresponding Is Not information? Ask this question for each pair of Is/Is Not facts in the problem specification.
- What change or changes have occurred in, around, or about this distinction? Ask this question for each distinction you have identified.
- How specifically could this change have caused our problem? Ask this question for each change you have identified.

Explain how each cause could create the problem.

If Smoothco's managers had used distinctions and changes to develop possible causes for the leaking BO-8s, they might have come up with the possibilities listed in the table opposite.

3. Evaluate possible causes.

Once we have a list of possible causes, our task is to determine which of them seems most probable and whether or not it is the

Describe Problem

State problem (object/defect) BO-8s leaking (in the field)

Specify problem

	Is	Is Not	Distinctions	Changes
WHAT	BO-8 containers	ST or HH-4 containers	Roughened translucent plastic	New suppliers — BO-8 and ST:
				5/1 – 5/10 XYZ; 5/11 – 5/25:
				Thin Plastic and No Seam
	Leaking, cracked	Misshaped, mislabeled	Packaging	Now XYZ and Thin Plastic:
				96 — 48-Pak, ca 4/15
WHERE	Around the neck	Cap, body of bottle	Sealing operation	Higher temp. sealing: 5/14
	In the field	In plant	After shipping	
	Districts 1, 3, and 8	Districts 2, 4, 5, 6, 7, and 9	Shipping method in peak season	Change in shipping method in
				peak period; new loading
	Random within districts	Specific dealers		One-product truckloads, plus
				76 more boxes side stacked
WHEN	Third week in May	Before		
EXTENT	District 1 — 200 complaints			
	District 2 — 300 complaints	More or less		
	District 3 — 150 complaints			
	800 – 1,000 cases	Fewer; all		
	"Small" crack	Large crack		
	Increasing trend	Decreasing or staying level		

true cause. This could be done by following conducting extensive—and expensive—tests. But there is a much faster, easier, and cost-effective way to test possible causes.

Once again, careful questioning is all we need. By asking, in turn, how each cause explains both the Is and Is Not of each dimension of the problem specification, we can test how well the hypotheses fit the facts.

Testing Possible Causes: Key Questions to Ask

- How could this cause explain both the Is and Is Not information? Ask this question for each pair of Is/Is Not facts in the problem specification.
- What assumptions must be made to explain the Is and Is Not if this is the true cause? Ask this question at each line of the problem specification.

In the figure that follows we have listed possible causes for the leaking BO-8s and the conclusions that might have been reached if each had been tested against a careful description of the problem. Notice that it is often necessary to make assumptions when testing possible causes. The number and kinds of assumptions may vary for each cause. The most probable cause is that which most best accounts for the data in the specification, while requiring the fewest and most reasonable assumptions. In this case, the combination of the extra weight and the side stacking appears to be the most probable cause of the leaky BO-8s in the field.

Identify Possible Causes	Evaluate Possible Causes	
Develop possible cause statements	**Does not explain**	**Explains only if**
Material from new supplier is weak	Only around neck Only Districts 1, 3, and 8	
48-Pak doesn't protect containers, neck is damaged	Only around neck Only Districts 1, 3, and 8	
New heat seal since 5/14 not strong enough	Complaints as of third week in May*	
Change of shipping method to side stacking and 76 extra cases creates stress on bottle's neck		Peak period shipping began at least 2 – 3 weeks before complaints (It did: peak on BO-8 begins in April) Leakers are at bottom of stacks

* Leakers caused by heat seal could not reach customers in one week: 8 days shipping to East Coast, 7 days in field warehouse, ? shipping to dealer, ? dealer inventory, ? dealer to customer.

4. CONFIRM TRUE CAUSE.

To this point, the developing and testing of causes have been based on the information in our problem specification. We now need to confirm that what we think is the most probable cause is indeed the true cause. A logical place to begin verification is with the assumptions we made during our testing.

Verifying and Monitoring: Key Questions to Ask

- How can we verify the assumptions we made during our test for most probable cause?
- How can this cause be observed at work?
- How can we demonstrate the cause/effect relationship?
- When corrective action is taken, how will results be checked?

Use the safest, easiest, quickest, cheapest, surest way to verify the true cause.

Testing has shown that the most probable cause of the leaking BO-8s is the combination of the added weight from shipping seventy-six more boxes per load and the side stacking, assuming that the leaking containers are found near the bottom of the loads. How can we verify that assumption? We might ask the people who unload the trucks to check the next load for leakers, and if they find them in the cases near the bottom we can be pretty sure we are correct. Other relatively fast, cheap actions might include conducting some physical tests on the current 48-Pak to see how well it withstands the added pressure when laid on its side. Leaking in this position would lend support to our most probable cause. These types of verification focus on experiments or simulations that confirm the cause or look for new evidence to support the information already known.

The final form of verification is, of course, to take action against what we believe to be the problem's true cause. If the problem is eliminated by our action, we know that a rational process led us to the correct solution. To avoid needless expense, however, corrective action should be taken only after the other verification procedures have confirmed the most probable cause. Corrective action should always be followed by monitoring to ensure that the cause was truly removed. Corrective action should also be the result of a well-thought-out Decision Analysis, which is the next rational process we will summarize for you.

Decision Analysis

People often begin the decision-making process by considering alternatives. But, to use a very simple analogy, this is like getting on a highway without having any idea where you are going. Without a destination you can never be sure you're on the right road; without objectives you'll never know which alternative is the one for you.

Decision Analysis includes the following steps:

1. Clarify purpose.
2. Evaluate alternatives.
3. Assess risks.
4. Make decision.

1. Clarify purpose.

It helps to begin any Decision Analysis with a clear statement of the decision that is to be made: "Choose the location of the new branch office," "Select a new container supplier," "Select a new director of research," and so on. This is particularly important when making group decisions, so everyone involved is aware of the expected outcome of their efforts.

The following situation as outlined requires that the Smoothco Company make a decision. We will use it as an example to help clarify the steps in Decision Analysis.

> After verifying the cause of the leaking BO-8s, Smoothco's management decided that side stacking would not be used on full

truckload shipments to Districts 1, 3, and 8, as an interim action. A meeting was scheduled for June 14 to discuss possible corrective actions.

From the situation described here, what do you think is the fundamental purpose of the decision to be made? If you answered something like "To choose a permanent solution to BO-8 leakers in the field," you have effectively defined the action to be taken and the end result. Once the decision statement has been made, the next step is to set our objectives. We do this by listing, in as much detail as possible, all the things we would like to see happen as a result of the decision. At this point we also need to look at the resources we have available for this decision (money, people, time, facilities, equipment, etc.), along with any laws, policies, or regulations that may restrict the choice.

Not all of the objectives we set will be of equal importance to us. Some will be absolutely necessary, while others will be highly desirable, and still others would just be nice to have—icing on the cake, so to speak. For this reason we divide or classify objectives into MUSTs and WANTs. By identifying those objectives that are mandatory for the success of the decision (the MUSTs) we will be able to eliminate, early on, any alternatives that would prove unworkable.

The remaining objectives (the WANTs) will also vary in importance, and we will need to give some thought to how much weight each one will carry during the decision-making process. We find it convenient to assign a weight of 10 (on a scale of 1–10) to the most important WANT or WANTs and to assign weights to the remaining WANTs based on how important they are relative to these.

Developing and Classifying Objectives: Key Questions to Ask

- What specific goals should be met?
- What needs must be satisfied?
- What limitations are we operating under?
- What do we want to achieve in the short term? over time?

- Which of these objectives are absolutely critical to the success of the decision?
- Are the MUST objectives measurable, so that we will recognize when an alternative meets them and when it does not? Are these standards realistic?
- To which of the WANTs should we assign a weight of "10"?
- Relative to those with a weight of "10," what weights should we assign to our other WANTs?

A key objective in the Smoothco decision relates to money. No capital expenditures can be made. But it would also be highly desirable to keep any further operating costs to a minimum. This can be stated as an additional objective. It is often appropriate to do this when a resource objective specifies a limit in terms of money, time, or effort. The added objective will express the need to maximize or minimize the use of this resource.

Opposite is a sample list of objectives, divided into MUSTs and WANTs and with weights assigned to the WANTs. The managers of Smoothco would probably have been able to come up with many more, and their objectives would reflect their values, but this is what a quick review by an outsider might look like.

2. Evaluate alternatives.

At this point we are ready to look at the alternatives from which we will make our choice. In some situations we are presented with alternatives, while in others we are responsible for generating them ourselves. In either case we should search out all possible alternatives within the range defined by the decision statement. Generating alternatives is a creative step. We should, therefore, use any method or technique that releases our creativity and that of others who can assist us. The purpose of Decision Analysis is to find and select the best alternative, and any method that leads us to that end should be welcomed.

In the Smoothco case, those responsible for the decision identified five alternatives: continue using the current 48-Pak without side stacking; return to the old 96-Pak, no side stacking; use a re-

Clarify Purpose

State the Decision Choose permanent solution to B0-8 leakers in the field

Classify Objectives into MUSTs and WANTs

MUSTs

- Retain display feature
- Eliminate leakers
- Require no capital expenditure

WANTs	**Weight**
Minimize additional operating costs	10
Support employees' suggestion plan	6
Maximize good dealer and customer relations	9
Maintain good employee relations	4

inforced 48-Pak with side stacking; increase the heat and get a better seal; buy new equipment and get a better seal.

Once alternatives are established, we can begin the process of assessing them against the objectives, based on the best available information about each alternative. This information may include known facts, our best projections, or the opinions of experts. The objectives serve as our guide for data gathering. For each objective we must have complete information about all of the alternatives so that we can make a reasoned judgment.

Evaluating Alternatives: Key Questions to Ask

- Is the information we have about our alternatives as specific, complete, and up-to-date as possible? If not, how can we improve the information?
- Does each alternative meet our MUST objectives? If there are any that do not, there is no point in considering them further.
- Based on the information we have about each alternative, how well does it meet each of our WANT objectives?

We record our judgment about the alternatives using a numbering system to make the assessment visible. For simplicity, we use a 10–0 scale. For each objective, in turn, we compare the information on the alternatives to determine which one best meets that objective. This alternative receives a score of 10. The other alternatives are scored relative to the alternative that scored 10, based on our judgment of the information.

Once the scoring of the alternatives is complete, we can calculate the weighted score, a multiplication of the weight and score. The numbers help make visible our judgment of two dimensions: how important each objective is for the overall decision and which alternative best satisfies each objective. When the weighted scores are totaled, we have a clear comparison of the performance of the alternatives.

On page 267 is a sample Decision Analysis worksheet on which are recorded the available data about the five alternatives under consideration by the Smoothco Company. As you can see, all five alternatives meet the first two MUST objectives. But the 96-Pak has no display feature, and the purchase of new equipment to get a better seal does not satisfy the third MUST: no capital expenditure. These two choices can, therefore, be eliminated at this point, reducing the number of viable alternatives to three.

The remaining three alternatives have been given weighted scores, and the highest has gone to the reinforced 48-Pak.

Clarify Purpose

State the Decision Choose permanent solution to B0-8 leakers in the field

Classify Objectives into MUSTs and WANTs

Evaluate Alternatives

A: Continue using 48-Pak, no side stacking

B: Return to 96-Pak, no side stacking

C: Reinforced 48-Pak, side stacking

D: Increase the heat and get a better seal

E: Buy new equipment to get a better seal

MUSTs	A: Information	A: GO	A: NO GO	B: Information	B: GO	B: NO GO	C: Information	C: GO	C: NO GO	D: Information	D: GO	D: NO GO	E: Information	E: GO	E: NO GO
Retain display feature	yes			no			yes			yes			yes		
Eliminate leakers	yes			yes			yes — per mfr. and tests			yes, per tests			yes, per mfr.		
Require no capital expenditure	none required			none required			none required			none required			10,500 more needed		

WANTs	Weight	A: Information	A: Sc.	A: Wt. Sc.	B: Information	B: Sc.	B: Wt. Sc.	C: Information	C: Sc.	C: Wt. Sc.	D: Information	D: Sc.	D: Wt. Sc.	E: Information	E: Sc.	E: Wt. Sc.
Minimize additional operating costs	10	$48, 668 annual cost	8	80				6,000 conversion and 39,000 annually	10	100	$45,000 annual cost	9	90			
Support employees' suggestion plan	6	Side stacking was an employee suggestion	0	0				Retains side stacking	10	60	Retains side stacking	10	60			
Maximize good dealer and customer relations	9	3,000 cases in stock; no problem getting more, so no conversion time needed	10	90				2 weeks need to convert and get new packs	7	63	Need 1 month for research and testing	5	45			
Maintain good employee relations	4	Employees like side stacking, lighter 48-Pak	10	40				Would be only slightly heavier to handle	9	36	Same as A	10	40			
		Total Weighted Score		210						259			235			

3. Assess risks.

Considering the risks associated with our high-scoring alternatives is the third stage of the decision-making process. By imagining that the alternative we are considering has been selected, we determine what might go wrong in the future. We can draw on our experience or on that of others. The information we accumulated while comparing alternatives against objectives may also provide a source of adverse consequences.

Identifying Adverse Consequences: Key Questions to Ask

- What are the implications of being close to a MUST limit?
- Where might information be invalid?
- What problems could we have if we implemented this alternative? What are the implications?
- How serious would each adverse consequence be if it did occur?
- How likely is it that each of the adverse consequences would occur?
- What actions can we plan to prevent or minimize the effect of each adverse consequence?

One adverse consequence of choosing the reinforced 48-Pak is that the conversion could be delayed by several factors. We should also search through the rest of the data on this alternative to identify other inherent risks. The table opposite gives a sample of some of the risks the Smoothco management team might have identified for the top two alternatives: the reinforced 48-Pak and the increased heat on the seal.

4. Make decision.

The final step in Decision Analysis is to commit to a choice by weighing the benefits against the risks. The careful consideration of each of our alternatives results in the best balanced choice.

It is important to remember that the best balanced choice is

Alternative: Reinforced 48-Pak

Identify adverse consequences	Assess Threat P*	Assess Threat S†
If the reinforced pack is still too weak,	L	H
we may get leakers		
If we have problems converting our	M	H
machines, there may be a delay and		
added cost		
If we can't get new cases fast enough,	M	L
there may be a delay		
If we have problems changing pack,	M	M
dealers will resist future changes		

Alternative: Increased heat on seal

Identify adverse consequences	Assess Threat P*	Assess Threat S†
If the increased heat doesn't make a	L	H
better seal, we may get leakers		
again		
If testing takes more than a month,	M	L
there may be a delay		
If the material has other		
weaknesses, we may get leakers	L	H
again		

*P = Probability
†S= Seriousness

not "the right answer." In decision making there is never one answer that will be correct for everyone. The alternative we choose will depend on our experience, judgment, and values and on the degree of risk with which we are comfortable.

In the case of the Smoothco decision, a person who is not a risk taker by nature might opt for the increased heat on the seal in order to avoid conversion costs and introducing another new pack. Another individual might prefer using a new material supplier to lower annual cost and speed up implementation.

Making the Best Balanced Choice: Key Questions to Ask

- Are we willing to accept the risk(s) to gain the benefit of this choice?
- Can we live with the degree of risk that is inherent in this alternative?

One of the ways in which we can obtain a greater degree of comfort with our best balanced choice is by going beyond Decision Analysis and utilizing Potential Problem and Potential Opportunity Analysis.

Potential Problem and Potential Opportunity Analysis

Once a decision is made, we tend to assume that our job is completed. But the decision must be implemented, and it is unrealistic to assume that everything will go smoothly during the implementation phase. It makes sense to take a little extra time to analyze and improve our implementation plan before putting it into effect. Potential Problem and Potential Opportunity Analysis provides a systematic process to help us improve our planning and give greater assurance of successful implementation.

Potential Problem and Potential Opportunity Analysis can be used in a wide variety of situations: to complete an important task or plan; to monitor a plan in progress; to react to internal or external changes that affect the organization; to improve current operations. The amount of time we devote to Potential Problem and Potential Opportunity Analysis depends on the situation. In many cases, remembering to ask a few key questions is all that's needed. In complex and unfamiliar situations, on the other hand, we often find it necessary to conduct a formal, step-by-step analysis, drawing on the expertise of others in the organization and making the complete plan visible.

For this quick overview, however, we will concentrate on the four major steps in the process:

1. Identifying potential problems or potential opportunities.
2. Identifying likely causes.
3. Taking preventive or promoting actions.
4. Planning contingent or capitalizing actions and setting triggers.

1. IDENTIFYING POTENTIAL PROBLEMS.

As soon as we have a concise statement that describes the action we are planning to take or the decision we are about to implement, we are ready to begin asking questions to elicit information. The clearer and more specific the plan statement is, the easier it will be to develop a useful plan from it.

> It is now June 18, and the Smoothco managers stated their purpose as "Switch to the reinforced 48-Pak." Adding "by July 26" would have provided a clearer definition of the end result.

Now the details need to be completed: the series of actions or activities necessary to reach the goal and the checkpoints needed to monitor the plan's progress. One approach is to list the steps in the plan in chronological order. (For a relatively simple plan, listing the steps is usually sufficient. In more complex situations we may elect to use a planning technique such as work breakdown structures, network diagrams, or Gantt charts to construct a detailed plan. The purpose of using the critical thinking process is then to protect the plan.)

Some of the key steps in the Smoothco Company's plan are listed in the figure on page 273. Assigning the person or persons responsible and having a completion date for each step of the plan are good habits to get into. They ensure that there will be checkpoints at which progress can be monitored, particularly in a case such as Smoothco, where the deadline is critical.

With the basic steps in place, we can now step back and look for areas where problems (or opportunities) might arise. If we can foresee these negative or positive deviations, we can plan actions to either neutralize or take advantage of them, respectively, and, by so doing, improve our plan.

Where do we look for these potential deviations? If we had unlimited time, we could review and analyze each detail. More often, however, we must rely on our experience to concentrate on those steps where potential problems or opportunities are likely to arise.

Problems tend to occur where several people or departments share responsibilities, where deadlines are tight, where there has been little previous experience, where the step cannot be easily observed and monitored, or where there is a complex interface between people and machines. Planning techniques such as network diagrams help identify the time-critical tasks or those areas that must be carefully coordinated.

Once we focus on the areas most critical to success, we need to identify specifically what might go wrong. The more specifically we can define potential problems, the more likely we will be able to identify effective actions to eliminate them or minimize their negative effect (or, in the case of potential opportunities, to maximize the positive).

Listing Potential Problems and Opportunities: Key Questions to Ask

- When we do this, what could go wrong? Ask this question at every critical step of the plan.
- What problems could this action cause?
- What specific opportunities might be found during the implementation of the plan?
- What unintended benefit could this action create?
- What else?

State Action: Switch to the reinforced 48-Pak by July 26.

Develop plan

Conduct employee meetings to explain actions and plans.	Plant Manager	June19
Order 200 48R-Paks for final test	PMT	June19
Test 200 sample cases by shipping to eastern distribution point and on to dealers by normal methods	DC/NO	June 22
Notify dealers about change to 48R-Pak	DM	June 22
Review and revise stacking and shipping procedures	BF	June 25
Check with dealers for any leakage to 200 sample cases	DM/BF	July 5
Place normal order for 48R-Paks to arrive Tuesday, July 10	PMT	July 5
Clean and ship all inventory of 48-Pak at plant and central distribution points	DC	July 21
Adjust production machines to 48R-Pak	NO	July 21 (until done)
Switch-over to production to 48R-Pak	SS	July 22
Start inventory of 48R-Pak production	SS	July 23
Ship 48R-Pak side stacked to appropriate districts and customers	BP	July 26
Sales to make detailed inspection for leakage at central distribution points and at dealers, and report to department manager	DM	on arrival

In the Smoothco plan two steps were considered critical to success: 1) checking with dealers for leakage to two hundred sample cases, and 2) adjusting the machines. Once the process questions were asked, several potential problems were identified at each of these critical junctures in the plan. The managers took one more recommended step. They set priority on each of the potential problems by assessing the probability that each would occur and the seriousness if it did, using a ranking system of "high," "medium," and "low." This type of assessment brings to light those potential problems that could derail the plan completely.

2. Identifying likely causes.

If we have set priorities in the previous step, we may want to limit our search for likely causes to those potential problems that are highly serious and highly probable. In the real world we are nearly always operating under constraints: time, money, personnel, and equipment are generally limited. It is simple common sense to concentrate our limited resources in the areas where they will have the most impact.

As always, when we begin to hypothesize about likely causes, we want to be as specific as possible. In order to take action against a cause, whether it has already brought about a problem or is likely to do so in the future, we must know as much as possible about that cause and the way in which it operates. Remember, there may be more than one likely cause for a problem.

Considering Causes for the Potential Problem (Opportunity): Key Questions to Ask

- What, specifically, would cause the potential problem (opportunity)?
- What other causes might bring about the same potential problem (opportunity)?
- Explain how each cause could create the potential problem (opportunity).

Some of the likely causes identified by the Smoothco team are listed in the figure on page 277. Note that one of them,

State Action: Switch to the reinforced 48-Pak by July 26.

Develop plan	List potential problems	Assess Threat P*	S†
Check with dealers for any leakage to 200 sample cases DM/BF July 13	Dealers don't check boxes	M	M
	Leaking BO-8s are found	L	H
Adjust production machines to 48R-Pak NO July 21	Machines can't be adjusted to take 48R	M	H
	Machines break down	L	H

*P = Probability
†S= Seriousness

"machines badly maintained," is not stated very specifically. If we were to ask why they would be poorly maintained, we might realize that maintenance people haven't had enough training on them. Knowing the cause of the cause, or root cause, as we call it, enables us to plan *specific* actions, which have a far greater chance of working than general, hit-or-miss ones.

3. and 4. TAKING PREVENTIVE (PROMOTING) ACTION AND PLANNING CONTINGENT (CAPITALIZING) ACTION AND SETTING TRIGGERS.

There are two types of action that we plan in Potential Problem and Potential Opportunity Analysis: preventive (promoting) action and contingent (capitalizing) action. Actions that reduce the probability that a problem will occur are preventive in nature; actions that facilitate the occurrence of a desirable deviation are promoting actions. Both preventive and promoting actions are directed at a specific likely cause and are designed either to keep the cause from happening or to encourage it to do so.

On the other hand, contingent (capitalizing) actions are not directed at the causes of potential problems (opportunities). They are designed to deal with the effects of the problem or opportunity once it has occurred, minimizing its negative, or maximizing its positive, impact on our plan.

A simple, easy-to-understand example, which makes clear the distinction between the two kinds of action taken in Potential Problem Analysis, is the way in which we fight fires. Checking electrical cords, keeping combustible materials in tightly closed containers, making sure children don't get their hands on matches—all of these are preventive actions, things we do to keep a fire from ever happening in our home. But we also keep fire extinguishers handy, post the number of the fire department in a conspicuous place, and perhaps even have a sprinkler system installed. These actions are contingent ones, designed to minimize the damage a fire would do to our home and loved ones if it did break out. Finally, triggers are needed to tell us that the potential problem has happened and that a planned contingent action should be taken. A smoke detector could trigger the use of a fire

State Action: Switch to the reinforced 48-Pak by July 26.

Identify Potential Problems	Identify Likely Causes
Dealers don't check boxes	Dealers don't know to check
	Dealers not motivated to check
Leaking BO-8s are found	Reinforced design not strong enough
Machines can't be adjusted to take 48R	Design of 48R doesn't consider machine limits
Machines break down	~~Machines badly maintained~~
	Maintenance people need training

extinguisher. If the fire is large enough, the fire department would be called. Every contingent and capitalizing action requires a trigger to be effective.

Taking Actions to Address Likely Causes: Key Questions to Ask

- What can we do to prevent this likely cause?
- What can we do to reduce the chances of this likely cause from happening?
- How can we keep the cause from creating the potential problem?

If we have identified the likely causes for a potential opportunity, ask:

- What can we do to ensure that this likely cause will happen?
- What can we do to increase the chances of this likely cause happening?
- How can we ensure that this likely cause will create the potential opportunity?

Ask these questions for each likely cause you have identified. Select cost-effective and effective actions.

Preparing Actions to Reduce (Enhance) Likely Effects: Key Question to Ask

- What action(s) can we take to minimize the damage or maximize the benefits if the likely cause, and consequently the problem or opportunity, does occur?

Ask this question for every potential problem (opportunity) that you have identified.

Setting Triggers for Contingent (Capitalizing) Actions: Key Questions to Ask

- How will we know the potential problem (opportunity) has occurred?

- What will activate each contingent (capitalizing) action?
- When should the contingent (capitalizing) action begin?

Following are two lists that might have been developed during the planning sessions at Smoothco. Note that the first enumerates likely causes and preventive actions, because preventive action works against the cause, not the problem. Each of the contingent actions on the second list relates back to the potential problem, since contingent actions are not directed against cause.

The tools of Potential Problem and Potential Opportunity Analysis can be used to develop and protect a complicated plan from beginning to end. But they are also extremely valuable in dealing with any situation in which we believe problems—or opportunities—might crop up and catch us unaware. When we are faced with such situations, it is always in our best interests to take a few moments to ask ourselves, "What could go wrong?" or, "What opportunity might arise?" and, "What can I do to mitigate the damage or seize the moment?"

Summary

In short, the Kepner-Tregoe critical thinking processes can be used to handle any or all of the concerns that managers face every day.

Situation Appraisal, done individually or as a team, can bring order into what often seems like unmanageable chaos. Identifying concerns, then stating them as clearly and specifically as possible, enables us to develop a list of issues requiring action. After quickly setting priorities, we can move into the action phase by asking three critical questions about each issue:

- Is this a positive or negative deviation for which we don't know cause and need to find it?
- Does a choice need to be made or an alternative evaluated?
- Are we going to take action or implement a plan?

The answers to these questions will direct us toward one of the Kepner-Tregoe modes of analysis: Problem Analysis, Decision Analysis, or Potential Problem and Potential Opportunity Analysis.

State Action: Switch to the reinforced 48-Pak by July 26.

Identify Likely Causes	Take Preventive Actions
Dealers don't know to check	Notify dealers prior to shipment
	Provide instructions for checking and reporting on shipment
Dealers not motivated to check	Provide discount on future shipment for prompt reporting
Leaking BO-8s are found	Conduct laboratory experiements on 48R prior to shipping
Design of 48R doesn't consider machine limits	Test prototype in machine prior to production
Maintenance people need training	Assess maintenance people capabilities and condition of equipment

State Action: Switch to the reinforced 48-Pak by July 26.

Plan Potential Problems	Plan Contingent Actions	Trigger
Dealers don't check boxes	Phone dealers for reports	If insufficient reports don't arrive after delivery date
Leaking BO-8s are found	Continue with interim action	Dealer report of leaking
	Redesign 48R	Problem Analysis shows same cause
Machines can't be adjusted to take 48R	Continue with interim action	Production reports 48R won't run
	Redesign 48R	Reinforced neck shown as cause
Machines break down	Continue with interim action	Production reports machine is down
	Find cause and repair machine	

Problem Analysis provides managers with the tools they and their employees need to find the root cause of deviations quickly and inexpensively. The process questions enable us to define clearly the limits of a deviation: what and where it is, when it was found, and how it is progressing. By carefully studying everything the problem is, every place it occurs, and every time it has been noticed, then contrasting these data with other situations, places, and times that are problem free, we will find relevant distinctions in the former. These distinctive areas can be examined for relevant changes and, from these, possible causes can be developed. By testing and verifying these causes against the facts that we have gathered, we can identify the true cause. No time will have been wasted on hit-and-miss actions; no costly, ineffective fixes will have been applied.

Decision Analysis is the thought process we use when we are faced with a choice. When we must make a decision, having a structured, visible process can be an invaluable way of avoiding endless, unproductive discussions. By forcing us to slow down and make sure we know what we want before we start looking for it, Decision Analysis keeps us focused. The development of a list of specific objectives, divided into MUSTs and WANTs and with weights assigned to the WANTs, gives us something concrete to evaluate alternatives against. People's pet alternatives can no longer be justified if they don't pass the acid test of the MUSTs and WANTs. Gathering accurate data on all the available alternatives before judging them is another way to temper biases or emotional feelings. Finally, when all the information on our objectives, alternatives, and risks is clear and visible, we can use our experience, knowledge, and judgment to decide what is best for us or our organization.

Potential Problem and Potential Opportunity Analysis is the future-oriented thought process that has saved many organizations from disaster and made many others into overnight successes. By taking the time to look ahead for threats and opportunities that might arise—and to determine what might cause them—managers can get a jump on the competition and protect or improve their own future. Identifying the most likely causes of future events, then planning actions to prevent or promote those events, gives us a much-needed advantage in today's highly competitive environment. Finally, no matter how hard we try to protect our plans, we should always expect the unexpected. By doing so, we can plan contingent or capitalizing actions to minimize the bad or maximize the good effects of events that we can't entirely control.

By applying the Kepner-Tregoe critical thinking processes on a day-to-day basis, managers can move their own agendas ahead and get their subordinates on the same track, at the same speed. Try it. We think you'll see a "positive deviation" in a very short time.

Acknowledgments

Twenty years ago we had the good fortune to join Kepner-Tregoe, where we learned nearly all we know about problem solving and decision making. Dr. Benjamin B. Tregoe, founder of Kepner-Tregoe, not only provided the concepts in problem solving and decision making that shaped our careers and this book, but also created the organization in which the learning that is the basis of this book took place. For your wise counsel and support, thanks, Ben.

The concept for the book required that top executives in some of the world's best companies meet with us and discuss at length their views about problem solving and decision making. The list of people willing to take the time to do that is, in our opinion, an honor roll of business leadership. In addition to the executives we cited in the Introduction, we owe a real debt of gratitude to: Van C. Campbell, Vice Chairman, Corning Incorporated; George B. Cobbe, Vice President, Hewlett-Packard Company; Scott Davidson, CEO, ICI Acrylics Inc.; Robert L. Ecklin, Sr., Vice President, Corning Incorporated; George Anthony Edgar, Group General Manager, Long Products Division, BHP Steel; Daniel L. Hale, Executive Vice President and CFO, USF&G Corporation; Jean Halloran, Human Resources Manager, Hewlett-Packard Company; Joseph Keilty, Executive Vice President, Human Resources, American Express Company, Inc.; Martin R. Mariner, Director, Quality Management, Corning Incorporated; Dennis H. Mason, former Plant Manager, Chrysler-New Castle Plant, Chrysler Corporation; Daniel W. Patterson, Sr., former Vice President and Launch Site Director, Lockheed Martin Space Operations and currently President, Lockheed Martin Aircraft Center; John Perkins, former Chief Engineer, British Airways Plc; David R. Sheffield, Group Controller, Worldwide Pharmaceuticals, Johnson & Johnson; Amy Williams, former Senior Vice President, USF&G Corporation; Marvin L. Woodall, President, Johnson & Johnson Interventional Systems Co.

In early 1994 Debbie Mather, executive vice president and partner of Kepner-Tregoe, Inc., informed us that we should write a book. Since Debbie controls all the administrative functions in our business, including finance, she's not a good person with whom to disagree. Her drive and unparalleled project management skills probably kept us from putting this far enough down in the priority queue for a 2014 publishing date. Debbie, thanks for the idea and the encouragement to carry it to fruition.

One of the pivotal decisions we made early in this project was that we wanted to write the book ourselves. After all, how hard could *that* really be? By the time we had completed the fourth page, however, we realized we were in deep water and couldn't swim. Our friend and colleague Peter Tobia coached us patiently through the rigors of writing. Peter, a far better writer than either of us, offered critique and counsel in an amazingly effective blend. He encouraged our efforts and pushed us when we couldn't get moving again. He even endured our tortured syntax without once asking about our grades in primary school English grammar. While many people aided in this book, without Peter it would never have been written. Peter, you're a jewel! Many, many thanks for getting us this far.

The manuscript also needed the sort of help that two busy consultants turned authors require. Linda Cuilla and Nancy Ogan at Kepner-Tregoe headquarters had to interpret our scroll and integrate dozens of edits, a task only slightly less difficult than deciphering hieroglyphics from the Rosetta stone. Thanks! Our friend Jim Fairbrother did preliminary editing, without which we might have been unceremoniously booted from the offices of Simon & Schuster.

Once we had enough of the book completed to turn over the printed page to our publisher, we realized how lucky we were to have Fred Hills of Simon & Schuster as our editor. Fred gave us tremendous encouragement and expert editorial advice. We also owe a great debt to the eagle eye of Simon & Schuster editor Burton Beals.

Three final groups must be mentioned. While we have highlighted a number of companies that deserve special mention because of their attention to problem solving and decision making, had it not been for writing limitations, we could have added many more companies to that list. The ideas in this book are really a reflection of our partnership with dozens of clients throughout the world. To all of you, thanks for allowing us to work with you.

We don't work alone. Our names on the dust jacket of this book represent several hundred of our Kepner-Tregoe colleagues around the world who work tirelessly to help organizations build the critical thinking proficiency we describe in this book. To our twenty-three partners and hundreds of colleagues in the firm, thanks for being the reason that there is something to write about.

Finally, we want to thank our family—our parents: if we don't "do you proud" it wasn't your fault; and our children: the Spitzer family—Andrew, Matthew, Maggie, Michael, and Emma—and the Evans family—Kate and Tim. This book is why you haven't seen us for many weekends over the last eighteen months. We owe you for our absence and recommend reading the section on Potential Opportunity Analysis.

Index

About the Authors

QUINN SPITZER is chairman and chief executive of Kepner-Tregoe. He is also a partner in the firm. Mr. Spitzer makes regular television and radio appearances throughout North America, including interviews on CNN and National Public Radio. He is frequently quoted in major publications including *Fortune, The Wall Street Journal,* and *The Economist.* Mr. Spitzer is a member of a number of boards of directors including the National Alliance of Business. He resides in Bucks County, Pennsylvania.

RON EVANS is a practice leader for Kepner-Tregoe. He is also a partner in the firm. Dr. Evans maintains an active personal consulting schedule with top executives in a number of Fortune 500 companies. He has consulted with business groups in Europe, Asia, and Australia. Dr. Evans has written articles on a variety of subjects in business and management. He received his B.A. from Duke University and his master's and doctorate of psychology from North Carolina State University. He resides in Camp Hill, Pennsylvania.

For more information on how to make your company a Thinking Organization, contact William Hextall, Managing Director of Kepner-Tregoe's UK headquarters in Windsor, at 01753 856716 or ktuk@attmail.com.